WOMEN IN AMERICAN HISTORY

Series Editors
———————

Mari Jo Buhle
Nancy A. Hewitt
Anne Firor Scott

THE WORKING CLASS IN AMERICAN HISTORY

Editorial Advisors
———————

David Brody
Alice Kessler-Harris
David Montgomery
Sean Wilentz

A list of books in the series appears at the end of this book.

THE COMMON GROUND OF WOMANHOOD

The Common Ground
of Womanhood

CLASS, GENDER, AND
WORKING GIRLS' CLUBS,
1884–1928

PRISCILLA MUROLO

UNIVERSITY OF ILLINOIS PRESS

Urbana and Chicago

1 2 3 4 5 C P 6 5 4 3 2

This book is printed on acid-free paper.

The frontispiece photograph is from the Special Collections,
Milbank Memorial Library, Teachers College, Columbia University.

Library of Congress Cataloging-in-Publication Data
Murolo, Priscilla, 1949–
The common ground of womanhood : class, gender, and working
girls' clubs, 1884–1928 / Priscilla Murolo.
p.   cm. — (Women in American history)
(The working class in American history)
Includes bibliographical references (p.   ) and index.
ISBN 0-252-02107-X (cloth : acid-free paper). —
ISBN 0-252-06629-4 (pbk. : acid-free paper)
1. Working-women's clubs—United States—History.
2. Working class women—United States—History. I. Title. II. Series.
III. Series: The working class in American history.
HQ1904.M87   1997
96-45787
CIP

ISBN 978-0-252-06629-0 (pbk. : acid-free paper)

For Ben, Max, and Tony,

my own "men of promise"

Contents

Illustrations follow page 54

Acknowledgments

My work on this book began so long ago that I'm embarrassed to count the years. It was inspired by one of the research topics David Montgomery recommended at the first meeting of his spring 1981 graduate seminar in U.S. labor history: "What were working girls' clubs?" A simple question, I thought; surely I'd have the answer by the end of the term. I was wrong on both counts. Straightforward questions are not necessarily simple, and I have lived with this one for well over a decade, as the seminar paper expanded into a dissertation and the dissertation became a book. Efforts to reconstruct the club movement's history absorbed many unforeseen hours, partly because its forty-five-year life span turned out to be longer than I had guessed but mainly because the documents it left behind so thoroughly captured my imagination. Attempts to explain the movement's various phases propelled me time and again to study contextual issues I had not expected to explore. Translating complex findings into lucid prose proved difficult to say the least. And the joys and chores of family life and teaching competed for my attention at every turn. For all of these reasons, I couldn't have produced the book without a lot of help, which it is now my pleasure to acknowledge.

My research was funded by a Yale University Fellowship, a Graduate Fellowship and Dissertation Grant from the Danforth Foundation, a grant from the Josephine deKarman Fellowship Trust, a Lena Lake Forrest Fellowship from the Business and Professional Women's Foundation, a Whiting Fellowship in the Humanities from the Mrs. Giles Whiting Foundation, and a Simpson Faculty Development Grant from Sarah

Lawrence College. The Mary McEwen Schimke Fund at Wellesley College helped me cover child-care expenses.

The quest for club documents took me to so many libraries that I became a connoisseur of user services. My blue ribbons go to the staffs of the Sterling and Mudd libraries at Yale University, the Milbank Memorial Library at Columbia University's Teachers College, the Chicago Historical Society, the Pennsylvania Historical Society, the Schlesinger Library at Radcliffe College, the Rosenthal Library at Queens College, and the Esther Raushenbush Library at Sarah Lawrence College. For help well beyond the call of duty, I am especially indebted to David Ment and Bette Weneck at Teachers College, Archie Motley at the Chicago Historical Society, Marie-Hélène Gold at Schlesinger, and the late Susan Steinberg, who assisted my research at Yale.

A large collection of friends, colleagues, and teachers contributed to the dissertation by aiding my research, sharing their own, reading portions of my work-in-progress, and smoothing my path in many other ways. For such gifts I thank Jean-Christophe Agnew, Eric Arnesen, Susan Bennett, Jeanne Boydston, Cecelia Bucki, Hazel Carby, Elizabeth Nickinson Chitty, Nancy Cott, Michael Denning, Ileen DeVault, John Ernst, Tara Fitzpatrick, Joyce Freedman-Apsel, Joanna Bowen Gillespie, Toni Gilpin, Julia Greene, Valerie James, Mickey Jarvis, Barbara Kaplan, Marta Kusic, Ruth Leonard, James Maffie, Martel Montgomery, Lee Ornati, Kathy Peiss, Stephen Schultz, Karin Shapiro, Amy Dru Stanley, Amy Swerdlow, Olivia Taylor, Alan Trachtenberg, Richard von Glahn, and Danielle Zora. One of my greatest debts is to Francine Moccio, whose sympathy, counsel, and exemplary perseverance carried me through many a difficulty. Nancy Cott and Laura Wexler supplied helpful critiques of the dissertation's final draft.

The dissertation also owed a great deal to my students at Sarah Lawrence, whose influence on my historical imagination pervades this book from beginning to end. Special thanks to Rachel Brickman, Avin Lipsky, Megan Parke, Sara Robledo, Deirdre Schifeling, and Kate Shaughnessy for reminding me by their actions just how much labor history matters in the "real world." I'm grateful to Deirdre for something else, too: the fresh, passionate questions she brought to sophomore-year studies of Marxist and feminist theory made her the reader I envisioned while struggling to turn the dissertation into a book useful to younger scholars.

My numerous debts to Sarah Lawrence friends and coworkers multiplied as I put the book to bed. Jim Cullen, Daniel Garrett, John Harris,

Carole Kenny, and Noah Sheldon supplied crucial help with the photographs. Encouragement from many colleagues—Paola Bacchetta, Bella Brodzki, Mason Gentzler, Barbara Hickey, Judith Kicinski, Leah Olson, Marilyn Power, Charlotte Price, Judith Serafini-Sauli, William Shullenberger, Fredric Smoler, Pauline Watts, and Komozi Woodard—went a long way to ease my last-minute jitters. Lyde Sizer and Elisabeth Perry read the final manuscript with extraordinary care, and I thank them for especially generous cheerleading as well as eagle-eyed editing. I also wish to acknowledge some old friends from Sarah Lawrence who made it possible for me to go to graduate school in the first place: Joan Furio, Cynthia Gale, Barbara Kaplan, Micheal Rengers, and, in particular, Sol Resnik. To explain what these five did for me would take a book in itself, so I'll simply say that they have my gratitude and love.

I owe a great deal to people who shepherded the book through its various stages at the University of Illinois Press. Thanks to Richard Wentworth for his faith in the book and patience with me, to Mari Jo Buhle for a discerning reading of the first draft and very useful suggestions for revision, and to both Mari Jo Buhle and Alice Kessler-Harris for encouraging responses to the revised manuscript. Karen Hewitt, Theresa Sears, and Mary Vavrus oversaw the publication process with skill and remarkably good humor in light of my marginal computer literacy. Margie Towery's first-rate copyediting smoothed out my prose and prompted me more than once to clarify my thinking. My gratitude to one and all.

For moral and material support and for welcome diversions from research and writing, I am profoundly indebted to my family. Elizabeth Bailey, Sarah Pesillo, Rebecca Reale, Valerie Murolo, Alyssa Chase, Valentina Sykes, Suzanne Robertson, George Schwenk, my Podgwaite and Owen aunts and uncles, my Albetski relatives, and members of the Chitty clan: all helped more than most of them realize to keep me going and relatively sane. My mother, Elizabeth Schwenk, my sister, Mercedes Murolo, and my brother, Fred Murolo, were wells of generosity, faith, and good advice. Memories of my father, Frederick Murolo Sr., and my maternal grandparents, Frank and Augusta Podgwaite, provided crucial inspiration; and so did the two youngest Murolos, Lily and baby Fred. My sons, Max and Anthony Schultz, have my deepest gratitude for forgiving my preoccupation with working girls' clubs, for making me laugh when things looked bleak, for being proud of me, and for their ferocious love.

Finally, I thank three people without whose collaboration I would have produced a very different book or, more likely, none at all. Dana

Frank shared my analytic concerns, listened to my personal worries, and showered me with wisdom and emotional support. Her insights clarified my thinking about working girls' clubs and many other topics; her generosity taught me a great deal about the meaning of friendship. David Montgomery was a stellar dissertation advisor—enthusiastic, skeptical, patient, and demanding in just the right quantities. I'm especially grateful for his detailed responses to my work, his skill at linking my micro-concerns to big issues in labor history, the example he sets as a scholar and activist, and the fact that he is in every way a mensch. My husband Ben Chitty, with whom I fell in love at age thirteen, has come through for me so consistently that my crush on him is stronger than ever. He has my thanks for countless hours of housework and child care, for assistance with typing and citations, for reading every word I wrote and helping me find quite a few of them, for rescuing me from computer disasters and, most of all, for believing in me. The best advice I can give anyone is to hook up with a friend like Dana Frank, a mentor like David Montgomery, and a life partner like Ben Chitty.

THE COMMON GROUND OF WOMANHOOD

Introduction

In February 1884, twelve silk weavers from New York City's West Side met to wrap up plans for a club where they and other "working girls"— young women employed in factories and stores—could gather after hours for conversation, study, and fun. The only question yet to be settled concerned the club's name. Its organizers were bitterly aware of bourgeois culture's contempt for the working girl: charities seeking to uplift her morals, public officials investigating her sexual behavior, and journalists with lurid tales about her family life, workplace, and neighborhood. Given this drumbeat of insults, some of the club's founders hesitated to choose a name that would identify the membership as working girls. In the end, however, pride triumphed over caution in the unanimous adoption of the following resolution: "Our organization is truly the child of the daughters of labor. Our fathers and mothers work; before them their fathers and mothers worked; and we, too, work. Let us call ourselves the 'Working Girls' Society' and show New York that we are not ashamed of *work*."[1]

While pride demanded a rejection of polite society's attitudes toward work, it did not rule out cooperation with leisured women, one of whom attended the founding meeting of the Working Girls' Society. In the fall of 1881, Grace Hoadley Dodge—the daughter of one of New York's wealthiest families and a rising star in local charities—had joined with a silk weaver in her Sunday-school class at Madison Square Chapel to organize a group of about fifty working girls who met weekly to discuss homemaking under her supervision. Twelve veterans of that project, which had fallen apart in 1883, now pressed Dodge into a more democratic mode of service. The discussion group had offered working girls instruction from above; the Working Girls' Society would promote their organization on the basis of cooperation, self-government, and self-support.[2]

It was a propitious time for such alliances. Within a year of its birth, the Working Girls' Society had rented and furnished meeting rooms on West 38th Street, recruited several more women from Dodge's social set, reached its target of two hundred wage-earning members, and made contact with similar clubs springing up in and around New York City, Philadelphia, and Boston. Branching out from these centers, the club movement soon took root in dozens of northeastern cities and mill towns, as thousands of working girls and hundreds of sympathetic ladies came together on much the same basis as the founders of the 38th Street Society. By 1890, when the first convention of working girls' clubs took place in New York City, the movement had extended to Chicago, St. Louis, and other midwestern cities. Northeastern clubs had meanwhile grown so numerous that interclub associations were operating in Manhattan, Brooklyn, and greater Boston and about to be formed in Connecticut and eastern Pennsylvania. In 1894, when the movement's second convention met in Boston, these associations—which included scattered affiliates in Baltimore, the Pittsburgh area, New Jersey, Rhode Island, and upstate New York—represented nearly one hundred clubs with a combined membership of over eleven thousand, and a count of the midwestern groups would have added at least twenty clubs and two thousand members to these rolls.[3]

Moreover, working girls' clubs exemplified a much larger trend. As they proliferated, so did other settings where working women joined forces with women of more privileged classes. The biggest network of meeting places was the Young Women's Christian Associations, whose genteel staff supervised an array of evening activities for Protestant workers: Bible study, entertainments and lectures, discussions of moral issues and current events, and courses in academic subjects, domestic crafts, and trade skills. Similar programs operated under the auspices of religious organizations such as the Episcopal Church's Girls' Friendly Societies of America, national missionary societies of African Methodist and African American Baptist women, Roman Catholic sodalities like the Sisters of Mercy, and numerous ladies' guilds in Protestant, Catholic, and Jewish congregations. And in cities both large and small, working and genteel women were increasingly in touch on more secular grounds too. They met through projects sponsored by charities such as the Children's

Aid Society and Charity Organization Societies, settlements such as Chicago's Hull House and Boston's Denison House, middle-class club networks such as the Women's Educational and Industrial Union and the National Association of Colored Women, and ethnic associations such as the German American *Vereine*, the National Council of Jewish Women, and female auxiliaries to the Ancient Order of Hibernians. Most of what historians know of these contacts between working and genteel women concerns the genteel group, which authored most of the documents left for posterity. This bias in the historical record speaks volumes about the typical balance of power when women allied across class lines. In every case, though, workers elected to participate; the alliances were voluntary, however unequal, and belong as much to workers' history as to the history of genteel reform. With that in mind, this book probes working women's attitudes toward two premises widely embraced by their genteel allies: the idea that womanhood supplied a strong basis for cross-class cooperation and the idea that women united could usher in a better world.[4]

Working girls' clubs are instructive here, not because they typified kindred movements but thanks to features that set them apart. They *were* typical in one important way that restricts what they can reveal. Though workers of various races took part in cross-class women's alliances, they very seldom allied with each other in the process; and working girls' clubs demonstrate that rule. Save for two African American clubs that passed through interclub associations in Philadelphia (in the mid-1890s) and Boston (a few years later), the movement was exclusively white—a limited window on a multiracial trend. Within these confines, however, the clubs were unusually diverse, democratic, and revealing. Unlike YWCAs and church-sponsored projects, they recruited Catholics, Protestants, and Jews. Unlike ethnic associations, they comprised much the same amalgam of groups as did late nineteenth-century working girls in general: mostly Irish Americans, German Americans, and other descendants of northwestern Europe. While factory and retail workers predominated, the movement also included domestic servants, dressmakers, milliners, office workers, and teachers. And whatever their religions, ethnic backgrounds, and occupations, club members had unique opportunities to speak up. Theirs was the only cross-class women's movement that invited workers to organize on the basis of cooperation, self-government, and self-support; and despite imperfections in practice, those principles gave club members considerable room to articulate and implement their own organizational agenda. Club programs offer exceptionally broad, clear perspectives, then, on white working women's goals as they allied with genteel women in the Gilded Age.[5]

Club members' ability to realize their goals depended of course on club sponsors' complicity. This book focuses therefore on members' relations with sponsors, which underwent many changes between the club movement's birth in the mid-1880s and disintegration forty years later. Patterns in club and interclub governance are a key theme. At every point in the movement's history, the class distribution of governing authority had a critical impact on club members' priorities. Their agenda hinged not only on their circumstances outside the clubs but also on their level of control over the movement and on club sponsors' pliability as allies.

The relationship with sponsors influenced club members' thinking about their external circumstances, too. Cross-class discourse was a central feature of club life, and it covered much more than organizational business. The documents that working girls' clubs left behind also hash over issues such as womanhood, respectability, democracy, class hierarchy, male supremacy, wage work, trade unionism, race, and nationality. These documents do not straightforwardly reflect the tenor of discussion in club meeting rooms, for they consist for the most part of material designed for public consumption: club journals and newsletters, for instance, along with publicity pamphlets, official reports on the proceedings at club conventions, and the like. Club members' sensitivity to public opinion undoubtedly made them more guarded when speaking "for the record" than on most occasions; and since sponsors edited club publications and presided over interclub gatherings, upper-class women's ideas loomed larger in these forums than at the movement's grass roots.

If the surviving record privileges sponsors' voices, however, members are certainly audible and sometimes quite loud. They clearly cared a great deal about the social issues that club documents highlight, and they were by no means simply an amen chorus for sponsors. Yet the way club members construed these issues had everything to do with the way club sponsors construed them. This was to some degree a rhetorical strategy; members tailored their statements to appeal to sponsors—to tell them in language they could understand about working girls' experiences and needs. Words were not the whole of it, though. Sponsors' presence also shaped members' self-identity by inviting them to compare their lives and worldviews to those of upper-class women and to interpret experiences and calculate needs accordingly.

Club discourse was not a hermetically sealed text, however, and its twists and turns cannot be explained without reference to contextual factors. Bourgeois culture's defamations of working girls in the late nine-teenth century made club members more radical thinkers in that era, for example, than they were a generation later, when American society's racialism had intensified to the point where they enjoyed considerable prestige as descendants of northwestern Europe. These and other exter-nal factors—including genteel reform trends, the labor movement's at-titudes toward working women, and discussions of the "woman ques-tion" in the popular press—had significant impacts on club life.[6]

This book's chief purpose in exploring the club movement and its contexts is to bring labor history and women's history together in ways that get at the interplay of class and gender systems. My use of gender as an analytic category differs from that of most women's historians, who conceive it as a matter of sexual difference—a category that distinguish-es women from men. The clubs' history prompts me to problematize sexual sameness: the extent to which women of different classes are sim-ilarly situated by virtue of their sex, the subjective grounds for sisterhood across class lines, and the structural conditions under which sisterly consciousness flourishes or fades. Moreover, my perspectives on class differ from those of most labor historians, who zero in on workers' rela-tions with their employers and the self-identities rooted therein. Work-ing girls' clubs are one of many sites where workers have interacted with upper-class people other than their employers; and as the clubs' history demonstrates, this aspect of class relations can have important repercus-sions for workers' concepts of "us" and "them." Conceiving the club movement as a shaper as well as an expression of its members' identi-ties as working women, this book asks what they made of their sexual sameness with club sponsors, what came of class differences between the two, and what these things reveal about class-gender systems in the larg-er society.

The book owes a great deal to the proliferation over the past two decades of scholarship on U.S. women's labor history. Research in that field has come a long way since the 1970s, when Alice Kessler-Harris, Barbara Wertheimer, Leslie Tentler, and other pioneers were struggling to locate women in the history of labor activism or explain their absence. There is now a relatively large and fast-growing body of literature on these issues and much more: housewives' relationship to the labor move-ment, sexual divisions of labor in the workplace, female occupations and work cultures, the roots and ramifications of racial divisions among working women, and a host of related subjects. This literature has also provided a springboard for recent attempts to integrate gender analysis into all of labor history—studies of working men, production methods, labor markets, managerial strategies, and so forth. The new scholarship addresses innovative questions about intersections of class and gender and has generated many insights on which I draw. As a study of working women's world beyond the workplace and labor movement, however, this book explores realms that have not yet received as much attention as they deserve.[7]

The literature in women's labor history includes several rich testaments to the benefits of widening its research agenda. Especially notable are Christine Stansell's history of sex and class in antebellum New York City and three books that focus on U.S. working women in the late nineteenth and early twentieth centuries: Sarah Eisenstein's study of their social consciousness, Kathy Peiss's study of their leisure patterns in New York City, and Ardis Cameron's study of their community networks in Lawrence, Massachusetts. These researchers offer extraordinarily perceptive analyses of gender's meaning along and across class lines—partly because they explore social locales labor historians typically ignore but also because they conceptualize gender identities as products of class hierarchy as well as sexual difference. Building on this foundation, I have tried to write a book relevant to both of the fields that overlap in women's labor history. Consider it an argument for broader visions of the social terrain where workers' class and gender consciousness takes shape and for closer attention to women's relations with one another across class lines.[8]

Chapters 1 and 2 provide an overview of the working girls' club movement in the 1880s and early nineties. They examine the creation and status of "working girls" as a distinct social group; compare club members' and sponsors' backgrounds, investment in the movement, and interpretations of club principles; and describe the various activities initiated under club auspices in this period. A central theme here is the tension between club members' desire to prove themselves respectable by bourgeois standards and their demands for respect as working women.

Chapters 3 and 4 focus on club members' and sponsors' relationship in the 1890s, when the initial client-patron arrangement gave way to an experiment with cross-class sisterhood. A grassroots drive to democratize club governance supplied the catalyst for sisterhood. Its program derived from parallels in club members' and sponsors' experiences of "woman's place" and ideas as to what it ought to be. While cooperation and commonalities take center stage in these chapters, however, disunity and difference are important themes, too. In particular, I examine club members' and sponsors' conflicting codes of feminine etiquette and explore the ways in which class differences became part of the very fabric of cross-class sisterhood.

The most ambitious project under the rubric of sisterhood began in the mid-1890s, when the club movement's agenda expanded to include labor reform—a cause whose discussion had earlier pitted club members and sponsors against each other. Chapter 5 traces club discourse on labor issues prior to this shift in the movement's reform program. Chapter 6 examines labor reform's rise as a movement goal, its brief tenure as an arena for cross-class cooperation, and its new directions when cooperation ceased. The club movement's relations with labor activists and employers, economic and reform trends that shaped club members' and sponsors' thinking about labor issues, and shifts in the distribution of power and authority within the club movement all played important causal roles in the developments these chapters recount. Against this backdrop, I analyze the distinctly gendered nature of the "labor question" as the clubs defined it in the mid-1890s and the utter disappearance of sisterly discourse once cooperation on behalf of labor reform fell apart.

Chapter 7 surveys club life in the opening decades of the twentieth century, exploring developments that set the stage for the movement's demise in the 1920s. I focus especially on three issues: an expanding pan-movement bureaucracy that curtailed rank-and-file power, a rise in club members' ascribed status in the larger society, and their tendency for both of these reasons to treat the club movement as a vehicle for nothing more than recreation. The chapter closes with an analysis of the movement's slide into decay after financial crises accompanying the depression of 1921–22 forced cutbacks in the clubs' recreational offerings.

The conclusion summarizes members' uses of the club movement, links their shifting priorities to their relationship with sponsors, and periodizes the movement's history on that basis. The patterns that emerge underscore the historical contingency of class and gender identities as well as their interdependence. The appendixes include some writings by club members as well as data on club programs and inter-club projects and leadership. Here and throughout the book, I have tried to make the club movement's history meaningful not only to women's and labor studies scholars but also to readers committed to building women's alliances across class lines. My central message to all is that the success of such alliances depends on their ability to unleash working-class women's energies and imaginations.

CHAPTER 1

Daughters of Labor

When the 38th Street Society's founders declared themselves proud "daughters of labor," they struck a note that echoed time and again in working girls' clubs. Anxiety about the working girl's public image abounded among club members of the 1880s and nineties, and so did the idea that their families' honor was as much at stake as their own. This mirrored upper-class discourse on working girls, which repeatedly disparaged their upbringing. But polite society's prejudices were not the only source of concern. The working girl was also a problematic figure in club members' own communities, where economic and cultural crises were redefining a daughter's proper place.

THE WORKING-GIRL PROBLEM

Bourgeois culture regarded the late nineteenth-century working girl in much the same way it regards "welfare mothers" today. She was part Jezebel, part wretch, part victim of depraved environments, part contributor to their depravity—and on all of these counts a sign that something was terribly wrong with moral standards in society's nether regions. That made the genteel public intensely curious about working girls' lives, and a slew of creative writers, journalists, and public officials went out to investigate. The results ranged from lurid, fictional studies of girls gone wrong—Stephen Crane's *Maggie: A Girl of the Streets* (1893), for instance—to prim-and-proper government documents packed with statistical tables. But virtually every text included an evaluation of working girls' morals, their sexual code in particular.

In 1875, for example, Azel Ames, a physician commissioned by the state of Massachusetts to survey women wage earners' health, published a treatise entitled *Sex in Industry: A Plea for the Working Girl.* The burden of its argument was that young women's industrial employment produced "physical deficiency and immoral tendency, the latter acting reflectively upon the physical forces to their greater detriment." Five years later, a *Harper's Magazine* article by William Rideing refined Ames's analysis by separating the victims of material deprivation from hussies who seemed to work by choice. The poorest working girls, women living on their own, deserved pity; the daughter who took a job so that she could have more than her father provided ought to be scorned. "Those who are familiar with the pert manners of . . . shop girls and their tawdry affectation of finery," Rideing concluded, "will not be disposed to bestow much sympathy upon them. Many of them live with their parents, dress well, and are fairly educated. . . . But those who are dependent upon themselves have a struggle which palliates their incivility." In 1891 the popular novelist Edgar Fawcett offered another variation on Ames's theme. Writing for the *Arena,* a journal addressed to Christian social reformers, he claimed that it was only natural for the working girl to trade her virtue for finery, since her parents were so often shiftless and her work so exhausting and unrewarding. "The more one observes the joyless life of working-girls," Fawcett mused, "the more he wonders that so many of them should be jealous of their good names. In losing these they not only relinquish a possession about which no one, for the most part, cares much whether it be lost or kept, but they obtain material comforts which must fall upon their jaded spirits like some magic mantle woven of starlight and sea winds." Representing somewhat different schools of thought, all three gentlemen agreed on one essential: working girls were predisposed to vice. That was the crux of the working-girl problem as the upper classes defined it.[1]

In club members' communities, on the other hand, the working girl embodied a new, and to some people distressing, pattern in the lives of craftsmen's daughters, who had just recently gone out to work in significant numbers. In working-class households headed by women, unskilled men, and others at the bottom of the labor market, girls had typically become wage earners in their early teens for as long as anyone remembered. The daughters of craftsmen, on the other hand, had traditionally stayed at home, devoting the years between grammar school and marriage to housework under the direction of their mothers. These apprenticeships in housewifery had sometimes included training in craft production, for the custom in some trades—printing, tailoring, and shoemaking, for instance—was that wives assisted their husbands. Craftsmen's daughters had very rarely labored outside the family circle, however, and their households had regarded that as a badge of respectability.[2]

By the mid-1880s, when working girls' clubs first appeared, new patterns were taking shape amid the quarter century of depression and recession ushered in by the Panic of 1873. Speaking for craft communities, William Cannon, president of the Cigar Makers' Union, described the panic and the six-year depression it triggered as a "whirlwind" that made "ghastly inroads into the prosperous and happy homes of the working people." His metaphor hardly exaggerated events. Manufacturers throughout the country suspended production, some permanently; factories that remained open reduced their workforces; unemployment became a national problem for the first time; and wage cuts so outstripped deflation in the cost of living that even in 1880, the year of "full recovery," the average industrial worker's wages purchased 5 percent less than in 1872. Families responded by maximizing the number of earners contributing to household coffers, and a host of craftsmen's daughters traded apprenticeships in housewifery for jobs in factories or department stores. This trend carried into the 1880s, when the inflow of European immigrants reached high tide for the nineteenth century, glutting an already crowded job market, and manufacturers' cutthroat competition for customers generated constant fluctuations in prices, wages, and demand for labor. Though the depression was over, household economies remained extremely precarious throughout the working class, and the ranks of wage-earning daughters continued to grow.[3]

Families headed by craftsmen confronted another problem as well: the accelerating diffusion of new technologies and work processes that displaced highly skilled labor. Craftsmen's diminished job security pushed even more of their daughters into wage work; and manufacturers' demand for female labor grew as craftsmen's displacement created multitudes of new, semiskilled jobs. Since women could be hired more cheaply than men, employers filled these new jobs with women whenever strength requirements or the force of gender customs did not preclude such a move. By 1890, roughly a third of all industrial workers in the United States were females.[4]

While mass production fostered the feminization of manufacturing, mass distribution through department stores feminized sales work.

These giant retail outlets became part of the American scene in the second half of the nineteenth century, as more and more cities grew large enough to supply the requisite number of customers. Appearing first in New York, Boston, Philadelphia, and Chicago, department stores had by the 1880s spread to cities throughout the United States and multiplied in the largest metropolitan centers. Since their profits depended not on markup but on a high volume of sales, department stores took full advantage of falling wholesale prices after 1873. They competed for customers by passing along savings. A Macy's advertising slogan encapsulated the strategy: "We Do Our Very Prettiest To Buy Low and Sell Cheap." The same credo characterized department stores' labor policies: all endeavored to hire cheap. And if that created a demand for female salesclerks, so did the fact that most department-store shoppers were women, who preferred to consult with clerks of their own sex. As these stores grew larger and more numerous, women's share of all retail sales jobs expanded from under 4 percent in 1870 to 16 percent twenty years later, and saleswomen's numbers increased from approximately 9,000 to 98,000.[5]

These developments created the social group known as working girls, a term that entered common usage in the 1870s and referred not to all female wage earners but to factory and department store workers in particular. The term also carried connotations as to a woman's age, marital status, residence, race, and ethnicity, for women employed in factories and department stores were in each of these respects a mostly homogeneous group. An 1888 federal survey of over 17,000 working girls in twenty-two cities across the United States provides a composite portrait. Three-quarters of the respondents were between the ages of fourteen and twenty-five; nine out of ten had never been married. Virtually all of them were white, and the vast majority were of northwestern European ancestry. The immigrants—about 20 percent of the total—hailed for the most part from Ireland, Germany, or England. So did the parents of another 55 percent who were native-born children of immigrants. At least 85 percent of the unmarried respondents lived with their families.[6]

In an article inspired by this survey, the *Chautauquan* attributed the working-girl phenomenon to cultural trends as well as economic imperatives.

> While new industrial conditions often have made the woman necessarily a wage-earner, the change in public thought in regard to the propriety of women doing work has stimulated numbers to seek employment. The increase in the wants of the family unquestionably has recruited the

ranks of women wage-earners. . . . Girls have gone to work that they and their families might have better clothing, more bric-a-brac, a piano, and books, as well as that they might have a roof to shelter and food to eat.[7]

The raw need that created the first wave of working girls now combined with new values to open the floodgates.

Tradition died hard in some quarters. Some craftsmen clung to the idea that respectable families kept their daughters at home as apprentice housewives. "Teach them to make bread," Pittsburgh's *National Labor Tribune* recommended in 1879, and the craft-union press continued to voice such opinions for many years. By the late 1880s, however, new outlooks were definitely gaining ground. Wage-earning daughters were by then so legion in craftsmen's households that there was little need to worry what the neighbors thought about one's daughter going out to work; their daughters were probably doing the same. And while stay-at-home daughters remained something of a status symbol, the wage earners could enhance their families' status as well. In households headed by men who earned enough to cover all or most of life's necessities, daughters' earnings purchased the trappings of gentility: good clothes, parlor furniture, a home library, or that sine qua non of refinement, a piano. Craft unions continued to call for a "family wage" that would pay working men enough to support their womenfolk, but more and more craftsmen's daughters were opting for other arrangements.[8]

The Order of the Knights of Labor, most of whose leaders were craftsmen, exemplified their slow and ambivalent acceptance of daughters' wage work. The order was founded in 1869 as an all-male organization of skilled garment workers. Ten years later, when a Knights of Labor convention first entertained a resolution calling for the admission of women, the order was twenty thousand strong and included all sorts of working men. The Knights were not yet ready to let women in, though; the resolution was tabled pending discussion by the rank and file and skirted again at the conventions of 1880 and 1881. At that point, Harry Skeffington, a Knights of Labor leader in Philadelphia, moved ahead on his own and inducted the order's first female assembly, composed entirely of shoe factory workers. Their successful organization convinced delegates to the 1882 convention to pass a resolution inviting women to join the order under the same rules that governed the admission of men. Though many male Knights thought this a wrongheaded move, women were officially welcomed; and since the order was by then open not only to wage earners but to all individuals deemed productive members of society, both women workers and housewives streamed in. In 1886, when the order's membership peaked at about 700,000 and Knights of Labor assemblies could be found in all parts of the country, about a tenth of the Knights were women.[9]

Male Knights' ambivalence about admitting women reflected mixed feelings about women's presence in the labor market. Knights of Labor spokesmen idealized domestic life, identified man as the natural protector of woman, and called for the establishment of a "cooperative commonwealth" in which women would not have to labor outside the home. At the same time, however, the order promoted equal pay for men and women doing equal work and became the first U.S. labor federation to endorse woman suffrage. Leading Knights' dreams of a purely domestic role for women in the cooperative commonwealth of the future went hand in hand, moreover, with support for working women's right to their jobs in the here and now. As Terence Powderly, the order's Grand Master Workman, declared: "The rights of the sexes are co-equal. Their privileges should be the same and I can see no reason why women should not be entitled to share in giving to the world its products as well as men."[10]

A similar mixture of domestic ideology and equal rights doctrines influenced working girls' behavior and attitudes. Family obligations loomed large in their lives. The 1888 federal survey shows that up to three-quarters of the respondents living in parental households regularly assisted with domestic chores, and an even larger proportion contributed to family finances. More than half handed over every penny they earned, and all but a few of the rest paid room and board. Sketchy as these statistics are, thanks to the investigators' methods of aggregating data, it is nonetheless clear that the typical working girl not only resided with her family but also served it in many ways.[11]

Yet domestic ideals do not seem to have led working girls to question the propriety of leaving home to earn a living. To judge from the hundreds of first-person testimonies collected by state labor bureaus in the 1880s and early nineties, women working in factories and department stores wholeheartedly shared Powderly's sentiments regarding their sex's right to "share in giving to the world its products." The women interviewed by state investigators voiced a host of job-related grievances: low wages, long workdays, poor sanitation, the grueling pace of labor, and the fines supervisors so often used to discipline women workers. Some interviewees added complaints about the forces driving women into the labor market, but the women they had in mind were invariably wives and mothers. A Rhode Island textile weaver offered the following lament:

In all the branches of trade women are not paid equal pay for equal work. Under this system women are employed to the exclusion of men. Quite often we see the wife and mother at work while the husband walks the streets—manly pride gone, home and children neglected. After working hard all day many women stay up to do cleaning and washing. There is no denying the fact that conditions are growing harder each year, with a puny race coming up not able to stand the strain. No thoughtful man or woman can look these facts square in the face and not tremble for the future of our country that we love so much.

No one suggested, however, that unmarried women's employment outside the home posed a danger to the family or the republic; and none of the working girls interviewed said that she would rather stay at home.[12]

Nor did working girls wish to earn a living in other people's homes. That put them right in the mainstream of women wage earners, who snapped up alternatives to domestic service whenever possible. The group with the most alternatives—native-born white women residing in cities—hardly ever took domestic jobs any more. Almost anything was preferable to work that required you to live with your employers, wait on them personally, and be at their disposal from the moment you got up in the morning until you went to bed at night. As the upper classes saw things, however, servants enjoyed unbeatable benefits: bed and board in respectable surroundings, the opportunity to earn money while learning to keep house, and close contact with people of exemplary virtue and refinement. Working girls' job preferences thus seemed quite irrational, not to mention impudent. They had, as one writer mourned, "imbibed the foolish idea that the position of a girl who does housework is inferior in gentility to that of one who works in a factory, or a printing office, or a milliner's shop." And whatever their reasons for passing up housework, it rankled the upper classes that working girls would troop off to factories and stores when so many ladies were searching in vain for white, native-born domestics. That "servant problem," which got endless attention in the genteel press, made the working girl an object of resentment as well as contempt. To a gentry agonizing over the shortage of "good help," the charge that she was immoral—maybe even a prostitute—made perfect sense.[13]

Such charges provided much of the impetus for the 1888 federal survey of working girls and the many smaller surveys conducted by state labor bureaus. Introducing his pathbreaking 1884 report on Boston's working girls, Massachusetts Labor Commissioner Carroll D. Wright noted, "One of the chief reasons for undertaking this investigation was, to determine whether the ranks of prostitution were recruited from the manufactory." Many upper-class Bostonians surmised that working girls with fancy clothes could afford to dress that way only because they picked up extra money by moonlighting as prostitutes. Wright's report, which included a detailed discussion of his subjects' "moral conditions," was an attempt to put this rumor to rest. He took up cudgels again when as U.S. Commissioner of Labor he summarized the findings of the 1888 federal survey. "From all that can be learned," he wrote, "one need not hesitate in asserting that the working women of the country are as hon-est and as virtuous as any class of our citizens. . . . Virtue and integrity belong to the individual. Either may be stimulated by surroundings or destroyed by them." There was the rub. Even as sympathetic investiga-tors congratulated the working girl for her virtue, they often described her social environment as one that was hardly conducive to morality over the long haul. Consider, for example, the following passage from an 1885 report on wage-earning women in New York City: "When virtue is only heard of or thought of once a week at Sunday-school—and the whole tenor of daily existence is against its observance— . . . it is no wonder that the young resort to out-door dissipation and the elders sink into apathy and hopelessness; and yet, with all this, there is a very large number of worthy, honest women who do their duty as they understand it, and per-severe in trying to make head against such adverse conditions." Praise of this sort did more to confirm than to challenge polite society's suspi-cion that a working girl who was not already doing wrong was proba-bly about to start.[14]

Genteel reformers concerned with this problem proposed to solve it by guiding working girls to righteousness under the auspices of organi-zations like YWCAs, Girls' Friendly Societies, and working girls' clubs. These movements were not merely upper-class initiatives, however. Working girls joined such groups in droves, far outnumbered the gen-teel participants, and influenced the roster of activities. This influence appeared especially in the club movement, where majority rule was the ideal if not always the reality. To make the movement work, then, club sponsors and members had to compromise, and that was no small or-der for women who came from such different backgrounds.

CLUB SPONSORS AND CLUB MEMBERS

The ladies who sponsored working girls' clubs belonged as a rule to the cream of genteel society. The most famous fictional representation of a club sponsor—Gerty Farish in Edith Wharton's *House of Mirth* (1905)—is deceptive in this regard. Gerty has more breeding than money and lives in "a horrid little place," a rented flat where her cook doubles as a washmaid. In real life, club sponsors generally lived in opulent households. They were the daughters of wealthy merchants and manufacturers, prominent clergymen, high-ranking politicians, and their peers. Many of these women were carrying on a family tradition of social reform, in some instances a deeply conservative tradition. Chicago's club sponsors included, for example, the daughters of George Pullman, the railroad sleeping-car magnate who built a company town where saloons, labor unions, and anything else that might undermine industrious habits were strictly forbidden. In most cases, however, sponsors had inherited a more liberal sense of mission. Florence Kelley, who helped to organize Philadelphia's New Century Guild, was the daughter of William Darrah Kelley, a Republican congressman among the most resolute proponents of equal rights for African Americans. Grace Dodge's grandfather, a partner in the Phelps, Dodge, and Company metals empire, was famous for his contributions to the Young Men's Christian Association, Dwight Moody's evangelical campaigns, freedpeople's schools, and the American Bible Society. Other club sponsors included the daughters and niece of New York's Episcopal Bishop Henry Potter, a strong advocate of trade unionism and capital's cooperation with labor; Arria Huntington, whose father and brother were also among the Episcopal priesthood's most vigorous supporters of labor reform; and Carlotta Lowell, whose mother, Josephine Shaw Lowell, was a pillar of New York's Charity Organization Society and Consumers' League.[15]

While their relatives often had rich credentials as reformers and philanthropists, however, sponsors rarely came to the clubs with lengthy credentials of their own, for the vast majority took up club work in their twenties. The most notable exceptions to this pattern were the New Century Guild's Mary Grew, a veteran of the abolition and woman suffrage movements, and Eliza Sproat Turner, who had been a Fourierist in the 1840s and in 1869 helped Grew establish the Pennsylvania Woman Suffrage Association. Under their leadership, sponsors associated with the New Century Guild were quicker than those in any other corner of the club movement to promote working girls' education for better jobs as opposed to domestic roles.[16]

Left to their own devices, sponsors of the younger set were more conservative than reformers of Grew's and Turner's vintage; religious sensibilities meant more to them than women's rights doctrines. As their

social status implies, most were Protestants, with Episcopalians particularly numerous. They viewed club work as a Christian duty, and many
combined it with church activities. Connecticut's Emily Malbone Morgan, perennial president of the United Workers of Hartford and an associate editor of the club movement's monthly journal *Far and Near*, was
also, for example, the founder of Episcopal laywomen's Society of the
Companions of the Holy Cross, a group devoted to prayer for the poor.
Most Philadelphia clubs began as church-supported projects, meeting in
Protestant parish houses under the sponsorship of ladies of the congre-
gation. And many a lady who took up club work in this and other cities
was also a Sunday-school teacher. "She is a strange being; such a mixture of the society girl and the saint": that description of a fictional club
sponsor in William Dean Howells's novel, *A Hazard of New Fortunes*
(1889), fit her real-life counterparts as well.[17]

Devout and imbued with a sense of noblesse oblige, they traded the
world of the debutante or fashionable matron for the more ascetic,
though no less elitist, realms of benevolent work. Club sponsors devoted enormous amounts of time and care to organizational duties that no
wage earner could undertake. They searched for suitable meeting rooms,
recruited teachers for club classes, and saw to a host of other tasks that
had to be handled during business hours. Many identified with club
members, referring to themselves as working girls whose wages had
been "paid in advance" by providence; but the idea that heaven had
appointed them to be rich often made sponsors smug, too. Grace Dodge
wrote in 1885, "Has not the Master given us our larger homes and separate bedrooms, our good localities, our greater education and knowledge,
all the purifying and refining influences in our lives, as a trust for the
good of the many, in order that we may diffuse a higher standard of living?" Generous and sympathetic as they were, club sponsors could also
be officious and preachy. They were especially condescending in the
1880s, when they repeatedly exhorted club members to reach for higher
standards of refinement, purity, and domesticity. But if sponsors initially mimicked the charity movement's "friendly visitors" who dropped in
on working-class households to dispense moral guidance, ladies who
remained with the clubs over time revised their agenda considerably.[18]

Club members demanded revision by refusing to be treated as objects
of charity. They were not that sort, they declared; and if this expressed
their pride, it also stated economic fact. The vast majority came from the
middle to upper levels of the female labor force. The factory workers, the

largest contingent, labored for the most part in book binderies, shoe factories, carpet and silk mills, and other workplaces where female earnings matched or exceeded the average reported in the 1888 federal survey of working girls. Sales clerks, whose wages and status surpassed
those of most factory women, were the clubs' second largest constituency.
Women in even more remunerative and prestigious occupations—dressmaking, millinery, office work, and teaching—were also present in small
numbers. There were, to be sure, some clubs where women near the
bottom of the occupational hierarchy predominated—a small band of
domestic servants in Ithaca, New York, for example, and several clubs
of cotton mill workers in New England. Such groups were very short-
lived, however. The lone exception to that rule—a cotton workers' club
in Fall River, Massachusetts—could never have survived but for meeting rooms provided free of charge by the Union Mill. In the typical club,
members could afford to rent their meeting rooms and insisted on doing just that. As a worker from New York City's 38th Street Society wrote
in 1891, "Why should we, as a club, do what, as individuals, we would
scorn to do? Why should we allow ourselves to be placed in the position of the recipients of charity when we have proven our ability to support ourselves?"[19]

Club members' claims to be self-supporting individuals had ambiguous connotations. Most of them lived in parental households and could
not otherwise have made ends meet. Some club members gave their
parents room-and-board money; others handed over unopened pay en-
velopes and received an allowance in return. Those members whose families were especially well off might keep all of their wages for pocket
money, and those who lived on their own might have very little to spare
after paying for necessities. In virtually every case, though, there was
surplus enough in family or personal budgets to meet the cost of club
dues, and most members paid additional fees for admission to club classes, tickets to special entertainments, or stays at the vacation lodges maintained by interclub associations. There is evidence, moreover, that the
typical club member could also afford to dress in a relatively fashionable
manner and to experiment with fancy home cooking. The club journal
Far and Near aimed its dressmaking and cooking columns at readers who
had at least something to spend on luxuries, not at "those very poor who
have no choice about clothing or food." Yet some club members complained that a number of the dresses recommended were "horrid and
cheap." And club sponsors sometimes complained that their pupils in

the cooking classes that tried out *Far and Near*'s recipes were extravagant in habits and tastes. Though club members were hardly well off, neither were they so poor as to save every bone for soup.[20]

Another sign of club members' economic status can be found in their stance toward very young working girls, those compelled by poverty to take a job before completing grammar school. No club admitted members under age fourteen, and in some cases the minimum age was as high as sixteen; but many recruited younger girls into "junior" divisions, where club members offered instruction in sewing, spelling, and so on, along with advice they hoped would save the juniors from "a life of ignorance and temptation." In return for this guidance, club members expected deference, and they protested when their pupils seemed, as one critic sniffed, "endowed with the fact that they know more than their superiors who have an excellent education." Sympathy for the juniors blended with a sense of superiority to the daughters of families so poor that they sent children of grammar-school age into the labor market.[21]

Club members' ethnicity also invited them to count themselves among the aristocracy of white working women. Workers of old Yankee stock usually steered clear of the movement, reportedly because they did not wish to mingle with Roman Catholics, who were there in force, or with Jewish women, who predominated in a few clubs. The rank and file of club members were native-born children of immigrants from northwestern Europe. The German American presence was particularly strong. A number of clubs conducted German classes, raised money with *Kirkmesses* (German fairs), or held public entertainments in Turn Verein halls. Surnames printed in movement publications show that daughters of other "old immigrant" communities—Irish and English in particular—regularly joined club members of German parentage. According to an investigator for the U.S. Bureau of Labor, these ethnic groups were by the 1890s clustered at the top of the manual labor market open to women. To judge from their behavior in the clubs, women in the best factory jobs identified more with saleswomen, milliners, teachers, office workers, and such than with the mass of female industrial workers.[22]

In principle, working girls' societies welcomed any wage earner who could afford the dues. Club members did not go out of their way to attract those of lower status, however, and they resented the presence of entrants deemed "rough." In a few cases, exclusivity was official policy. The Noon-Day Rest, a lunch club in downtown Chicago, admitted only office workers, milliners, and teachers and students in art and business schools, for example. In other instances, club programs designed by and for the better-skilled and better-paid did not appeal to less fortunate workers. The sponsor Eliza Turner regarded this as a major problem in Philadelphia's New Century Guild; but the guild's members apparently disagreed, for they resisted her suggestion that activities be amended so as to attract the "other sort." This was not the only club whose members and sponsors differed as to the desirability of outreach to more disadvantaged workers. Sponsors' articles for *Far and Near* sometimes chided club members for their prejudices against wage earners of certain nationalities or from neighborhoods or occupations where rumor had it that the girls were not "nice." One New York City club split in two when a sponsor tried to unite tobacco factory workers earning an average of $3.50 a week with a mixed group of longtime members whose wages were in the $5.00–$9.00 range. The newcomers did not meet what the old-timers saw as requirements for club membership: stylish dress, refined speech, and ladylike manners. Resentment on both sides gave way to open hostilities, and within a month the tobacco workers broke off to form their own group, which had no official relationship to other working girls' clubs.[23]

Club members were regularly more discriminating than sponsors in identifying appropriate recruits. An anecdote from Jane Addams's *Twenty Years at Hull-House* helps to explain why. A debating society for teenagers of both sexes seceded from the Hull House settlement to protest the presence of "toughs" in its men's club. Addams attended the deserters' first meeting in their new quarters and scolded them for snobbery. Her audience, she later recalled, "contended with much justice that ambitious young people were obliged for their own reputation, if not for their own morals, to avoid all connection with that which bordered on the tough, and that it was quite another matter for Hull-House residents who could afford a more generous judgment." Similar dynamics operated in working girls' clubs. Sponsors could rub elbows with the least fortunate, least cultivated workers without ever being mistaken for their peers. Quite the contrary held for club members, whose desire to maintain respectable appearances made them keenly sensitive to status gradations within the working class.[24]

Snobbery was not the only factor at play here. The next chapter explores an ethic of solidarity that undergirded all of club members' bids to be recognized as respectable, even those designed to differentiate them from less privileged workers. They displayed sexual purity to elevate working girls' collective reputation, for instance, as well as to distinguish themselves from the "rough" girls; and they made a point of asserting their families' respectability in addition to their own. Exclusivity went hand in hand with a vigorous mutualism that led many club members to style themselves as spokeswomen for all working girls and, in some cases, the whole working class.

CHAPTER 2

Quests for Respectability, Demands for Respect

Working girls' clubs gave their members a chance to share what one described as "a separate human piece of life between working and sleeping." The factory or department store where the typical club member earned a living employed scores or even hundreds of young women; but the social networks they formed operated under heavy constraints on the job, where the glares of supervisors and the rush to keep up with production or sales quotas put a constant damper on conversation. There were also plenty of hindrances to sociability once the workday was done. Cramped living quarters often made it difficult, if not impossible, to accommodate visitors. Neighborhood sidewalks and stoops were common meeting spots but not very comfortable, and quite a few parents forbade their daughters to socialize on the street. Parental restrictions also combined with a shortage of spending money to keep many young women from patronizing dance halls, theaters, and other commercial amusements as often as they would have liked. Working girls' clubs offered a solution. Located in industrial-residential neighborhoods or downtown commercial districts and open in many instances on all but Sunday nights, club meeting rooms provided a convenient and, what was more important, parentally approved gathering place—a "safe place," one club sponsor observed, for working girls whose "mothers are careful in regard to where they go in the evening." These were not the clubs' main attractions, however. What their members most valued was the opportunity to combine sociability with self-improvement.[1]

"Let us encourage social life," declared a wage earner at the clubs' 1894 convention, "for it is the centre, the heart, of the club; upon it the very existence of the club depends, for unless a club is social it is not co-operative, and until it is thoroughly co-operative it is not successful." Most club members agreed that sociability was not only a desirable end in itself but also a springboard to other goals. Club parties and entertainments invariably attracted the largest turnouts; such gatherings were described in loving detail when members reported their doings in the club movement's monthly journal, *Far and Near;* and workers enumerating the benefits of club membership usually placed sociability at the top of their lists. It was, however, frequently noted that young women interested in recreation alone rarely joined working girls' clubs and, if they did sign up, soon dropped out. For the stalwarts, club social life provided an impetus for cooperative efforts to make themselves more respectable, in their own eyes and those of society at large. According to Brooklyn's Good Will Club, the member who built the closest "heart relations with other girls" was also the quickest to call for collective efforts at self-improvement, because "she long[ed] to have all working girls respected." Testimony from other clubs indicates that she also encouraged recreational activities in hopes of bringing more wage earners into the club fold, where they could be enlisted in the struggle for respectability. As the United Workers of Roxbury, Massachusetts, explained, "The clubs offer great opportunities for *social* intercourse, and this may be the 'drawing card' which shall lead the members to a fuller use of their mental powers."[2]

THE MEANINGS OF SELF-IMPROVEMENT

Self-improvement had many meanings for club members. With that goal in mind, they united with sponsors to organize classes in subjects ranging from cooking and sewing to literature and calisthenics, to form committees to aid impoverished neighbors, and to hold group discussions, or "practical talks," on working girls' moral responsibilities, especially obligations to their families and to one another. Such activities composed the core of every club's program in the 1880s and early nineties. The largest and most numerous classes were in do-it-yourself dressmaking and hat trimming, whose mastery enabled wage earners to acquire more fashionable wardrobes as they increased their domestic skills. Committees to assist the needy encouraged their members to "live nobler and truer lives." Practical talks meanwhile made participants "purer and stronger" and prepared them for marriage and motherhood. "In after years," a member of the 38th Street Society predicted, "we will look back with pleasure to our pleasant and profitable practical talks, and . . . think how much better we have been as wives and mothers and how our children have been . . . [taught] the true way of life and living." These formal efforts to nurture feminine virtues were supplemented by the more casual enforcement of refined behavioral codes. Club members regularly urged one another not to use slang, chew gum, speak loudly in public, wear flashy clothing, or adopt a "fast" style in their dealings with men. Like relief committees, practical talks, and classes in needle-work and cooking, such admonishments were designed to help club members live up to polite society's vision of the ideal woman. The ex-emplary club member resembled the consummate gentlewoman: both were tastefully dressed, accomplished in domestic crafts, sympathetic to the less fortunate, sexually pure and modest, and spiritually oriented toward hearth and home.[3]

While striving toward this ideal, however, club members repudiat-ed the very heart of elite beliefs regarding womanliness: the notion that respectable femininity was incompatible with wage labor and that harsh material conditions destroyed working-class daughters' moral fiber and intellectual capacities. As Lucy Warner, a member of the Help Each Other Club in Danielsonville, Connecticut, declared in *Far and Near*:

> We have the brains. Give us the time and opportunity to use them. . . . Are working girls, as a class, virtuous? . . . Yes, we are as proud of our hon-or, we are as careful of our reputations as our sisters who dress in "pur-ple and fine linen and fare sumptuously every day." . . . Dear sister work-ers, we who work in shop and store and factory, and in countless homes all over the United States, if it is because we work that people look down on us, then let us pray that the Lord will change their opinion, and go quietly about our business, for, among the "nobility of labor" there is an illustrious company, at whose head stands the Carpenter of Nazareth, by Whom labor was forever glorified.

This conscious working-class pride suffused club members' embrace of upper-class standards for womanly behavior and sensibilities. Measur-ing themselves against those standards, they readily admitted a short-fall in terms of accomplishments; but they bristled at the suggestion that they lacked the potential to measure up. To Warner and most other club members, self-improvement involved more than acquiring the attributes of a "lady"; it also entailed a struggle for recognition as her equal inso-far as natural endowments were concerned.[4]

Self-improvement, as club members practiced it, was also a doctrine of loyalty to sister wage earners, family, and community. At the 1890 convention, for example, a series of statements in response to the question "What do working girls owe one another?" identified individual virtue as a means of enhancing women's collective lot on the job. Most speakers defined the virtuous working girl as a follower of the Golden Rule: she treated her peers as she would have them treat her. If she was working for pocket money, she nonetheless demanded a living wage, so that she would not undercut the less fortunate girls whose earnings had to cover necessities. She also helped newcomers to her workplace learn their jobs, instructed, rather than reported, women who made mistakes in their work, tried to avoid costly strikes but refused to work once a walkout was underway, and endeavored to rid her workroom of the "great evil of hurting the feelings of our fellow-beings."

There was no call for self-sacrifice, for, as a member of Philadelphia's New Century Guild remarked, "it is hardly common sense to esteem others *above* self where the stake is livelihood." But, this speaker immediately added, "a recognition of what is due other people, as well as what is due one's self, is necessary, lest in the place of sympathy will be found a hard forbearance, wearing on her who holds it quite as much as on her toward whom it is held." While unbridled individualism stunted a working woman's morals, individual displays of high moral standards served the group. Nowhere was this clearer than in the area of sexual conduct. As a member of New York City's Second Street Society declared, "When we come into contact in any way with men, whether socially, or casually, or in our work-rooms, we owe it to every working-girl to be true to our womanhood; to so impress them with a sense of true, noble womanliness, that they cannot think lightly of us." "We should strive to lift all," she continued, "by lifting up our own lives into their highest possibilities." Every club member who took the floor agreed.[5]

At the 1890 convention and in numerous reports to *Far and Near*, club members also associated self-improvement with service to their families. "Our Society," announced a member of New York's Endeavor Club, "endeavors to teach its members how to make the best use of life, how to use their time and talent to the best advantage, so that if they learn this themselves they cannot help benefitting those by whom they are surrounded in the home circle." Other club members testified, by way of example, that skills acquired in cooking, dressmaking, and millinery classes were used at home to lighten mothers' housekeeping burdens and stretch household budgets, that books borrowed from club libraries broadened families' cultural horizons, and that lessons learned in calisthenics classes were passed on to siblings so that they would know how to carry themselves in a manner commanding respect. Calculated in part to mollify parents, who sometimes complained that club members spent too much time in their meeting rooms and too little helping out at home, such testimony was in the main designed for public consumption. Club members, that is, displayed respectability by announcing their love of home—and, in many instances, exaggerating their enjoyment of housework. Not that they merely pretended to care about family obligations; ample evidence shows that they took them quite seriously. But for this very reason they felt obliged to tell anyone who cared to listen that their families reared virtuous daughters dedicated to domestic roles—that their families, in other words, were no less respectable than those whose daughters did not go out to work.[6]

For club members, moreover, a proper love of home went hand in hand with concern for neighbors in need of aid and sympathy. The clubs' relief committees delivered both. Flowers, Christmas and Thanksgiving baskets, fresh fruit and eggs, homemade jellies, and other delicacies were distributed to households where the incapacitation of a breadwinner or homemaker was playing havoc with the budget. Layettes were stitched in club meeting rooms and given to destitute mothers. Children were invited to holiday parties where club members passed out sweets, toys, and more practical gifts. In all of their relief work, clubs laid great stress on the community ties binding them to the recipients of their largesse. Describing a New Year's Eve party for "*very* poor children," for example, Roxbury's Amaranth Club reported that each member of its relief committee "brought children whom she really knew about and was responsible for them for the time being. . . . It was not a wholesale invitation to unknown children, whose names had been provided by a city missionary, but personal knowledge came in, and in consequence a personal interest was shown by each member in her own children." Nor did club members draw a hard and fast line between helping the less fortunate and helping themselves and their families. Guests at Christmas parties organized by the Lucy E. Tilley Club of St. Louis included members' younger siblings as well as other children. The Helping Hand Society of Allegheny, Pennsylvania, featured a millinery class whose participants trimmed hats not only for themselves but also for "mothers, sisters and friends, never forgetting the poor, who we may know to be in need of hats." Members of the Flower Circle of Hartford's United Workers held entertainments for their families in addition to preparing bouquets and food baskets for the poor. Workers belonging to the Second Street Society's Lend a Hand committee trained for better jobs in the garment industry as they made clothes for the needy. And while club treasuries regularly allocated money to relief committees, the committees organized many a fund-raising event whose proceeds went into the general fund.[7]

It is hardly surprising, then, to find that club members rarely described their relief work as "charity"—a term implying moral as well as social distinctions between donors and recipients. Unlike Charity Organization Societies, which oversaw most upper-class exercises in benevolence in the late nineteenth century, working girls' clubs did not dispense advice on "right living" when they distributed material aid. To the extent that moral improvement entered the picture, club members deemed relief work a form of self-improvement. As a member of Boston's Shawmut Avenue Club explained, "not only would we help others, but we would help ourselves, for I think Lend a Hand [committees] lift us up. . . . And surely the thought that we are going about In His Name keeps us from sin, and helps us to resist temptation a great many times." Club members treated relief work as a means to strengthen their own morals, not to correct those of other people.[8]

Linking the struggle for respectability to solidarity with workmates, family, and neighbors, club members' ethic of self-improvement embodied what the historian Temma Kaplan has defined as "female consciousness": women's acknowledgment of obligations that fall to them by virtue of their sex and their demand for the rights these obligations imply. Club programs stressed the fulfillment of obligations stemming from domestic roles, which seem to have been quite near and dear to the members. They signed up for classes that enhanced their homemaking skills. Their relief committees replicated women's work in the family by distributing food, caring for the sick, and seeing to the needs of children. Club members also brought family values to bear on the question of working women's duties to one another. They identified working girls as sisters and urged them to act like a family unit, the stronger helping the weaker and the older teaching the younger while everyone endeavored to promote internal harmony and guard the collective reputation.[9]

In return for fulfilling female obligations, club members of the 1880s and early nineties demanded one right above all others—the right to respect commensurate with that accorded ladies. Efforts to secure that prize rested to some degree on adherence to genteel gender conventions, especially the notion that respectable women's lives revolved around the home. As a member of the 38th Street Society declared, "Education and wealth help a little to make my ideal woman, but she may be found without either in the working girl that takes pleasure in learning all the household duties that a woman ought to know." The impulse to earn respect by proving one's domestic mettle played second fiddle, however, to a sense of entitlement rooted in class pride. Though club members often welcomed the counsel of ladies who offered to instruct them in the ways of "true womanhood," they also exuded what one observer termed an "'I'm as good as you are' feeling." Working girls' clubs, announced a wage earner at the 1894 convention, "must be *free from 'bossism'* . . . since all possess equal rights and privileges." And the energy members poured into democratizing club life outstripped that devoted to meeting genteel standards of femininity.[10]

SELF-GOVERNMENT, SELF-SUPPORT, AND THE PURPOSES OF COOPERATION

In theory, members and sponsors agreed that their clubs should be cooperative enterprises governed and financed by those they served. The two groups had divergent ideas, however, as to what kind of cooperation was most needed and how working girls' clubs should practice what their constitutions preached with regard to self-government and self-support. These differences of opinion reflected different stakes in club members' struggles for respectability and demands for respect.

Club members were far more sensitive than sponsors to imbalances of power between the two groups. In virtually every club, policies and programs were adopted and officers chosen by members' votes. Most clubs could also boast that from the very outset wage earners held various offices. Were it not for these features, which distinguished working girls' clubs from charities, most of the members would never have signed on. Democratic forms did not guarantee democracy, however. In the club movement's early years, the lion's share of power was usually vested in club presidents—and they were almost always upper-class women, elected in appreciation of their willingness and ability to devote so much time and energy to club affairs. A club's members voted on the proposals presented at monthly business meetings, but it was the president's responsibility to set the meetings' agendas.

Under such conditions, self-government was often reduced to the right to respond to questions ladies deemed important. "As matters stand," observed an anonymous letter to *Far and Near* in 1890, "our clubs are monarchies which it pleases us to call republics, and in which our queens masquerade, with more or less skill, as presidents." Club members, the writer hastened to add, had a great fondness for their presidents, but this only compounded the problem: "The president who is most popular and most beloved is the very one who has the hardest time discovering her mistakes, for in reigning over the hearts of the other members she involuntarily gains too much ascendancy over their minds, and *because* they love her they do not disagree with her." Rank-and-file affection for club sponsors precluded revolt, but it did not rule out pressures for more democratic arrangements.[11]

The result was a widespread switch to the council form of government, first adopted by New York City's Endeavor Club in 1888, three years after the club's founding. Under the council plan, clubs were administered by twelve-woman boards, eight of whose seats had to belong to wage earners, and committees set the agendas for business meetings. The plan had such appeal that, after copies of the Endeavor Society's bylaws were distributed at the 1890 convention, *Far and Near* reported their adoption by many other clubs. Emma Illwitzer of New York's Progressive Club outlined the features that most endeared council government to club members: "It will be much easier for twelve to find out the desires of all the members than for one. . . . Especially so as eight members of the council are to be working girls, and they are more apt to hear the ideas and opinions of the different members expressed freely during the month than the president ever could." Programs more nearly representing the wishes of the membership were the premier benefit of the council plan.[12]

While some club sponsors reacted defensively to insinuations that, out of ignorance or arrogance, they neglected the interests of the membership, most gave their blessings to council government and analogous power-sharing schemes. Their reasoning, however, was very different from that of club members. At the 1890 convention, for example, Jane Potter—the sponsor who served as president of the Endeavor Club— identified the council plan as a means of giving club members "systematic training in the art of government" and "a growing sense of responsibility." At the same gathering, Mary Storrs Haynes, the sponsor of a Brooklyn club, announced that self-government enhanced club members' domestic virtues. Club sponsors, she said, had always recognized that "only a system of government which should permit free expression, and should teach with all that is practical and educative, that *higher* education of self-government and responsibility as *woman* would tend to the better building up of the *home.*" Taking a very different tack, L. E. Ackerson, a wage earner from the Endeavor Society, described the council plan as a necessity if the club movement was to help working girls win the respect they deserved. "We must show to the world," she argued, "that working girls have higher ideas of life. . . . We must so act and live that society may be benefitted by the working class. May we be such that we will be treated with respect." Such sentiments lay at the heart of club members' enthusiasm for democratization.[13]

Discussions of self-support as a club principle revealed a similar mixture of unity and division across class lines. Club members held fast to the ideal, and so in most instances did club sponsors. For the members it was a badge of respectability, one that distinguished them from the recipients of charity and buttressed their claims to equality with people of means. For the sponsors it was a strategy for reaching the legions of working girls who would not accept assistance under openly charitable circumstances. The New York *Evening Post* observed in 1890 that "half the energies of the women promoting the . . . clubs seem directed to disseminating the declaration that they are not a charity." Club members and sponsors alike participated in that effort.[14]

In some instances, however, the sponsors' desire to extend the club movement encouraged the conclusion that self-support was not the most useful tenet. In 1891, when a prominent Boston clergyman complained that the dues and fees demanded of members minimized the clubs' usefulness to working girls, *Far and Near* received a flood of letters on the subject. Nearly all of the writers took aim at the assumption that club members would be better off if someone else financed club life. As a worker from the Perseverance Club in New Haven, Connecticut, explained, "We girls want to stand on a level with any other self-supporting or independent people, whether they be wage-earners, salary-earners, or professional men and women. It is a poor way to begin by asking them for pecuniary assistance. . . . If we want to keep the respect of the community in which we are placed, let us try to observe the first rule of financial morality and live within our income." Not everyone agreed. A lady from Boston's Fraternity Club wrote, arguing that, since the club movement's overriding goal was to unite women across class lines, it should seek financial aid from wealthy sisters and use that money to open its doors to those who could not afford to pay their own way. "It will be most unfortunate," she warned, "if any feeling of class distinction is raised and intensified." To club members, however, there were distinctions and there were distinctions. They wished, as a rule, to preserve the line dividing them from the recipients of charity and to eradicate as nearly as possible that which divided them from gentlewomen. Neither could be accomplished if working girls' clubs accepted patronage.[15]

A satirical story that circulated in New York City clubs in the early 1890s illustrates members' attitudes toward the idea of a cross-class sisterhood founded on charity. The heroine of the piece is Mrs. Jones, a member of the Needle Eye Society formed by working-class women determined to save the rich from eternal damnation. The story describes her visit to the wealthy Mrs. Titlow. After reminding her hostess of Christ's words in Matthew 19:24—"It is easier for a camel to go through the eye of a needle, than for a rich man to enter the kingdom of God"—Mrs. Jones offers sympathy and moral support. "Let me be your friend," she says, "I want to be your sister." By the end of her visit, though, it is clear that Mrs. Jones is actually there to pry and meddle. "Tell me about yourself and your family," she urges. "What is your husband's business? Is he honest in it? Does he treat you kindly? What are your own besetting faults?" As this story implies, club members knew something about the smug, officious ways of friendly visitors from Charity Organization Societies, and they were not about to countenance financial arrangements that would make them the objects of charity.[16]

"I have noticed," announced a wage earner at the 1894 convention, "that those who fail to favor the 'effort toward self-support' forget that we are self-governing." She was arguing against the idea, advanced by some club sponsors, that since colleges accepted donations without pauperizing their students, working girls would not be demeaned if their clubs acquired endowments. Were that to happen, she maintained, members would have no more voice in club management than students had in the administration of their colleges. As she pointed out, self-support was not only a matter of status and pride for club members; it was also essential to their control of organizational affairs. If the club movement solicited charity, the balance of power would tip more than ever in club sponsors' direction, for they would bring in bigger donations than the members ever could. Thus, in the vast majority of clubs, members established a strict ban on "public begging"—asking for gifts from the rich. Sponsors were prohibited from organizing charity balls and such on behalf of the movement. They might occasionally lend or donate their own money to a club whose treasury was momentarily depleted, but shortfalls were usually made up by club members: when their dues and fees did not cover all the expenses, they held fund-raising events to which they invited their families, friends, and neighbors.[17]

Cooperation—the last of the club movement's three official tenets—had cloudier meanings than self-government or self-support; club members and sponsors did not debate its application in the straightforward way they discussed the merits of council government or various possibilities for raising money. Nevertheless, two schools of thought with regard to cooperation are discernible. Club sponsors generally stressed cross-class cooperation in service of working girls' moral improvement while members emphasized mutualism among working girls struggling for respect. The Three P's Circle provides a sterling example of the former strategy, and the club convention of 1890 illustrates the latter.

The Three P's Circle was a cooperative endeavor organized by Grace Dodge in November 1889. The Ps stood for "Purity, Perseverance, and Pleasantness"; the purpose of the circle was "to rouse in its members a sense of the true dignity of womanhood, especially in purity of life and sunniness of temper." Members signed a card bearing the following pledge:

I _____ PROMISE BY THE HELP OF GOD,
1. To try to be modest in language, behavior, and dress.
2. To try as far as possible to avoid all conversation, reading, art, and amusements which may put impure thoughts into my mind.
3. To try to guard and promote the purity of others, especially of companions and friends.
4. To uphold the law of purity as equally binding upon men and women.
5. To strive after the special blessing promised to the pure in heart.
6. To try to cultivate a cheerful spirit, and to diffuse sunshine whenever possible.

This document was countersigned by one of the group's special "cooperating members"—Dodge, another club sponsor, or an especially virtuous working woman—who would then help to see that the pledge was met. Members of the Three P's Circle received monthly "messages" from Dodge: religious pamphlets, lists of behavioral "Don'ts" for respectable women, and such. Beginning in the 38th Street Society with a charter membership of fourteen, by 1890 the Three P's had a fifty-member branch inside that club and smaller groups operating in three other New York City clubs. Within a few years, however, enthusiasm waned and membership shrank to a handful, though the project limped along until Dodge's death in 1914.[18]

As Dodge was launching the first Three P's Circle, club members were hatching plans for a movement-wide assault on insulting stereotypes of working girls. Intensive discussions got underway in the 38th Street Society in June 1889, when local newspapers reprinted a charity leader's broadcast of such stereotypes at a public meeting. For several months, 38th Street members hashed over possibilities for a counteroffensive. In October they adopted resolutions that in some respects bear a striking resemblance to the Three P's pledge but also go far beyond that strategy for self-advancement.[19]

Though they called in part for cooperative efforts to promote purity, good manners, and morally uplifting leisure pastimes among all working girls, the resolutions were, at base, a statement of pride in labor. They ended with the following declaration:

> All should try to promote the work of the societies, for the fundamental principle of working girls' clubs is to make girls and women respect themselves, and to make them realize what they can secure by co-operation. People will respect working-girls when they show what they can accomplish for themselves and others. We, as such, therefore will force others to respect us because we respect ourselves, even though we are only factory and shop girls. We can do it for ourselves, and strengthen one another by co-operation, and by recognizing the dignity of labor. In this matter we will agitate, educate, and co-operate.

Whereas the Three P's Circle promoted cross-class efforts to make working girls become more virtuous, the assault on stereotypes invited working girls to cooperate with one another in a struggle for public recognition of the virtues they already possessed. And whereas the Three P's—also known as the Homebuilding Group—aimed "to make through girls and women happier, brighter homes," the 38th Street Society's resolutions called for working girls' elevation outside the domestic sphere.[20]

The first concerted attempt to implement these resolutions was the club convention of 1890, which New York City clubs organized amid a winter's worth of rank-and-file discussions of the proposals from the 38th Street Society. Club members' convention statements regarding working girls' obligations to each other emphasized one side of the struggle for respect: efforts to persuade the public that working girls were already well endowed with the feminine virtues most valued by the genteel gender code. The speakers' calls for sexual decorum and observance of the Golden Rule outlined a strategy for winning respect on polite society's terms. Working girls who heeded these calls would demonstrate that they and, by implication, their peers were no less modest and altruistic than the finest lady. The fact that virtually every speaker focused on the need for sisterly solidarity on the *job* suggests, however, that club members also wanted respect on their own terms—not as ersatz ladies but as *working* women claiming the right to respectable conditions of labor.[21]

This was confirmed at the convention's final session, where delegates from several New York City clubs addressed the question, "Toward what are we tending?," and proposed new ways of winning respectful treatment for working girls. "Why," asked the Steadfast Club's speaker, "are so many of our sisters working for such very small salaries? . . . While our fathers and brothers who love us dearly have the privilege of voting, why cannot they elect men to the law-making halls who will do justice to all people?" A member of the Far and Near Club continued in the same vein, expressing the hope "that the mighty co-operation of the girls, with the help of the club [sponsors], will rouse the uninterested of this city and of others, to a sense of a needed reform in wages and rules of shops and factories." "What people want," concluded an Endeavor Society member, "is justice alike to employee as well as employer; a better understanding between the two; [and] no difference on account of sex in regard to positions in any of the ranks of labor." Respect entailed more than public recognition of the working girl's feminine virtues. Working men, legislators, and employers, as well as upper-class women—club sponsors in particular—also had to recognize her rights to equal pay for equal work, protective labor laws, and workplace reforms beyond the letter of the law.[22]

In claiming these rights, club members recognized no division between working girls' entitlements as women and as wage earners. They spoke as daughters and sisters whose menfolk ought to look out for them in the political arena, as women calling upon more fortunate members of their sex to show solidarity by taking a greater interest in labor affairs, and as wage earners demanding equity with working men as well as employers. Separable in theory, female and class consciousness were inextricably interwoven in club members' minds, where both were decidedly mutualistic.

The mutualism derived to some degree from the grievances working girls shared. Sex discrimination in the labor market, degrading treatment at the hands of employers, and disparaging stereotypes of working girls: all of this imposed a collective identity on club members and their peers. The strong sense of "us" that club members articulated—sometimes in regard to one another, sometimes in regard to all working girls—did not depend entirely on grievances against "them," however. It sprang more fundamentally from both the job-based social networks the clubs institutionalized and the new networks formed in club meeting rooms. As club members so often pointed out, sociability prompted cooperation; and the better they got to know one another, the bolder their assertions of collective rights. The problems working girls confronted provided the basis for cooperative struggles for respectability and respect, but it was a mutualism rooted in sociability that gave these struggles their dynamism.

As time wore on, moreover, and club-based friendships proliferated, respect increasingly overshadowed respectability as a rank-and-file goal. Bids for recognition as virtuous women took more and more of a back seat to rejections of standard definitions of feminine virtues. And during the depression of 1893–97, members tried with unprecedented vigor to make club discussions of work life springboards for labor reform projects. Asked in the early 1890s to identify club life's most important benefit, a member of the 38th Street Society replied that it had "elevated the working class in the minds of the world in general." A few years later, she would probably have pointed instead to the movement's defiance of gender conventions that cramped working girls' leisure, and she might well have predicted that the clubs would prove an equally powerful agency for reforming conditions on the job.[23]

CHAPTER 3

Patrons and Friends

Different as they were in so many regards, club members and sponsors also came to see each other as sisters. Irene Tracy, a charter member of the 38th Street Society, attributed this "oneness" to personal friendships that crossed class lines. "We all meet on the common ground of womanhood and sisterhood," she wrote in 1892. "The Club working girl does not feel that she is looked down on, but feels that she has gained the respect, love, sympathy, and loyalty of a stanch friend, while the woman of leisure feels she has gained a true friend in the girl who has to go out in the world alone day after day, who has learned so well how to help herself, and is such a true, womanly woman; for there is something strong and self-reliant about her; she is to be trusted." This assessment of class relations in working girls' clubs was repeated often in the 1890s, by members and sponsors alike.[1]

There was, to be sure, a disingenuous side to the claim that friendship erased class divisions. A group of Boston club members complained that "though [sponsors] are willing to come to our clubs and be pleasant and friendly they would never welcome us to their homes and treat us as one of themselves." This pattern extended throughout the movement, and the exceptions merely proved the rule. The 250 New York City club members whose presence was requested at an Endeavor Club sponsor's high-society wedding in 1891 did not get invitations to the reception, for instance. On those rare occasions when club members were invited to a sponsor's home, the party was invariably for them alone, not one where they rubbed elbows with her fashionable friends.

Just as club sponsors' inner circles as daughters of polite society were closed to working women, moreover, the most intimate corners of club members' lives were off limits to ladies befriended in club meeting rooms. Home visits from club sponsors were assiduously avoided. In some clubs, members even refused to supply a home address, for no self-consciously respectable household wanted callers whom the neighbors might easily mistake for "friendly visitors" dispatched by charities. A sponsor's knowledge of a club member's personal affairs derived almost entirely, then, from the members' self-presentation in the meeting rooms; and there is considerable evidence that candor did not always prevail.[2]

Forthright expressions of rank-and-file opinion on questions of etiquette were especially rare, for club sponsors discountenanced any defiance of behavioral codes that reigned in upper-class milieus. Working-class rules of conduct were, by sponsors' lights, not simply different from their own but distinctly inferior as well, and sponsors found numerous ways of making that insulting judgment obvious, despite their ever-gracious demeanor. Club members responded by constructing a gracious facade of their own; they typically adopted an uncharacteristically refined manner in club meeting rooms.

Friendships of the sort Irene Tracy described flourished nonetheless, thanks mainly to the spread of council government and other democratic reforms following the 1890 convention. As discussions of etiquette so clearly demonstrate, the client-patron relationship between working women hoping to establish their respectability and ladies sharing their expertise on respectable ways remained intact. That formerly central relationship was now overshadowed, however, by a feeling of oneness or, as most club activists put it, "sisterhood," for democratization created numerous forums where club members and sponsors came together on a relatively egalitarian basis. It was here, in an atmosphere conducive to sociability as well as teamwork, that they became friends.

THE PROBLEM OF ETIQUETTE

> When on the street, take my advice,—
> You'll find it worth the pay—
> If you should meet a man, girls,
> Just look the other way.
>
> For it is better far, you see,
> To be distinctly cold;
> You'll find it inconvenient, girls,
> To be considered bold.[3]

Far and Near regularly carried such warnings against behavior that breached refined rules of etiquette, especially where sexual decorum was concerned. Most of the admonitions came from upper-class women who equated feminine respectability with the maintenance of an unfailingly ladylike demeanor. Club members occasionally joined the chorus, too, arguing that dainty manners would help to raise working girls' status in the public mind and in the eyes of working-class men. As the steady drumbeat of advice and exhortation suggests, however, many a club member did not consistently practice what her movement preached with regard to etiquette. Though refinement was de rigueur in club meeting rooms, the behavioral standards workers embraced there did not necessarily hold sway in other settings. In fact, according to Lillian Betts, an upper-class social reformer intermittently involved in several New York City working girls' societies, the disjuncture between members' conduct within and outside the meeting rooms was "the most difficult problem in club life."[4]

Betts illustrated the problem with an anecdote about a club member named Molly. Exuberant and extremely popular with her peers, she readily assented to a sponsor's request that she set a good example by toning down her boisterous behavior at club gatherings. But outside the club, she followed her own decidedly unladylike formula for personal dignity. When a passing ragpicker muttered obscenities at a group of women enjoying a dinner break in front of her factory, Molly jumped onto his back, grabbed hold of his hair, and rode him like a horse up and down the block until he knelt and apologized to her workmates. They were delighted with his comeuppance, as was Molly—until she realized that the scene had been witnessed by the lady to whom she had made that pledge of decorum. Pride immediately gave way to a shame-faced explanation: "I could not help it. You don't know what he said. He won't never speak to another girl minding her own business as he spoke to us. I won't tell you what he said; it was too bad."[5]

From sponsors' vantage point, discrepancies between club behavior and street behavior bespoke working women's tendency to backslide when ladies were not there to guide them toward respectability. As club members saw it, respectability required flexible standards of conduct. Unlike sponsors, who called for allegiance to genteel conventions no matter what the setting, club members generally treated respectability as Peter Bailey has recommended labor historians regard it—"as a role (or cluster of roles)" whose demands on the actor depend on the prejudices of the audience. It seems safe to assume, for instance, that Molly did not hesitate to tell her workmates what the ragpicker had said; the fuller their knowledge of his offense, the more they would applaud her for paying him back. Repeating his words to a club sponsor was unthinkable, however, for the lady would surely be scandalized to hear even secondhand obscenities fall from another woman's lips. The net effect of gossip about the ragpicker incident on Molly's reputation among club members is difficult to gauge, but those dismayed by her immodesty were probably outnumbered by those impressed by her daring. According to Betts, young women like Molly were popular within the clubs precisely because they were bold on the outside; and their popularity suggests that most club members saw nothing wrong in altering one's demeanor to fit the audience.[6]

This when-in-Rome attitude heartened myopic sponsors—ladies who neglected, that is, to look beyond club meeting rooms. Kate Noble, wealthy founder of the Young Women's Friendly League of Waterbury, Connecticut, supposed, for instance, that sponsors could cure club members of all roughness by setting a fastidious example. "Let the more favored [club] sisters . . . always take the utmost pains to have their own speech and demeanor irreproachable," she declared at the 1894 club convention. "No girl likes to appear conspicuous, or unlike the companions whom she respects and loves, and she will insensibly modify her defects of speech and manner, and in time become as quiet and modest as they." Quiet and modest at her club, yes. But in a host of daily milieus where she was surrounded by companions who did not practice genteel etiquette, the same adaptability Noble applauded was bound to discourage refinement.[7]

Indeed, this was a chief complaint of M. E. J. Kelley, a Newark, New Jersey, club sponsor who regularly dispensed advice on matters of etiquette to readers of *Far and Near*. An active supporter of the labor movement, Kelley knew far more than most sponsors about working women's lives outside the clubs and understood clearly that the decorum so readily adopted in some settings was just as readily discarded in others. A recurrent argument in the monthly column she authored under the pen name "Aunt Jane" was that her readers should carefully mind their manners no matter where they might be or who might be watching. It was wrong, she insisted, that so many club members who were admirably modest when dealing with men from their neighborhoods—where parents could keep an eye on things—flirted and went buggy-riding with the country boys they met when staying at club vacation lodges. It was also improper for girls to write letters they would blush to show their mothers or to build friendships based on mutual resentment of parental restrictions on daughters' behavior. And it was especially lamentable that workers whose doings in club meeting rooms suggested devotion to self-improvement should so often fail to display this trait in other environments. If "Aunt Jane" had not observed these workers in their clubs, Kelley wrote, "she would sometimes be tempted to think they were living solely to munch caramels, read silly novels, go to dances, and get a beau." Since conduct approved by parents and club sponsors was far more decorous than that which working girls condoned when left to their own devices, "Aunt Jane" constantly urged her readers to internalize voices of authority and follow their prescriptions at all times.[8]

Self-policing of this sort could not, however, promote the behavioral consistency Kelley recommended, because working- and upper-class authorities—parents and sponsors—measured club members' respectability with different yardsticks. While "Aunt Jane" told her readers that refined girls relied on maternal guidance regarding questions of sexuality, numerous club members declared that their mothers flatly refused to talk about such things. The sensational literature abhorred by sponsors and foresworn by workers in Three P's Circles was regular fare in many club members' households. And crowded conditions in working-class homes frequently ruled out the bodily modesty endorsed by sponsors. As a member of the 38th Street Society confessed during a practical talk on "Purity and Modesty," she and quite a few of her club sisters had "grown accustomed to more or less exposure before mothers and sisters, alas! often before fathers and brothers." These and other differences between family practices and the "new and nobler standards" sponsors promoted precluded simultaneous bows to parental authority and the authority of "Aunt Jane" and company. To place a higher premium on the latter, moreover, was to risk family conflict. "I know," a club member exclaimed in *Far and Near*, "how difficult it is to introduce new ideas into the home. . . . Yes, it is hard, often impossible to change father and mother, and it is also hard to be called 'Princess,' 'Fine Lady,' etc., when we who mingle more with the outside world than mother does . . . try to correct our manners." Daintiness, invariably applauded by club sponsors, might simply annoy the folks at home.[9]

It could also isolate a club member at work. The culture working women constructed on the job typically condoned gum chewing, slang, risqué jokes, and countless other violations of ladylike canons of good taste. The worker who conformed to more refined standards might be a paragon in club sponsors' eyes, but workmates generally viewed her as a prig and made her days hellishly lonesome. "Aunt Jane" admitted as much when she chided club members for going along with vulgarity in the workplace "rather than have anyone think they are setting themselves up as better than others." She promised that women who declined to go along with the crowd would be vindicated over the long run: "Supposing you are thought a crank; there's nothing very bad about that. Just think of all the people you've heard of as having made history, and if you read their personal lives you'll find that somebody thought them cranks." Inspiring words for someone hoping to make history as a missionary of refinement, perhaps. Club members laid a greater emphasis on making friends, however, and incessant displays of refinement did not jibe with that goal.[10]

While club members' desires for peace at home and popularity at work discouraged consistently dainty behavior, their self-respect deterred compliance with club sponsors' prescriptions regarding dress. At the heart of these prescriptions lay the idea that a working-class woman's clothing ought to signal her acceptance of a lowly station. "Don't wear an imitation of some expensive thing," warned *Far and Near*'s fashion column. "Anything which does not claim to be costly is in good taste, but imitations are the essence of vulgarity." Echoing this message, an editorial on "The Vulgar Girl" identified stylishness as one of her chief crimes: "She dresses as near the height of fashion as her income allows, and is fond of large, striking hats, showy cloaks, [and] dresses of bright colors." To set the proper example, sponsors wore plain clothing to club gatherings. As club members realized, however, that clothing was usually made of finer materials than they could ever afford; and as they also knew, many a lady who dressed austerely in club meeting rooms decked herself out in the fanciest of fashions when circulating in high society. Sponsors' pronouncements on clothing smacked of hypocrisy, then, as well as arrogance. In effect, they advised club members to leave stylishness to ladies and choose garments befitting the so-called "worthy" poor who did not waste money on frippery. If such garments made a working woman seem more reputable to elite spectators, it was only because they looked down on her kind. Most of her class peers were certain, moreover, to regard humble clothing as a badge of shame—and to admire the very outfits ladies deemed vulgar. To become a faithful follower of club sponsors' advice on dress would be to capitulate to upper-class snobbery on the one hand and to lose face in working-class circles on the other.[11]

Club members' primary response to that advice was passive resistance: practical neglect tempered by verbal acquiescence. They very seldom sent queries to *Far and Near*'s "Fashion Department," for example, much to the consternation of the lady in charge. Workers who arrived at club gatherings in outfits fancy enough to make sponsors cringe were quickly surrounded by admiring club members. Observers of the club movement noted that its rank and file, like most unmarried working women, made every effort to keep up with the latest styles and, when family budgets permitted, spent the better part of their earnings on clothes. When members and sponsors held formal discussions about dress, however, the general consensus was that respectability required simple attire and ruled out passions for self-adornment.[12]

Given the clubs' dependence on sponsors' participation and the irk with which many a member undoubtedly received their sermons on etiquette, one might conclude that workers' affirmation of genteel values in club meeting rooms was a pretense calculated to quiet the ladies without alienating them. Club members, to use Bailey's formulation, may have been "playing *at* roles," showing sponsors what they wished to see in order to preserve and improve an alliance that offered working women considerable benefits. It is unlikely, though, that club members were entirely detached from the refined roles they assumed in sponsors' presence, for those roles could be played to great advantage outside club meeting rooms, too.[13]

As *Far and Near*'s stanzas on street behavior asserted, working women did indeed find it "inconvenient"—and worse—"to be considered bold," to be treated, that is, as if they lacked respectability. Sexual insults from foremen were a constant complaint and precipitated more than a few strikes, such as the 1885 walkout at the Stearns silk mill on New York City's West Side. Advertising that action as a "Strike for Good Morals," the women who walked out won the backing of New York's Central Labor Union, a local priest, and even a few employers. The offending foreman was soon ousted.

If appeals for protection against sexual corruption could strengthen women's hand on the job, bearings that offended genteel standards of rectitude could have the opposite effect. Carpet weavers from New York's Higgins mills—a group that included many members of the 38th Street Society—discovered this during their 1889 strike against wage cuts. When the secretary of the Carpet Weavers' Union appeared before a conference of ladies interested in ameliorating factory women's conditions, her fashionable outfit undercut her plea for aid. Voices from the floor argued that, if the strikers could afford such fine clothes, they could easily make do with lower pay. Failing to win support from this assembly of potential sympathizers, the walkout eventually ended in defeat.

While these and similar incidents showed that public manifestations of sexual modesty and thrift could pay off in terms of workplace clout, club members' daily experience taught that a genteel demeanor widened a woman's employment opportunities. Plain dress was required of salesclerks; and it rivaled good grammar and stenographic skills as a prerequisite for office work, which generally offered shorter hours and higher yearly earnings than jobs in factories or stores. Aware of the advantages of clerical employment and of public opinion's effect on workplace battles, club members surely had more than a feigned interest in mastering the etiquette sponsors propounded.[14]

While club members often chose to ignore sponsors' pronouncements on good taste, then, they also expressed appreciation for such advice. As Jane Russell, a member of New York City's Endeavor Club, wrote to the ladies who edited *Far and Near:* "We want a great deal of help about our clothes; we want to study our styles and get hints about becomingness. . . . We want points on etiquette, how to treat our young men friends, how much to accept from them, what we ought to decline." To the extent that working women's dress and sexual demeanor determined their access to elites' sympathy and aid, club sponsors were an immensely rich mine of useful information. Their recommendations could help club members play the lady with finesse, thoroughly knowledgeable as to what would please a bourgeois audience that included prospective employers, potential strike supporters, and others whose judgments of working women had economic ramifications.[15]

It is also important to recognize that the ideal of female sexual purity, which suffused sponsors' behavioral prescriptions, was widely shared in working-class communities and among club members themselves. In New York City, sixty members of a factory lunch club demonstrated their devotion to this ideal by striking to force the discharge of a workmate who, according to neighborhood rumor, had been arrested—probably for prostitution. The strikers knew the story was false; but the accused's reputation had been so damaged that they refused to risk their own good names by working with her. Discredit, even by association, not only reflected poorly on a young woman's family but also impaired her matrimonial prospects. Behavior and companions indicating high sexual standards, on the other hand, attracted the right sort of suitor, one who could be expected to provide a comfortable home. This, at least, was many club members' hope, embodied in and fueled by stories like "The Modern Cinderella," written for *Far and Near* by the Connecticut cotton mill worker Lucy Warner. The heroine of the piece is a mill operative inspired by a wealthy friend to organize a working girls' club whose members swear off slang, alcohol, and men who drink. The happy ending takes place at a party where the heroine celebrates her marriage to an ambitious young machinist and two of her virtuous club sisters catch the eyes of eminently eligible college boys. However fanciful the notion that conspicuous purity might help factory women attract college-educated suitors, Warner's assumption that it pleased respectable, matrimonial-minded working men was well founded.[16]

As suggested by that machinist's presence in the Prince Charming role, when club members heeded sponsors' counsel regarding sexual conduct, they were not necessarily trying to endear themselves to elite observers. The intended audience was more likely composed of class peers, whose opinions determined a working woman's standing in her community and consequent desirability as a bride. Certainly there was a difference between the sexual etiquette prescribed by sponsors and that prevailing among working-class youth—especially in big cities, where most of the clubs were located. As Jane Russell's letter hints, though, it was precisely this difference that made sponsors' advice to club members valuable.

Why would this be true? The remarks of a clergyman ministering to tenement families on New York's Lower East Side help to explain. The young women of his parish, he noted, "sometimes allow young men to address them and caress them in a manner which would offend well-bred people, and yet these girls would indignantly resent any liberties which they consider dishonoring." Thanks to her acquaintance with sponsors' fussier rules of conduct, a club member could exhibit such outstanding sexual decorum that her beaus would not dare take offensive liberties nor would neighborhood gossips smear her name. Where sexuality was concerned, displays of refinement could be quite rewarding even when the elite were not watching.[17]

On the whole, however, it was more risky than rewarding to play the lady in working-class milieus, where a stickler for polite standards was sure to win at least some admirers but equally sure to strike a greater number of people as a snob or prude. There is no record of any club dialogue about the limited utility of the manners sponsors prescribed. Club members' when-in-Rome attitude permitted unseen deviation from the prescriptions but precluded face-to-face dissent. And sponsors, in their haste to "share what we consider our real advantages with our less fortunate sisters," did not pause to consider that, for working women, fastidious manners could be as costly in some ways as they were advantageous in others. The risks of refinement—the source of that "most difficult problem" identified by Lillian Betts—thus went unexamined. Club sponsors dispensed advice based on the naive supposition that refinement was universally rewarding; and club members, declining to challenge this supposition, extracted whatever useful pointers they could from a barrage of often inappropriate recommendations.[18]

If sisterhood required understanding, candor, and a roughly equal distribution of authority across class lines, club discourses on etiquette were decidedly unsisterly. Since the rules of "good etiquette" derived from upper-class mores, club sponsors were automatically arbiters of politesse and club members merely probationers. Sponsors' upbringing in environments where starchy manners were obligatory led them, moreover, to equate the drawing room's code of proprieties with common decency; the logic of working women's departures from this code escaped ladies. Club members were in no position to explain, for their own code of proprieties ruled out frank replies to sponsors' advice. Friendliness could not erase these problems, which were, if anything, exacerbated by goodwill: sponsors' desire to share their wealth of refinement and club members' reciprocal desire to gratify their benefactresses. Durable as this patron-client relationship was, however, sisterhood became the dominant trend, for club life entailed a lot more than discussions of manners.[19]

"WOMANHOOD IS EVERYWHERE THE SAME"

"I have often been surprised," a member of Hartford's United Workers told the 1894 club convention, "to see how genuinely some women of leisure are in touch and sympathy with the working girls who are so practical and sensible." The women she had in mind, of course, were club sponsors, who had indeed come through in some surprising ways since the first club convention in 1890. Back then, their main objectives had been to imbue working girls with domestic skills and reform their moral standards; now they stood foursquare behind club programs with other, more pertinent aims. From the sponsors' standpoint, club members were a surprising lot, too. Four years ago they had not seemed nearly as practical and sensible as they did now that sponsors had gotten to know them well. The new programs and sponsors' new respect for club members were both products of club life's democratization.[20]

As members advocating the council form of government had predicted, rank-and-file opinion carried more weight when most club officers were wage earners. Workers' control of the clubs thus took a quantum leap forward with the widespread establishment of governing councils following the 1890 convention. Even where the council plan was not adopted there was a significant increase in members' influence. Physicians and other professionals began to join sponsors' ranks and to serve as informed spokespeople for the wage-earning rank and file, who talked more candidly with career women than with women of leisure. A number of clubs elected working-class presidents whose social ties to the membership facilitated a freer flow of opinion from the bottom up and guaranteed a sympathetic ear at the top. *Far and Near*, which debuted six months after the 1890 convention, helped produce a similar atmosphere in clubs entirely officered by sponsors. Its frequent articles on self-government and self-support spread calls for greater reliance on working women to every corner of the movement, while its pages gave club members a movement-wide forum for airing their views as to the clubs' social purpose. Many clubs meanwhile grew so large and their programs so elaborate that the sponsors could not possibly oversee every activity. Rank-and-file committees formed to take up the slack and became arenas for the exercise of working-class leadership. Whatever the formal arrangement regarding a club's governance, then, working women were speaking up more loudly than ever before. Against this backdrop, club members and sponsors came to refer to each other as friends and sisters, rather than "the ladies" and "our girls."[21]

Reflecting and fueling that attitudinal change were significant changes in club programs, especially in the areas of recreation and education, where club members' demands for a greater emphasis on "good times" and for greater control of the learning process widened avenues of communication across class lines. Sponsors, who in the past had done most of the talking, now listened to what one described as "secrets hitherto unguessed—of what it means to keep a home safe, pure, and bright, with the wolf often scratching at the door," and their respect for working women vastly expanded in the process. The primary token of that respect—the one that meant the most to club members—was sponsors' increasingly active support for rank-and-file initiatives that flew in the face of many a lady's original vision of the club movement's purpose.

This turnabout integrated sponsors into club networks in which they had earlier been very marginal figures; members who had earlier regarded them as patrons now accepted them as friends. This was not a universal pattern. Some sponsors stuck to old ideas as to the clubs' purpose, and some members disliked "society women" on general principles, no matter how cooperative they might be. Friendship was most definitely the trend, however. Club programs were evolving in ways that gave sponsors ever more exposure to the realities of working-class life and supplied club members with more and more indications that, as one worker told the 1894 convention, "warmth of heart and breadth of sympathy are not confined to women who earn their own living." The developments that led to this conclusion were nowhere more evident than in the convention's sessions on education and recreation, which differed immensely from corresponding discussions at the convention of 1890.[22]

Delegates to the earlier gathering reported on three types of educational activities: weekly roundtables or "practical talks"; classes in literature and history; and "practical classes" in subjects such as dressmaking and millinery. Most speakers defined these ventures as efforts to make club members more womanly; and nearly all described educational settings in which working women were expected to imbibe lessons handed down from above. Grace Dodge struck the dominant note in her opening comments on practical talks, a fixture in the vast majority of working girls' societies. Club members, she noted, chose many of the topics covered, helping to set an agenda that typically ranged from methods of housekeeping to municipal politics. But sponsors chaired each talk, spoke far more than any of the workers present, and took pains to draw their attention, whatever the talk's topic, to "fundamental laws of health and domestic economy." By these means, Dodge explained, sponsors guaranteed that practical talks would train working women in the home-loving, refined ways of "true womanhood."

The clubs' numerous practical classes, and much rarer courses in literature and history, were discussed in similar terms. Speakers described them as remedial efforts to offset wage labor's bad effects on club members' domestic virtues and, one lady added, to combat the "unhealthy speculations" that seized young women "brought up by mothers . . . too ignorant or too busy to help them in their ponderings." Here, too, the concept of club education as a curative for defects in working-class femininity went hand in hand with an authoritarian learning process. Though their votes generally determined the subjects taught, club members were assigned to passive roles in the classroom. Ladies monopolized the teaching. The students' job was to show up regularly, sit quietly, follow instructions, and strive for the womanly virtues embodied by their genteel mentors.[23]

The notion that working girls should model themselves after ladies shaped club education even in those few instances where it promoted working women's advancement on the job. Arguing that practical talks should rouse club members to seek parity with men in the labor market, a lady from Boston's Shawmut Avenue Club outlined the benefits of studying upper-class career women and inviting them to lecture. A similar orientation shaped policies at the trade school run by ladies from Philadelphia's New Century Guild, whose sponsors believed that "women . . . ought to be as carefully trained to their trades as men." The guild's convention delegate described a broadly appealing curriculum: "professionally thorough" courses in dressmaking, millinery, and male-dominated trades such as typesetting and glasswork, all of which offered better pay and more prestige than the typical working woman enjoyed. Yet course schedules combined with admissions criteria to place the school beyond the reach of most working-class daughters. Since classes met in the daytime only, wage earners who could not afford to quit their jobs were excluded; and the admissions committee regularly turned down applicants deemed too uneducated or unassuming to build successful careers. The school was designed, in effect, to serve working women who bore some resemblance to upper-class career women in their educational backgrounds, professional ambition, and access to leisure.[24]

Whether they promoted "true womanhood" or achievement in the workplace, the educational endeavors described at the 1890 convention were managed with a heavy hand by club sponsors and embodied upper-class strategies for working women's advancement. Club members' dissatisfaction with this state of affairs would later become obvious. But no member who took the floor in 1890 questioned sponsors' right to design the educational process and define its official goals.

The winds were blowing in a very different direction in 1894. At that year's convention, reports on educational projects came for the most part from club members. One of the things they reported was a distaste for any activity reminiscent of grammar school, "when the schoolroom seemed so unpleasant, the lessons such a task, and not a word [was] allowed to be spoken without demerits being added to the deportment." Clubs where such things remained a problem were very much in the minority, however, to judge from the delegates' statements. In most quarters, the membership had taken command of practical talks and turned them into gatherings so nondidactic in tone that they figured more prominently in the convention's session on social life than in the one on education. Members had also begun to teach classes in some clubs and, thanks to their nonauthoritarian methods, proved singularly popular instructors. Rank-and-file pressures had meanwhile inspired many a lady to adopt similar methods. The delegates' criticism of schoolmarmish behavior blended with much larger portions of praise for classes where everyone was encouraged to speak up and students learned not only from the instructor but also from each other. Sociable, democratic education was now the official ideal, and practices in line with that ideal predominated.[25]

There were corresponding changes in the stated purposes and typical contents of the various curricula. No club speaker at the 1894 convention described courses in domestic skills as a means of rescuing working women from the negative influences of labor outside the home. No one objected to the growing emphasis on trade education—the appearance of courses in clerical skills and of dressmaking and millinery courses designed to prepare students for jobs in those fields. None of the educational projects described was exclusionary. The New Century Guild's trade school, absorbed by Drexel Institute in 1892, was no longer a club undertaking. Its policies had not spread along with the enthusiasm for trade education. Nor did anyone at the 1894 convention suggest that club members model themselves after upper-class career women or home-oriented "true women." Touted in 1890 as a way to make working women more like ladies, practical education was now hailed as a way of "learning something useful"—something that would enrich club members' lives as daughters of labor.[26]

Once a rarity, courses in liberal arts and civics were now relatively common, moreover, and far less Sunday-schoolish than their forerunners. As a member of the Working Girls' Club of Cincinnati explained, "making the most of one's self" required "liberal education," the type acquired in colleges, not parish houses. Baltimore's Myrtle Club applied much the same rule in a proposal for movement-wide classes on municipal affairs. It was foolish, the Myrtle delegate argued, to suppose that female "moral faculties" furnished viable answers to urban problems: "Good intentions without exact knowledge will accomplish as little in politics as in the practice of surgery." What club members needed, then, were classes that armed them with facts about municipal elections, courts, tax structures, spending on public services, and so forth. The morality essential to good citizenship would presumably take care of itself. Educational programs had come a long way since the 1890 convention, where Dodge had reported that practical talks stressed the moral dimensions of every topic from elections to home cooking.[27]

Equally striking changes had occurred in club recreation. The 1890 convention's session on that topic was astoundingly brief: there were just two three-minute statements, both from members of New York City clubs. The Second Street Society's delegate announced that its monthly sociables helped to attract new members. The Far and Near Club's delegate argued that entertainments were a good idea because they encouraged the use of Sunday-best manners, made weary workers "pleasanter to live with," and, when tickets were sold to outsiders, raised money for the club treasury. Club sponsors' silence at this session explains why the two speakers took the tacks they did. As of 1890, most sponsors wished to keep recreation at the margins of club life, so that members would devote their best energies to self-reform. Just a few weeks before the convention, for example, Dodge had asserted in a public address that working girls' clubs were "not for amusement, but for intellectual and moral improvement." Challenging that idea in a roundabout manner, the Second Street and Far and Near delegates legitimized a greater emphasis on recreation by defining it as a means to impeccably sober ends: bigger clubs, fuller treasuries, "pleasanter" club members. But neither delegate dared to suggest that good times should be a staple of club programs.[28]

Four years later, this idea had not only been proposed but had also carried the day in the oldest northeastern clubs, where democratization was most advanced. At the 1894 convention, a dozen delegates, including several sponsors, spoke on recreation. The New England, New York City, and Philadelphia clubs they represented had all made good times central to their programs. Games, dancing, and sings were regular activities; Saturday nights brought all-club parties; and the guest lists for those parties sometimes included men. Recreation for its own sake no longer lacked legitimacy in these clubs, whose spokeswomen took pains to convince less convivial groups that women who gave most of their waking hours to routine labor desired, needed, and deserved lots of amusements.[29]

Good times were much more than salve for the weary, however. Citing mottoes like "each for all" and "union is strength," speaker after speaker described sociability as a seedbed for sisterhood. "Until we know each other we cannot work together," argued a member of Boston's Shawmut Avenue Club. "The so-called social evenings are the greatest factor in this development. . . . At these informal gatherings we have time to chat and to become acquainted, to learn of another's daily life and interests, to find out and appreciate the good qualities, and to be tolerant of others' opinions." As the workers who spoke at this session made clear, club members most valued getting to know each other. It was exciting to compare notes with working women from different firms, different occupations, different kinds of households, different religions and ethnic backgrounds, and different parts of town. Every participant heard ideas that defied conventional wisdom in her own workplace, neighborhood, or church. Everyone learned about labor and living conditions that contradicted patterns she'd taken for granted. And friendships that transcended these differences fueled an exhilarating sense of collective potential. The word from Springfield's Young Women's Guild, for example, was that sociability created "grand opportunities and possibilities" for club members to make history: "With our large numbers, which are constantly increasing, what a power we might be!"[30]

If club members found it especially inspiring to know a diversity of workers, it was also gratifying in very practical terms to *be* known by club sponsors. Getting acquainted with working women as individuals deepened a lady's sympathy for working women en masse, and that made her a wiser, more helpful ally. Edith Wharton describes the first step in this process with particular eloquence in *The House of Mirth*, whose upper-class Lily Bart rethinks her attitudes toward "obscure humanity" when she mingles with members of a working girls' club:

> Lily had never conceived of these victims of fate otherwise than in the mass. That the mass was composed of individual lives, innumerable separate centres of sensation, with her own eager reachings for pleasure, her own fierce revulsions from pain—that some of these bundles of feeling were clothed in shapes not so unlike her own, with eyes meant to look on gladness, and young lips shaped for love—this discovery gave Lily one of those sudden shocks of pity that sometimes decentralize a life.

The change in Lily is ephemeral; she visits the club just a few times before drifting away. But as Wharton probably realized—her philanthropist sister-in-law Mary Cadwalader Jones studied working girls' clubs in the mid-1890s—ladies who socialized with club members on an ongoing basis were profoundly altered by the contact. Was pity the catalyst? Maybe; but that's not what they said, nor club members either. The consensus, rather, was that cross-class friendship made club sponsors smarter, not more sentimental; it allowed them, as the Springfield club delegate put it, "to broaden their ideas of life," to see beyond what their own narrow experience taught. And the more they knew of working women's worlds, the quicker sponsors were to endorse recent changes in club governance, education, and recreation.[31]

This is not to say that cross-class friendship was merely an instrument. While club members used it to educate sponsors and sponsors used it to get educated, both groups genuinely identified with each other. That was unmistakable at the 1894 convention's opening sessions, where both defined sisterhood across class lines as club life's chief benefit. Virtually every speaker agreed with the lady who declared that club sisters had "come to know that womanhood is everywhere the same, and that forward movement means movement all along the line." What made this discovery significant and stirring, however, was the recognition that not everyone was the same in the same way; women were not all identical. As a Shawmut Avenue Club member said of club sponsors, "They must see life from our standpoint to know what we most need, and to do that they must be friends, not patrons, and in helping us they help themselves." Understandings of working women's situation did not come naturally to club sponsors, in other words; they had to listen very hard to figure things out, and their willingness to listen served them as much as it did club members. Sisterhood based on homogeneity was everyday stuff, but sisterhood amid class disparities—*that* was worth shouting about. It disproved the notion that workers were inherently inferior to the upper classes. A member of Springfield's club made that point: "We find the bonds of common humanity stronger than the surface division of caste." In addition to refuting conservative dogma, club members' and sponsors' unity suggested that they had it in them to remake the whole world. A lady from the Friendship Club in Troy, New York, thought, for example, that the club movement might someday spark a millennium that replaced class conflict, religious intolerance, and other social divisions with an "all-embracing religion of love." No one had imagined such things in 1890, but so much had changed since then that anything seemed possible.[32]

The idea that women were "everywhere the same" did not deny class differences. Rather, it expressed the conviction that both working- and upper-class women had something to gain from an alliance. Class differences seemed less significant than in the past, however, and not just because club members and sponsors were making friends. As chapter 4 explores, friendship illuminated significant parallels in their aspirations as daughters of labor and daughters of privilege, and therein lay the foundation for oneness of a more pointed sort than has been described thus far.

Grace Dodge, ca. 1910. (Special Collections, Milbank
Memorial Library, Teachers College, Columbia
University)

Club members at the 38th Street Society, New York City, ca. 1890.
(Special Collections, Milbank Memorial Library, Teachers College, Columbia
University)

A millinery class at the Progressive Club, New York City, ca. 1894. (*Scribner's Magazine*, May 1894)

Dressmaking at the Progressive Club, New York City, ca. 1894. (*Scribner's Magazine*, May 1894)

A typewriting class at
the Prospect Hill Club,
New York City, ca. 1894.
(*Scribner's Magazine*,
May 1894)

New York City club members at a music drill (calisthenics
class) in University Place Hall, ca. 1894. (*Scribner's Magazine*,
May 1894)

After the music drill. (*Scribner's Magazine*, May 1894)

Grace Dodge and members of the 38th Street Society assembled for a "practical talk." (Special Collections, Milbank Memorial Library, Teachers College, Columbia University)

Club sponsors from the Massachusetts Association of Women Workers, ca. 1910. Back row, left to right: Amelia Ames, Julia Frothingham, and an unidentified woman; front row, left to right: O. M. E. Rowe, Edith Howes, and Elizabeth Eustis. (Schlesinger Library, Radcliffe College)

Marion Niles (left), sponsor of the Community Club of Newton Lower Falls, and Ethel Hobart (right), administrative secretary of the Massachusetts Association of Women Workers, ca. 1914. (Schlesinger Library, Radcliffe College)

The cast of an historical pageant performed by members and friends of the Community Club, Newton Lower Falls, Massachusetts, September 14, 1914. (Schlesinger Library, Radcliffe College)

Leaders of the National League of Women Workers at the NLWW convention held at Wellesley College, June 1918. Left to right: Sarah Ollesheimer (retiring president, incoming first vice president), Jean Hamilton (chief administrative secretary), and Fannie Pollak (incoming president). (*Club Worker*, July 1918)

A party at the Valley Girls' Club, Arctic, Rhode Island, ca. 1921. (*Club Worker*, April 1921)

CHAPTER 4

The Woman Question

No social question garnered more attention in working girls' clubs than the "woman question," and on no front did club members and sponsors stake out richer common ground. The potential for unity had seemed slight as long as upper-class women dominated club governance and used every platform at their command to promote "true womanhood." Club members of that era had called themselves "true women" to signal their respectability; but sponsors' version of the ideal—its overweening emphasis on domesticity in particular—had never acquired much of a following. Once the members started to govern, a more radical and, as it turned out, unifying set of concerns emerged. Challenges to orthodox opinion on woman's proper place abounded in club publications; club programs promoted working women's violations of gender conventions; and the new agenda got active backing from ladies who had just recently been marching to a very different beat. These patterns came most strikingly to the fore in regard to three issues: housework, marriage, and club experiments with mixed-sex recreation.

HOUSEWORK

Club members' comments about housework nudged sponsors away from their initial efforts to make training for housewifery the center of club education and drew them toward members' negative views of domestic service. Out of this came a general consensus in defense of working women's right to choose extra-domestic activities over housework.

The new climate encouraged the expression on club members' part of more daring opinions as well.

In the 1880s and early nineties, ladies associated with working girls' clubs devoted their best energies to upgrading the membership's home-making skills through practical talks on housework, cooking and sewing classes, and regular *Far and Near* articles on domestic topics. Club members responded with little enthusiasm. Those who intended to marry in the near future flocked to cooking classes; and the promise of better wardrobes made dressmaking and millinery classes quite popular. To sponsors' dismay, though, there was very little rank-and-file interest in studying the proper way to make a bed, use a washboard, embroider a pillowcase, and so on. When *Far and Near* invited club members to suggest household topics they might study at the clubs' summer vacation lodges, the call went unanswered. And the scarcity of letters received by the author of *Far and Near*'s column on home decoration with fancy needlework moved her to ask, "What is the matter with you girls? Why don't you talk, either to ask or to give some facts?" No one replied, it seems; but an earlier letter to the journal's editors suggests one answer to the question. "Mother makes the beds and does the cooking," a club member wrote, "and if I wipe the supper dishes before going to the club, I think I do well enough, and mother thinks so, too, and realizes that bed-making and dish-washing are a weariness to the flesh after a long day at a machine or behind a counter, and that the daughter who is supporting herself and helping to support the family is doing quite her share." This family division of labor—the typical arrangement in club members' households—gave domestic training a very limited utility, at least in the short run.[1]

But what of the future? How would club members handle their prospective responsibilities as housewives and mothers? This was the sponsors' main worry, and it led many of them not only to proselytize on behalf of domestic education in the clubs but also to recommend that the members exchange industrial and sales jobs for work that would presumably prepare them for homemaking. In some cities, sponsors established employment bureaus that steered club members toward domestic service, as ladies throughout the movement set out to eradicate the members' belief that domestic service was undesirable. A few, such as the anonymous author of *Far and Near*'s "Household Corner" for October 1891, urged working women to abandon wage labor altogether and become stay-at-home apprentices to their mothers.[2]

These zealous attempts to domesticate club members certainly harmonized with orthodoxies regarding woman's place; but sponsors' dedication to the cause was less an expression of deference to gender orthodoxy than a sign of their faith in upper-class nostrums for working-class problems. The notion that resourceful housekeeping could make poverty cozy was tirelessly promoted in charity societies, where some sponsors had worked for a short spell before joining the clubs. In the early 1880s, for example, Grace Dodge had drawn the following lessons from her mentors at New York's State Charities Aid Association: "What the poor need is to be taught providence, thrift, cleanliness, and management. The women do not know how to spend money properly nor the science of making happy homes. They need to be taught these necessary things." In the early 1890s, the same maxims were taken up by the nascent home economics movement, whose adherents—soon to win national fame with an 1893 World's Fair exhibit that claimed to show how a family of six could live comfortably on five hundred dollars a year—were invited by club sponsors to pen lessons in domestic science for the initial issues of *Far and Near.* Bowing to conventional wisdom as to how the "other half" could best be helped, club sponsors endorsed any and all schemes for increasing working women's homemaking skills.[3]

Sponsors had the capacity, however, to look at the question of domestic education through a very different lens. As women who had chosen alternatives to the sheltered, home-centered life led by most of their class sisters, they knew firsthand what it meant to be deprived of educational opportunities consistent with this choice. In the late nineteenth century only a handful of ladies associated with working girls' clubs enjoyed the benefits of higher education; and the barriers that kept most club sponsors from emulating this group stand out clearly in its members' personal histories.

Consider, for example, Florence Kelley and Dr. Eliza Mosher. Kelley, a founder of Philadelphia's New Century Guild, managed to enter Cornell University, where she earned a bachelor's degree in 1882, only because her parents consented to hire a battery of home tutors. "There was," she later recalled, "no school in Philadelphia equipped to fit a girl thoroughly for college, low as the standard of entrance requirements then was." Her year's work with the guild filled time she had hoped to devote to graduate study at the University of Pennsylvania. Its classics department, where she wished to prepare for law school, rebuffed her application with the explanation that men and women did not belong together in the classroom. Encouraged by her family to study overseas if necessary, Kelley finally earned a law degree at the University of Zurich.

Eliza Mosher, a regular speaker in Brooklyn's working girls' clubs, ran a similar obstacle course complicated by a lack of family encouragement and some burdensome family responsibilities. After attending a Quaker academy instead of a college, she studied medicine over the vociferous objections of kin. Since no medical school would accept her, she apprenticed herself to the interns at a Boston women's hospital but was compelled to leave after a year, when the family summoned her to nurse her dying mother. Still ineligible for medical school, she followed the stint at home with a second apprenticeship, this one to a woman doctor in private practice. Only then did Mosher meet entrance requirements for course work leading to an M.D., which she earned at the University of Michigan in 1875. Whatever their desires with regard to higher education, precious few club sponsors had the wherewithal to match such exemplary achievements.[4]

The vast majority—whose families were less supportive than Kelley's and whose temperaments were less rebellious than Mosher's—made do, then, with schooling designed to create charming mistresses for upper-class homes. Grace Dodge's experience was typical. While her brothers prepped for Princeton University, she studied letter writing, music, and the like with home tutors and spent one year at Miss Porter's famous Connecticut finishing school, where, as another alumna of her vintage later reported, "some of the teaching . . . received was the world's worst." The elder Dodges did not believe that women should go to college. Most club sponsors' parents felt the same; and their failure to provide daughters and sons with equal schooling gave club members a fertile field for changing sponsors' ideas as to the type of education appropriate for working girls.[5]

As New York City's Sarah Minturn suggested in an address to the 1890 convention, she and many other sponsors had been attracted to club work precisely because it afforded otherwise unattainable opportunities for intellectual growth. Homebound women, she argued,

> are said to be ever ready to take offence, to be petty in their judgments, and to look at life only from their individual stand-point. Do not all these faults develop naturally from their isolated position and narrow sphere, and do they not show how necessary it is that by some means women should come into closer contact with other minds, have some share in the training which

comes from acting with a number of people for a common purpose? It is indeed most important, not only for its effect on the character of women, but for the sake of any cause they may wish to further.

Ladies hoping to educate themselves for social usefulness were but one step away from conceding that working girls, too, should study things other than domestic topics; and by the mid-1890s, club members' calls for more liberal educational programs had won many a sponsor's support.[6]

The consequent deemphasis on preparation for housewifery drew fire from guest speakers at the 1894 convention's session on domestic service. Mrs. C. H. Stone from St. Louis argued, "An education in the rudiments of house and home keeping is one of the crying needs for every girl and woman, no matter what is being said to the contrary by many intelligent people; and it is the frequent absence of this idea in the working girls' clubs that mars this otherwise well-planned movement." The clubs, Stone contended, ought to downplay "book-learning" and provide instead a "wholesale education in the rudiments of housework," so that club members could train not only for housewifery but also for domestic service. Similar pleas came from Ellen Richards, the leader of the home economics movement, and from a lady representing the Boston YWCA's Domestic Training School for servants.[7]

Helen Iselin Henderson, a sponsor of New York City's Endeavor Club, delivered the reply. She began by observing, "One hears on all sides to-day, from unthinking and even from thinking men and women, such words as these: 'You say to us that the life of a factory girl is a hard one. . . . Why does not your factory girl go into domestic service where she will have a comfortable home, healthy work, and good pay?'" Club sponsors had wondered about that same question just a few years earlier. Now that they were talking *with* club members instead of *at* them, the answers seemed quite obvious. "One of the principal causes of repugnance felt by a factory girl to 'living out,'" Henderson reported, "is that the work is never-ending, and that she has no time each day to call her own." This was the main point the members made in virtually every club roundtable on domestic service. Pressing another of their favorite points, Henderson also noted that servants, who received a good part of their wages in the form of room and board, could contribute less than other working women to family coffers. The only thing she said in favor of domestic service echoed club members' opinions as well; she proposed, as they often did, that it could be a "blessing" to young women who would otherwise live alone. So much for the idea, once prevalent among club sponsors, that a household job was the best job for any woman worker.[8]

Sponsors' new visions of domestic service went hand in hand with a new sympathy for club members' preference for "book-learning" over domestic education. The expanding array of club classes in the liberal arts testified to that sympathy. Most of them were taught by sponsors, and club members organized quite a few of these classes at a sponsor's suggestion. This change in club meeting rooms was reflected in the pages of *Far and Near*, which was edited and largely authored by a committee of ladies prominent in the movement. From the journal's debut in the fall of 1890 to its demise four years later, there was a steady decline in the volume of articles on domestic subjects and increase in the number of pieces on literature, political economy, and natural science. The editorial stance underwent a similar change. *Far and Near* began as a diligent advocate of domestic virtues, but that theme was rarely sounded after the first year or so. In 1893, for instance, when the editors ran an essay contest on "How to Succeed in Life," they awarded the only prizes to a pair of club members whose lists of necessary virtues—curiosity, education, ambition—included not a single plug for domestic skills or love of home. There was now a general consensus in support of club members' formulas for self-improvement, in which domestic training played a negligible role.[9]

Sponsors also lent some support, or at least a respectful ear, to more radical thinking about housework. Echoing the argument a club member had made the previous year in *Far and Near*, M. E. J. Kelley told the 1894 convention that "families of working women . . . have no more right to expect the girls to assist with housework after they come home . . . than they have a right to expect it from the boys." A few months later, in the New Century Guild's newsletter, Eliza Turner—who had in the past missed few opportunities to tout homemaking—presented without editorial comment four letters in which guild members argued the advantages of newlywed couples living in boardinghouses. The chief advantage they identified was that the bride would not have to bother much with housework, which they saw as more tiring, isolating, and monotonous than in any way rewarding. Sponsors rarely voiced such iconoclastic views. Most continued to speak of housework as women's work; none went so far as to describe homemaking as mere drudgery. But their willingness to listen to club members' opinions, rather than preach about working women's need for more domestic know-how, created an atmosphere in which radical ideas could get a hearing.[10]

"THE TRAINING OF OUR FUTURE MEN"

Members' and sponsors' attitudes regarding men's involvement in club social life proved remarkably compatible as well. From the very start, club membership had reduced working women's need to depend on men for amusements. Building on this foundation, members and sponsors alike made female autonomy the cornerstone of all club experiments with heterosexual recreation—ventures that began in the early 1890s and multiplied steadily thereafter.

It was, as Lillian Betts noted, a "fixed idea" in club members' communities that young women should rely on men to treat them to amusements. This was in part a function of economic fact—women earned less than men and had less to spend on recreation—but it had the force of social custom, too. Daughters were expected to give their families a higher portion of their earnings than sons typically handed over. And any man worth his salt was supposed to treat the woman on his arm, even if she could afford to pay her own way. For all of these reasons, the arrangement Betts described was as fixed in practice as it was in theory.[11]

Club sponsors initially saw male treats as a threat to the recipients' sexual purity. As Dodge warned in an 1887 book of morally uplifting letters to working girls: "It is dangerous as well as wrong . . . to put yourselves in any way in a man's power." If he paid for your night on the town, she warned, he would probably expect sexual favors in return and might even drug your refreshments in order to break down your resistance. Many sponsors harbored similar fears in the club movement's early years. As they learned more about club members' lives, however, sponsors worried less about the sexual dangers of treating and more about its impact on working men's opinions of the opposite sex. Betts lamented, for example, "So small a matter as carfare will make a girl thrust herself on a young man's care. The girl will not resent indifference, even discourtesy, if only her aim is accomplished. The young men suffer the reflex of this attitude, and their estimate of women is regulated by these misconceptions." This new vision of treating's disadvantages was very much like club members' own.[12]

Describing the situation from their perspective, a member of the New Century Guild identified male pride as the treating problem's source and public disrespect for working women as its result. She wrote to the guild newsletter to quarrel with a brand of popular humor she called the "Great Ice Cream Joke"—newspaper caricatures of young women so hungry for

sweets that they soon emptied their escorts' pockets. "If we should pro-
pose to share the expenses," she complained, "the very cavaliers who go
home and grumble at the meanness of girls would feel, or profess to feel,
humiliated by such a proposition. What are we to do?" One answer to
this dilemma, and to the concerns voiced by Betts, was men's integration into club social life, for in that setting the women, via the club treasury, footed the bill.[13]

Assuming the financial burden, club members also claimed the right
to choose the amusements and determine the rules of etiquette that
would hold sway. In most cases, men were admitted to club sociables by
written invitation only. Chaperones were always present, and formal
receiving lines were common. These niceties went hand in hand with
refined entertainments. The typical gathering featured recitations, singing, dancing, lemonade, and ice cream. Sponsors were certainly pleased
with such arrangements, which appealed not only to their sense of propriety but also to their sense of obligation to share advantages custom-
arily reserved for daughters of the upper class. As the New Century
Guild's Eliza Turner proudly told the 1894 convention, the clubs' mixed
sociables gave members "the same opportunities for social intercourse,
and the same wholesome protection in that intercourse, as [are] provided for girls in society."

The staid atmosphere at these sociables was not only or even primarily a bow to sponsors' standards of decorum, however. Balls and pic-
nics organized by late nineteenth-century women's trade unions without the cooperation of genteel reformers were, by all accounts, similarly
restrained. When hostess roles gave them the power to set the tone of the
occasion, working women regularly opted for refinement, demanding
that the men behave in a more courtly way than usual. Club members
also expressed the hope that their demand for Sunday-best manners
would encourage boyfriends to mend their rowdy ways. Urging club
members to invite men to every one of their sociables, the Shawmut
Avenue Club's Lizzie Patterson declared at the 1894 convention: "Girls,
you have a great work before you—upon you depends the training of
our future men."[14]

The men responded ambivalently to club members' efforts on this
front. The steadily growing number of *Far and Near* reports on mixed
sociables suggests that it was not in most cases difficult to get men to join
the party, even when more raucous pleasures beckoned. A good crowd
showed up, for example, at the 1892 reception organized by Brooklyn's
Kindly Club to keep members' beaus out of the saloons on New Year's

Day. Yet some clubs complained that, despite warm invitations to various gatherings, men stayed away.[15]

That problem alarmed very few club sponsors. The eldest among them—ladies who had reached adolescence in the first half of the nineteenth century, when upper-class daughters' social lives were generally sex-segregated—promoted heterosexual recreation in hopes that it would discourage romantic escapades. According, for instance, to Eliza Turner (b. 1826), the more regularly young men and women got together, the less likely they were to succumb to the "insane glamour which wrecks so many lives,—the 'falling in love.'" Such assertions made little sense, however, to the younger majority of sponsors for whom club work provided an alternative to the heterosexual social whirl that enveloped Gilded Age debutantes. As this younger set saw things, the danger was not too little but too much mixing with the opposite sex, for constant contact with men seemed to make the debutante a lesser woman. She had, according to *Far and Near*, "no time for . . . quiet thought, sober reading, spiritual 'stock-taking,' no time for self-sacrifice, for usefulness." Sponsors who had become club activists to escape the fate of "society girls" were noticeably less enthusiastic than the older group about opening club sociables to men. Reluctance soon gave way to compliance, however, and even, in some quarters, devotion to the cause, for club members' postures toward the men whose company they sought in no way resembled those of obsequious society belles.[16]

Club members did, to be sure, press the invitations they issued and, despite some sponsors' wishes, made mixed-sex sociables weekly affairs in quite a few clubs. The norm, though, was to entertain men just once a month; and there were very few cries of discontent with all-female sociables or sorrow at rejected requests for men's presence. To the contrary, club members often strutted their enjoyment of get-togethers unattended by men. At the 1889 reunion of New York City clubs, for example, Dodge received thunderous applause when she said of their recent New Year gala in Madison Square Garden with women only: "We danced and had such fun, and there wasn't a man present! Wasn't it nice!" Her audience so clearly agreed that the *New York Times* printed its report on the reunion under the headline "Men Are Excluded." Even in the 1890s, when they were regularly inviting men to their sociables, club members took pains to show the public—the male public in particular—that it was easy to have fun without men. The message might be delivered in a humorous manner, as when Boston clubs sent *Far and Near* the following joke:

> Chair—"Any young women who like to ask friends to the excursion are more than welcome to do so. Bring as many as you like—sisters, cousins and aunts.
> From the Floor—"Any brothers?
> Chair—"Well—no—because there's a boycott, you know."

Behind such jokes stood a serious point, as the New Century Guild's Dressmakers' Association stressed in a newsletter report on one of its many all-female parties: "The thought is expressed that if some of the men who laugh at women's parties had been present they might have changed their opinion as to the dryness or lack of amusement at a party of the sisterhood." By broadcasting the idea that good times felt just as good when men did not participate, club members helped keep their pride intact when men were invited but did not show up.[17]

Something more was at stake, too. Such broadcasts enhanced club members' power to enforce their rules of etiquette for mixed gatherings by threatening that, if the men did not mind their manners, they would be barred from future get-togethers. When threats failed to do the trick, action followed. As one club reported, "If [men] are at all discourteous, the girls are offended and at the next business meeting suggest that that special group of young men be dropped from our invitation list." Brooklyn's Asacog Club seems to have banned all males after two used counterfeit invitations to attend a sociable that took place just days after an "indignation meeting" protesting men's coarse language at a previous party. It was rarely necessary to ban anyone, however. Given club members' obvious readiness to stick to parties "of the sisterhood," most men behaved themselves when they were included.[18]

Though they were hardly identical, club members' and sponsors' attitudes toward heterosexual recreation certainly harmonized. Male treats were a problem for working women in both groups' eyes: an injury to pride according to the members, a hindrance to decorum according to the sponsors. For similar reasons—members' wishes to be treated like ladies and sponsors' commitments to ladylike rules of conduct—both regarded the refinement prevailing at mixed-sex club sociables as a must. Elderly sponsors' formula for discouraging foolhardy love affairs meanwhile dovetailed with members' desire to open club entertainments to men. And though younger sponsors were more wary at putting out the welcome mat, their distaste for the man-centered world of debutantes guaranteed staunch support for club members' refusals to toady to male guests. Virtually everyone helped in one way or another to construct an atmosphere that promised to train men away not only from rowdiness but also from expectations of female deference.

MARRIAGE

The most explicit challenges to male privilege and strongest endorsements of female autonomy occurred in club discussions of marriage. Sponsors had used their old platforms as discussion leaders to set a very different tone, sermonizing on the joys awaiting a domestically skilled bride and inviting club members to respond in kind. Now that member-controlled roundtables were the rule, new themes emerged. Negative appraisals of the working-class housewife's labor conditions overshadowed testimony on the joys of skilled homemaking; and a bride's need for domestic know-how got far less heed than her need for a husband whose loving attentions would offset housewifery's burdens. If this disappointed club sponsors, they kept it to themselves, and most probably sympathized with the opinions that club members were now airing. Sponsors' constant reminders that marriage meant work had clearly taken root, albeit in an unexpected way; and members' consequent standards for judging prospective husbands—standards that might well price a woman out of the marriage market—paralleled the self-assertive attitudes that sponsors displayed as independent wives and proudly contented spinsters.

Hoping to whet rank-and-file interest in domestic education, club sponsors had in the old days bombarded the members with lectures identifying expert housekeeping as the key to marital happiness. Lillian Betts delivered one of the more eloquent testaments on that subject when she gave an 1888 reunion of New York City clubs the following account of her discoveries as a "friendly visitor" to working-class homes:

> The richest woman I ever saw had five children, and a husband earning one dollar and twenty-five cents per day. . . . I never saw more beautiful, healthy-looking children. The home is as clean as broom, soap and water can make it; the mother the picture of health and happiness. . . . What was the secret of her content, her happiness? She had the knowledge necessary to fill her position of wife and mother. She was the only mother, of two hundred and forty-four visited, that cut and made the garments worn by herself and children; one of five who could make bread, and the only one who did make it. She had used her every opportunity, and was reaping a full harvest.

From sponsors' standpoint, the moral of such tales was obvious: working women foresighted enough to acquire the requisite skills were sure to glory in their future roles as homemakers. This was not the moral that club members drew, however. The incessant talk about a housewife's workload did, by members' own accounts, win them away from romantic daydreams of matrimony as an escape from long hours of wearisome labor. They were hardly inclined, however, to replace fantasies of married ease with visions of brooms, suds, ovens, and such as the stuff of wedded bliss.[19]

They mused instead about the joys of a loving spousal relationship. Even those few club members whose statements on marriage echoed sponsors' calls for domestic education defined tending the home as a way of tending the husband. A member of the 38th Street Society declared, for example, that "a girl whose natural domestic tastes have been carefully and properly trained, whether at the Club or in the home circle, strives to make the home the most attractive of all places to her husband, and to carefully study his needs and moods, with an earnest aim to strengthen and help him with all the patience and charity that her nature is or can be made capable of." Though most club members probably agreed that husbands should be cherished, the typical commentator focused on the other side of the coin, emphasizing a man's obligation to compensate his wife for all the homemaking she did on his behalf. The predominant recipe for marital happiness was far less labor-intensive, then, than that proposed by advocates of domestic education; its main ingredient was neither elbow grease nor wifely "patience and charity" but an attentive and helpful man.[20]

A toast from the Girls' Union of Ithaca, New York, to newlywed club sisters—"The Girls Who Have Married and Left Us"—illustrates the connection between club members' awareness of wifely burdens and demands with respect to husbands.

> Girls, who wants to live in a room six by seven,
> And cook and fry for two?
> For my part I don't call it heaven
> To live in such misery; do you?
>
> I would rather work for one
> As long and as hard as I can,
> Than support myself before marriage
> And after support my man.

Then there is danger of marrying a drunkard,
A man who goes this way and that;
Who never will spare you a dollar,
To buy a new dress or hat.

Then while with your foot the cradle you rock,
He reads or sleeps at his ease;
And with cut and burned fingers you mend the socks
Your beautiful husband to please.

But the girls who have married and left us
Don't have such husbands as this;
Their husbands are men of promise,
Men the world would miss.

The reference to a wife supporting her husband was a half joke. Married women who earned money by taking in boarders, engaging in industrial homework, or holding jobs outside the home were plentiful in some sectors of the working class, but not in the strata from which most club members came. While she might reasonably count on being free from paid employment, however, a club bride knew she would labor hard and long. Though her home was probably more spacious than a "room six by seven," it usually lacked electricity and hot running water; and the household budget rarely covered many labor-saving expenditures, especially once babies started arriving. Housekeeping under these conditions was not only more hellish than heavenly but also more arduous as a rule than the husband's job. His workday, no matter how backbreaking, was finite; the housewife's was, as the old saying goes, "never done." Her work, moreover, could be just as strenuous as his. As a New Century Guild member told a man who came to the club to debate women's physical fitness for carpentry, "a day at the wash-tub was a pretty good test of muscular power." After such a day, an evening with a mending basket and a fretful baby was a pretty good test of stamina—a greater test than most men had to endure. Reviewing these facts of married life, club members might well conclude in all seriousness that homemakers, even if they never earned a penny, contributed more to their households than did wage-earning husbands.[21]

Only "men of promise," then, could make marriage attractive. It went without saying that the suitable candidate earned enough to keep his wife out of the labor market. What club members stressed were his qualifications as a companion. He had to be, as the toast implies, the sort of man who would spend his leisure hours at home instead of a saloon, spend his spare dollars on his wife as well as himself, put down his evening newspaper to help her mind the baby, and forgo a nap to keep her company while she darned his socks. He had, in short, to be the sort of man who would treat his wife as a cherished partner instead of a workhorse. This was a mighty tall order; and the men who did not measure up were hard to weed out because suitors generally did their best to seem as promising as possible. To settle knowingly, however, for a man who fell short of the standard was to volunteer for a truly miserable fate in light of the inescapable burdens of keeping house on a working-class budget. Acknowledging those realities, club members wanted husbands whose assistance would reduce the drudgery and whose respectful, affectionate ways would make it feel worthwhile.[22]

Rank-and-file pronouncements on matrimony almost always endorsed a spousal relationship that called for a lot more than wage-earning on the man's part. The most popular theme was that wives should beware of self-forgetfulness and husbands try hard to oblige and console. These were lessons club members drew from their mothers' lives as well as sponsors' reminders about housewifery's demands. As a member of the 38th Street Society commented in an essay presented at a practical talk on securing domestic happiness: "Instances have been known where the mother took too much responsibility on herself and so made the husband weak and careless. . . . There are cares which the woman alone must bear, but if her choice of a husband is a man willing to help and cheer her, he will brighten her life to such an extent that her cares will be forgotten in fond companionship with her husband."

A more radical stream of opinion surfaced as well. Some commentators flatly declared their unwillingness to put up with bossy husbands and typically added complaints regarding working girls' status in their families of origin. A member of the New Century Guild contributed the following in its newsletter, for example: "Independence is to be admired in women as well as men, and the woman who devotes a part of her time to work in preference to living in idleness at the expense of her male relatives deserves all the credit she can get and a great deal more, and when she marries she does not like to feel that she is, as it were, going into harness with a man to drive her but to feel rather that she is one of a double team." A double-team arrangement was a small thing to ask, perhaps, but as this writer clearly knew, it was more than a great many wives had. Whether "men of promise" were defined in terms of helpfulness and sympathy or a capacity to treat women as equals, club members applied a demanding standard.[23]

Demographic patterns in club members' communities did not support such choosiness on the part of would-be brides. In the industrial Northeast, where most clubs were located, the women of marriageable age well outnumbered the men, and the imbalance was greatest among American-born descendants of northwestern Europe. Given the undersupply of potential husbands in their neighborhoods, one might expect club members to ask for less in the way of manly charms or wifely independence. Club life encouraged a demanding stance, however, not only by reminding working women that marriage would mean even more work but also by putting them in touch with some enviably independent upper-class wives.[24]

Club sponsors' ranks included a significant minority of married women who, far from being harnessed to their homes and husbands, threw themselves into extra-domestic life. Chicago's Bonnie Winthrow, a founder of the Ogontz Club, was probably the most dramatic case in point. When she married Lynden Evans in the mid-1890s, physicians advised the bride that her husband, always in delicate health, was nearing death's door and would require painstaking care. She responded by giving herself a crash course in nutrition, which helped her keep the groom alive for another thirty years. Instead of retiring into the kitchen or sickroom, however, she expanded her activities away from home. In addition to continuing work with the Ogontz Club, Bonnie Winthrow Evans became a devoted member of the Fortnightly (an upper-class women's club), launched the Chicago School of Domestic Arts and Sciences, and served as founding president of a citywide association of working girls' clubs—all within the first few years of her marriage.[25]

Newlywed activists were relatively rare. Most of Evans's counterparts—sponsors who entered the movement as single women just recently out of school—retired from club work if they married. Matrimony did not necessarily douse the independent spirits that had led them beyond the haunts of debutantes; as one retiree's husband later recalled, "I never had any influence with her." But such things were invisible to club members if the lady in question dropped out of club work. In addition to rarities like Evans, though, there were a good many slightly older sponsors who came to the clubs already married and whose independence supplied the membership with considerable food for thought. Among the leading lights of the New York Association of Working Girls' Societies (NYAWGS), for instance, were Mrs. Henry Ollesheimer, president of the Ivy Club, chief organizer and executive of a sick benefit fund for members of NYAWGS clubs, and a pillar of New York's Society for

Ethical Culture; Mrs. Richard Irvin, secretary of both the 38th Street Society and the NYAWGS and an officer of numerous Episcopal Church
women's leagues and nursing homes; and Mrs. Archibald Alexander,
president of the Industrial Society of Hoboken, the New Jersey correspon-
dent for *Far and Near,* a director of the NYAWGS, a member of the boards
of several state asylums, and eventually a probation officer, too. Club
federations based in Brooklyn, eastern Pennsylvania, Connecticut, Massachusetts, and Illinois tapped the energies of similar cadres of impeccably respectable married ladies whose lifestyles suggested that there
was nothing disgraceful in a wife's devoting herself to something more
than housekeeping.[26]

If Ollesheimer and her cohorts refused to let matrimony prevent them
from getting out and about, then a self-consciously respectable club
member could aim without compunction to do the same. She could also,
according to some married club sponsors, expect a tenacious interest in
extra-domestic affairs to help her honeymoon last a lifetime. As Eliza
(Mrs. Joseph) Turner declared, "Every husband . . . likes to have his coat
kept whole and to be met with a smile, but as soon as he finds out that
the angel in the house can do nothing *but* mend and smile, he will want
to spend more evenings at his club than he would if she could make
herself good company; and to do that, to be a lively companion, an intelligent sympathizer, a judicious counsellor, she must sometimes get out
of her chimney corner." To daughters of the many working-class communities where saloons and lodges were nightly filled with men who had
left their spouses at home, the report that husbands were more endur-
ingly attentive to worldly wives made the independence enjoyed by ladies like Ollesheimer and Turner all the more attractive.[27]

A working-class woman wishing to follow their example confronted
some sobering realities, though. Unlike sponsors, who had servants to keep
the home fires burning, club members who wed were often so busy with
mending, mothering, and other chores that it was all but impossible to
stray far from the chimney corner. Brides almost always resigned their club
memberships, in large part because they preferred to spend evenings with
their husbands but also because housework absorbed so much time, energy, and attention. Its demands were certainly evident in the activities of
the housewives' groups formed in a few large clubs where "domestic circles" gathered one afternoon a week while sponsors looked after the children. To get away from housework and child care for a spell was one thing,
to get housework and child care off one's mind was quite another. The
agenda of the Domestic Circle of the 38th Street Society, for example, fea-

tured short courses in cooking, sewing children's clothing, and handmaking household decorations; lectures on childrearing and home nursing; and a series of roundtables on cleaning methods. The circles' members were clearly wrapped up in domestic life whether or not they liked it, and several of their discussion topics—"The Bright Side of Suffering," for example, and "What Does a Woman Need that She Does Not Receive"—suggest that some of them did not like it much at all. Aware of these discontents, unwed club members meanwhile organized talks on subjects such as "How to Be Pleasant though Married." While contact with married sponsors invited thoughts about the rewards of avoiding a domestic rut, reports on the doings of domestic circles highlighted the odds against a working-class woman grasping those rewards, no matter how independent her spirit.[28]

One could dream of beating the odds by wedding a man with the financial means to, as a New Century Guild member wistfully put it, "commence housekeeping on such a scale that the wife will not be obliged to take the position of a household drudge." That scale was usually beyond a couple's means, however; and no matter what the case at the start of her marriage, domestic drudgery was just about inevitable for a working-class housewife with children. All the more reason, then, to hold out for "men of promise," who were not only egalitarian enough to grant a wife's right to get out of the house on a regular basis but also considerate enough to remain attentive despite the inevitable reduction in her premarital allure as a woman with extra-domestic involvements aplenty.[29]

The expansion of club recreational programs gave an additional boost to members' standards for prospective husbands by making realistic images of housewifery more palatable and the wait for a promising man more enjoyable. As a member of the 38th Street Society explained,

> It is a sad truth that too many brides forget the seriousness of the marriage tie, and think chiefly of the change from labor to supposed ease. But how is it with us *now,* since we have become Club members? Oh, the happy, happy change that came with our initiation! At last we have found a place where we could spend pleasant evenings. Pretty rooms, music, dancing[,] reading, laughter, all help to throw off the burden of the day, and we return home rested and cheered, and surprised to find that we could be so young and gay.

Boredom and exhaustion on the job encouraged working women to think of any man who could support a housewife as a good catch. The more fun they had at the clubs, however, the more likely members were to consider the drawbacks of rushing into marriage.[30]

Some club members wondered, in fact, why they should marry at all. A number of the most prominent club sponsors—Grace Dodge, Massachusetts Association of Working Girls' Clubs Societies president Edith Howes, and *Far and Near*'s editor-in-chief Maria Chapin, to name a few— were confirmed spinsters. So were many of the working women who stepped forward as leaders when democratization broke up sponsors' monopoly on club governance. Occupying positions of authority and esteem within the clubs, such women supplied living proof that matrimony was not a girl's only route to prestige in middle age. These lessons-by-example were accompanied by verbal jabs at the conventional notion that spinsterhood was tragic and shameful. When critics predicted that working girls' clubs would turn their members into "old maids," unmarried sponsors responded by reporting that women could live quite contentedly without husbands. As one lady concluded in a *Far and Near* story about a spinster who enjoyed a successful career as a concert singer and an equally rewarding personal life: "Just now some old gentlemen and happily married women may be saying that our clubs . . . will soon be 'Old Maids' Paradises.' We hope that many a happy marriage of club members will prove them to be quite in the wrong, but we thank them for connecting the word 'paradise' with perpetual maidenhood, for it shows that we have, after all, fallen on liberal days when a woman, either as a 'spinster,' 'wife,' or 'relict,' can create, unaided, her own Earthly Paradise." Not only content but also proud to go it alone, wage earners in some clubs joined with sponsors to form "Ancient Orders of Spinsters," unabashedly advertising their supposedly humiliating marital status.[31]

In this conducive atmosphere, a few club members even went so far as to argue that "old maids" were actually much better off than wives— especially those with distinctly unpromising husbands. Unmarried women, declared one satisfied spinster,

> can say "Yes, I will do so and so," or "No, I will not do so and so," instead of "Well, you know, I can't say until I hear what my husband says," which is, of course, quite right when it is remembered that the husband generally supports his wife and children. . . . We are not kept to the grindstone of breakfast, dinner, and supper, making and mending, or sitting up nights with Baby teething, or Johnnie with the mumps, and then being told by Hubby in the morning that he will have to look out for a young wife. No going out evenings, because Hubby goes alone. He can't be bothered with waiting till all the children are in bed, and, then too, he couldn't have as good a time if wife was along. We single women can go anywhere we choose. . . . No longer ago than our late war [the Civil

War], it was mostly "old maids" who braved the horrors of the hospital tents, and our trained nurses and noble sisters of Charity are almost without exception single women; so hurrah for us!

These points, though rarely expressed so boldly, were nonetheless well taken by the mass of club members. While most clearly hoped to marry and were acutely aware of the man shortage that might deprive them of the chance, they still called for men more attractive than the "Hubby" described above. Those who became spinsters by choice or because a promising man never came along often struck outsiders as a pathetic lot. "One always grows sad when thinking about them," wrote Lillian Betts. In club meeting rooms, however, they were highly regarded.[32]

Club members' respectful views of spinsterhood and their demanding postures as prospective brides reflected trends at play outside the club movement. The rate of marriage among American women entering adulthood in the 1880s and nineties was the lowest ever: a little over one-tenth never wed. This is partially explained by geographical gender imbalances—an undersupply of men in the Northeast and women in the West. Since such imbalances were nothing new, however, attitudinal trends clearly entered the picture as well; and to judge from the divorce rate, women's critical thinking about matrimony lay at the heart of those trends. By the turn of the century, the annual number of divorces—most of them initiated by women—was expanding three times faster than the national population. Though investigators did not tabulate class-specific statistics on spinsterhood and divorce, they often noted that both were especially common in working-class communities, where women's "industrial emancipation" provided viable, even attractive, economic alternatives to marriage and imbued workers-turned-housewives with commensurately high expectations of their husbands. As Carroll Wright, the U.S. Commissioner of Labor, reported in 1892, "If a woman has the opportunity of supporting herself honorably while she is developing her intellectual and spiritual faculties, she is more likely to seek or to accept marriage relations which depend on the purest and highest elements of companionship." Club membership exaggerated this pattern in two crucial ways. It increased working women's opportunities to cultivate "intellectual and spiritual faculties," including a keen awareness of homemaking's burdens, and it invited them to ponder the lives of upper-class women who were remarkably independent wives or unapologetic spinsters. If club members' views on matrimony exemplified a larger wave of opinion, then, their associational life pushed them toward the wave's crest.[33]

"IDEAS WE NEVER THOUGHT WOULD
SEE THE LIGHT OF DAY"

Club members' and sponsors' oneness behind feministic positions on housework, heterosexual recreation, and marriage had several taproots. It derived in part from the fact that working women and those involved in volunteer activities were frequently classified as one by proponents of the idea that women belonged at home. By the mid-1890s, the popular press was avidly dissecting and, as a rule, disparaging the "New Woman" enthusiastically participating in extra-domestic life. Working girls, professional women, ladies active in women's clubs and reform causes: all came under fire as misfits and faddists. These criticisms lumped club members and sponsors together in a manner conducive to unity on the woman question. And the class prejudice that further undercut working girls' public image made this united front strategically useful to club members, whose departures from gender orthodoxy took on a more respectable air thanks to sponsors' cooperation. In the main, though, oneness emerged from members' and sponsors' discovery of common aspirations when democratization gave the working women a chance, as one of them observed, "to put into words the very ideas we never thought would see the light of day."[34]

Though oneness was new, the aspirations it reflected had always suffused both members' and sponsors' ranks. Working girls' clubs were from the very start a haven for women seeking alternatives to domestic confinement and subservience to men—two cardinal conventions of "true womanhood." Wage earners who declined household jobs and enjoyed getting out of the house after work mixed with ladies determined to make themselves useful and influential beyond the home. Just as club life reduced members' dependence on male-financed, male-dominated sociability, moreover, club work gave some sponsors substitutes for the man-centered activities of debutantes while increasing others' autonomy as wives. Unconventional opinions regarding women's proper place were quite literally unspeakable, however, until democratic club governance was not only a principle but also a practice. Sponsors' sovereignty within individual clubs and their corner on interclub communication muffled the voices of working women who, as later developments proved, had a great deal to say in behalf of nonconformity to the "true woman" ideal. Meanwhile, self-censorship stopped sponsors from articulating such ideas. Ruling over purportedly self-governing organizations, they had to present themselves as altruistic proxies for the wage-earning rank and file, and this precluded mention of the personal ambitions that propelled ladies out of their parlors and into club meeting rooms. Unable to speak their minds, members and sponsors could not come to a meeting of minds on the woman question, no matter how similar their attitudes in that regard.[35]

In fact, the very predilections they shared placed them often at cross purposes. Club members' distaste for housework stymied sponsors' efforts to make themselves socially useful by domesticating working girls. Though sponsors' behavior with respect to matrimony jibed with rank-and-file attitudes toward the opposite sex, their lectures on matrimony—the constant harping about the joys of fastidious homemaking—left club members cold. Men's absence from club sociables of that era appealed to sponsors critical of the debutantes' world but hampered members' ability to challenge male control of mixed-sex recreation. None of these contradictions could be resolved until democratization broke the silence veiling commonalities in members' and sponsors' definitions of woman's proper place.

Club members led the unveiling process. It was they who initiated club roundtables on domesticity's discontents, for instance; and their calls for female autonomy and gender equality were more bald-faced as a rule than those of sponsors. Candor proved contagious. Before very long, sponsors, too, let down their guard. "The club room is a place where we can be most truly ourselves," one of them told the 1894 convention. "We talk our hearts out there." The more freewheeling the discussions the clearer it became that many of the things in sponsors' hearts resembled ideas club members were finally bringing to light, especially ideas regarding housework, marriage, and men. From this common ground flowed programmatic reforms that vastly enhanced club life's value to workers: a reduced emphasis on the acquisition of domestic know-how, a host of new experiments with liberal education, and recreational activities that gave club members a means of "training . . . our future men," or as some might have said, building "men of promise." Here lay the most significant manifestations of cross-class sisterhood, whose practice depended on self-revelation by club members and sponsors alike. Sisterhood's origins went deeper than that, however; candor was unifying not in and of itself but thanks to the parallel concerns that working- and upper-class women had brought to the clubs in the first place.[36]

What more their common ground might yield remained to be seen. Club members had high expectations, for the changes afoot in club programs seemed to prove that, as one member put it, "the love of women for one another" could "walk straight through difficulties and accomplish anything." But attitudes toward domesticity, men, and marriage were not the most telling measure of sisterhood's strength. The real test would come when the club movement confronted social issues that did not affect members and sponsors in comparable ways—issues having to do with working women's lives on the job.[37]

CHAPTER 5

The Labor Question

Surveying the club movement in 1895, the journalist Helen Campbell predicted that this "sisterhood of women regardless of class or station" would soon place "the whole labor question . . . on a new footing." Campbell's credentials—she had published several renowned books on working women—gave her words an especially encouraging ring; but she was hardly alone in her optimism. Equally rosy forecasts abounded in club circles in the mid-1890s, when, after years of sponsors' foot-dragging, the movement's first labor reform projects were getting underway. While club sponsors provided the staff, the impetus for these projects came from workers, both the legions of club members whose labor conditions deteriorated during the depression of 1893–97 and various labor activists courting genteel allies in that period. Workers also determined each project's focus, pointing sponsors toward labor problems especially meaningful in club meeting rooms and toward cooperation with labor organizations. By the end of the decade, however, sponsors were laying plans on their own, and the projects they conceived had virtually nothing to offer club members or labor organizations. Shaped in part by trends in the labor movement, these twists in club history help to elucidate women workers' attitudes toward trade unionism in an era when they were notoriously difficult to unionize. What stand out most clearly, though, are the pitfalls of the organizational model embodied by working girls' clubs, where cross-class sisterhood yielded very little in the way of mutual answers to the labor question. Developments that brought the question to a head in club circles are the subject of this chapter; the results are explored in the next.[1]

SILENCES AND STALEMATES

As the Chicago labor activist Lizzie Swank Holmes observed, a great many late nineteenth-century working girls "preferred to . . . allow others to think that they were comfortably situated, quite well off, and needed no one's sympathy." Lunch boxes manufactured to look like books or scrolls of music were popular items; they promised to disguise a worker's identity as such when she traveled to and from her job. So did the fancy dresses or cloaks that covered quite a few travelers' workaday clothing. Especially anxious to keep up appearances, Holmes noted, were American-born daughters of families who had previously kept the womenfolk at home. When such workers—the backbone of the club movement—encountered club sponsors in the 1880s, they were exceedingly tight-lipped about material hardships.[2]

The reticence betokened not only pride but also distrust for ladies whose sermons in behalf of fastidious housekeeping made them sound suspiciously like emissaries from charity societies. By keeping mum, club members made it clear that they would not countenance the snooping and condescension for which "friendly visitors" were famous. At the initial meeting of the silk workers' discussion group that gave birth to the 38th Street Society, for example, the feeling from the floor was that Grace Dodge had organized the meeting in order to pry. As one worker reportedly told a companion, "She only wants to find out things to tell her rich friends. They'll laugh at us." Silence was the rule, then, in regard to poor working and living conditions; and in the 38th Street Society as well as other clubs, the silence lasted until sponsors' expressions of respect convinced members that it was safe to confide in them.[3]

Rank-and-file trust in sponsors grew very slowly at first, encouraged by the ladies' unfailing politeness but impeded by their presumptuous attempts to mold working girls into "truer" women. Given sponsors' control of club governance, moreover, workers no longer loath to speak up about material hardships did not necessarily have opportunities to do so. By the late 1880s, discussions of such things were regular fare in only a few clubs. Following the 1890 club convention, however, democratization and the steady subsidence of sponsors' propaganda in support of "true womanhood" untied workers' tongues movement-wide. Arrogant outsiders might still be told that working girls were doing fine. In 1892, for instance, the novelist Edgar Fawcett's insultingly melodramatic portrait of their "joyless lives" in New York City received the following reply from an Ivy Club member in *Far and Near:* "That New York City working girls are proverbially intelligent, moral and contented is conceded by all who are familiar with them, and if Mr. Fawcett will visit any of the working girls' clubs, where 2,000 of his so-called 'drudges from filthy tenements' assemble nightly, perhaps their sunny, cheerful and contented faces . . . may be a living contradiction to his exaggerated theories regarding them." It made sense to wear masks of contentment when confronting the likes of Fawcett; but in their talks with sponsors, "sunny, cheerful" club members had begun to voice deep dissatisfaction with their lives on the job and shortages of creature comforts at home.[4]

The programmatic result of this outpouring was a burst of cooperative efforts to help club members weather or escape the troubles they described. New York City clubs led the way, launching three such ventures in the winter of 1890–91: a garment shop, a sick benefit fund, and a job placement service. The Children's Dressmaking Company, a cooperative sewing room and retail shop organized by the Far and Near Society, eventually employed more than fifty club members who enjoyed an eight-hour day, freedom from the hated piece-wage system that paid workers according to output instead of hours on the job, training in custom clothing construction, and a third of any profits reaped. The Mutual Benefit Fund of the New York Association of Working Girls' Societies provided an income to subscribers out of work on account of illness. The association's Alliance Employment Bureau, which specialized in factory, sales, and clerical jobs, offered placement at a nominal fee to club members and other working women. Over the next few years, clubs throughout the movement, from its strongholds in the Northeast to its outposts in the Midwest, made material aid to the membership a vital part of their programs. By summer 1893, *Far and Near* had reported the establishment of emergency loan and sick benefit funds, downtown lunchrooms offering cheap hot meals to women who would otherwise make do with a cold snack, club bathrooms where workers living in cold-water homes could soak in a warm tub, employment committees that helped jobless club members find work, and "loan closets" that dispensed blankets, medical supplies, and healthful foods to those who took sick. There also appeared a host of new spelling, typewriting, and other classes that prepared club members to exchange manufacturing and sales jobs for office employment, where wages were higher, workdays shorter, the labor less grueling, and layoffs quite rare.[5]

Though most of these projects were organized, financed, and administered by club members, sponsors invariably lent a hand, and they supplied nearly all of the seed money and administrative energy for New York's elaborate flagship ventures and the lunchrooms opened in other cities. Backed by and in some cases dependent on club sponsors, the new activity deepened rank-and-file confidence in their potential as allies. It was not long, then, before club members were trying to stretch sponsors' concern with working women's economic welfare into a commitment to labor reform.

Very few sponsors doubted that labor conditions deserved their attention. As altruists accustomed to wealth, ease, and kid-glove treatment, most were deeply moved by club members' repeated complaints about low wages, sudden layoffs, ten-hour and longer workdays, violations of laws safeguarding workers' health, and the tyrannical rule of factory foremen and department store floorwalkers. Sponsors' concern with such problems did not automatically beget meaningful action, however. As Dodge confessed in a December 1891 newspaper exposé of labor problems that club members had recently brought to her attention, sponsors found it "difficult to answer the question as to how these wrongs can be righted." Indeed, they barely understood the question, for the knowledge that club members suffered wrongs on the job had not yet shaken sponsors' faith as moral reformers that virtue was ultimately rewarded in the labor market. Club members seeking help in their dealings with employers were regularly advised, therefore, to improve their performance as employees.[6]

Readers of *Far and Near* might well have concluded that it was pointless to ask sponsors for more useful types of assistance. The journal's first mention, in February 1891, of a club talk on labor conditions made the probability of rebuff quite clear. The Industrial Society of Hoboken, reported sponsor Caroline Alexander, had just discussed a new French law requiring employers to warn workers about impending layoffs. The club's members had unanimously agreed that such a law would be a great boon to American working girls, who in slack seasons opened every pay envelope in fear of finding a dismissal slip. Alexander conceded that the suspense was "horrible," but she felt obliged to speak in defense of employers, with whom she had conferred on the subject. "The girls," she declared, "do not seem to realize the inconvenience which they cause by leaving their places without giving any warning that they do not intend to return. . . . It cannot be expected that a contract so heedlessly broken by one party will be respected by the other." Women who be-

lieved as deeply as sponsors did in virtue's rewards and counted as many
businessmen as they did among their relatives and friends were likely
to counter virtually any complaint about working conditions with a complaint about workers.[7]

Underscoring that fact, an editorial in *Far and Near*'s very next issue
defined the improvement of working women, as opposed to their environments, as a vital club principle. Charges that the club movement did
too little to "make the daily struggle for existence any easier or safer for
its members" were entirely off the mark, the editors argued. "The answer
to this criticism is always the same and suggests itself at once. Our clubs
do not claim to solve all our problems or to smoothe away all our difficulties. We combine in them for our pleasure, our moral and mental improvement, but not with the hope of lessening the obstacles in our several paths, and only trusting that as we become better fitted to overcome
these obstacles they may seem to diminish." Did working women face
any obstacles too great for a diligent individual to scale? Not according
to an accompanying editorial assuring club members that "the outlook
is happy for the wage-earner who works with effort, concentration, thor-
oughness, attention to details and ambition." However questionable this
statement's veracity, the message behind it was irrefutably true: the outlook was bleak for any wage earner who hoped to turn club sponsors into
labor reformers.[8]

A wishful thinker might find reasons to believe they would soon come
around. Club sponsors were, after all, striving to ameliorate the effects
of bad working conditions; and during the spring and summer of 1891,
Far and Near published several articles in which sponsors proposed ways
of improving work life itself. One lady called for the appointment of
women factory inspectors who would look out for women workers'
health and safety. Another applauded the New York Consumers' League
campaign to get affluent women to patronize department stores where
salesclerks' wages were higher than average and workdays somewhat
shorter. A third writer urged *Far and Near* readers to "use their influence
everywhere to create the most powerful of all agencies—public opinion
in favor of paying men and women equal wages for equal work." And
an editorial quoting the German socialist Ferdinand Lassalle told club
members to reach for more than life's necessities, "feel most keenly the
pressure for higher wages," and thus form "an advance guard to help
the onward and upward movement of all small wage earners." As suggested by the editors' assumption that employers would automatically
meet the wage demands of workers who heeded Lassalle's advice to

"have as many wants as possible," however, sponsors believed that efforts to right industrial wrongs need not and should not set labor and capital at loggerheads. They deemed it quite proper, therefore, for the state, the general public, and genteel organizations like the Consumers' League to press for improvements in working women's terms of employment. Nonetheless, the thought of turning the clubs into instruments of labor reform still left sponsors cold, for that threatened to exacerbate club members' bitterness toward the employing class, not to mention their forgetfulness about working girls' shortcomings as employees.[9]

In fact, sponsors' fears of promoting worker unrest loomed so large as to make any club talk about labor reform scary; and discussions of reform strategies that would mobilize the clubs were just too frightening to be tolerated. This became clear in November 1891, when *Far and Near* published a letter in which Lizzie Burke, a member of New York City's Far and Near Society, proposed that the club movement become an "auxiliary to the formation of Trades Unions among women." Working women were poorly paid, she wrote, because employers were "hoarding their ill-gotten wealth with perfect adoration to the 'Golden Calf,' striving to accumulate millions at the expense of their 'industrial slaves.'" Since the clubs aimed to foster mutualism, she argued,

> therefore, to be consistent, they might go a step farther and say, Girls, your labor belongs to you, and justice demands that you should receive the highest possible wage in return therefor. And add that . . . the lesson to be derived from such teachings is one that would encourage girls to organize "Trade Clubs" of their respective calling, which would be of lasting benefit in aiding to ameliorate the condition of girls poorly paid and help release them from the grasp of grinding "capitalists" whose object is almost to own them body and soul.

Burke probably expected a mixed response from the journal's editors. Though she must have known that her hostility toward employers would raise hackles, she also had reason to think that her proposal would be taken seriously. Just one month earlier, *Far and Near* had printed an article in which the sponsor M. E. J. Kelley advised that ladies "interested in matters of general concern to women" join with like-minded working girls to promote trade unionism. Kelley was an anomaly, however. Other club sponsors did not wish to get involved with labor organizing; and the pugnacious brand of unionism Burke seemed to represent filled them with dread. Instead of addressing the substance of her letter, then, *Far and Near*'s editors simply ruled her out of order, decreeing that "labor questions, like politics and religion, must be left to each member to settle for herself, and our organizations exist for the improvement of the individual, not to deal with conditions of work and wages."[10]

This was an obviously hollow claim. Readers needed only to turn the page to learn that Boston's Shawmut Avenue Club—one of the oldest and largest of these organizations where everyone allegedly puzzled out labor questions on her own—was holding roundtables on trade unionism and the benefits of the eight-hour day. *Far and Near*'s "Club Notes" section would soon report that roundtables on labor issues were taking place in other clubs as well. No decree delimiting the clubs' purpose could prevent such discussions from inspiring additional rank-and-file calls for cooperative attacks on workplace problems.[11]

To judge from *Far and Near*'s contents for the next half year, sponsors thus turned to a second line of defense, based on the proposition that proposals like Burke's misapplied sisterly principles. M. E. J. Kelley was brought to heel, at least in her writings for *Far and Near;* making her debut as "Aunt Jane," she now concentrated on admonishing club members to mind their manners and added an occasional good word for "untiring effort" on the job. The editors ran no follow-up articles on factory inspection, the Consumers' League, or, needless to say, trade clubs. There were, however, several essays on work life, all of them penned by club sponsors and all sounding a common theme. One told the story of a woman who got a job in an office formerly staffed by men only and so distinguished herself as a hard worker that the boss soon hired other women. By going the extra mile for employers, the author concluded, club members could meet sisterly duties "to the woman of the future, she who will rejoice to find the world of work a better place because of the women who live in it today." According to a second article, club members also had a "moral obligation" to repay the kindness of bosses who went beyond the requirements of law in providing for women's comfort on the job. This writer—who had once seen a cloakroom mirror break because of a salesclerk's negligence and had heard that factory operatives sometimes littered their lunchrooms or let washroom basins overflow—warned that to mistreat an employer's property was to injure sister workers by discouraging the spread of employee welfare programs. Striking a more positive yet similar note, a third article advised the woman who cared about her workmates to please the boss in order to win a supervisory job that would give her "a chance to establish better relations between employers and employees." The cumulative message was that club members owed it to their sex and especially to other working women to become model employees. The hope behind the message, apparently, was that duties to employers would become a hotter topic of discussion than grievances about labor conditions.[12]

By spring 1892, *Far and Near*'s editors were ready to put this hope to the test. The sponsor Jane Newell's April letter to the "Correspondence Column" provided the occasion. "The other day," she wrote,

> I was present at a discussion of working girls' clubs, at which a very serious indictment was brought against us by a woman who is deeply interested in good things. . . . She said we read all the speeches at our annual reunions, and never read a word that would brace us up to more faithful work, would emphasize the right of an employer to faithful service and teach that this would surely bring respect where respect was due. . . . Let us hear from the workers on this point. Such statements show us that every member of every club should feel that she has the honor of all in her keeping, and if she is unfaithful and lazy every one of us suffer for it.

Seconding the request for workers' testimony, the editors announced that the topic for the next month's "Thoughts from Club Members" column—where club principles had often been hashed over in the past—would be, "Do our clubs stimulate us to more faithful work or not?" Had club members, in other words, been moved by sponsors' preachments on work life? The only response as of May was silence. "But Miss Newell's question is too important to be dropped," declared the slow-to-take-a-hint editors, "so please send in a great many answers to it for the June number." Once more, it seems, club members remained silent. Or perhaps they submitted answers unfit to print. At any rate, the question was finally dropped, and the "Thoughts from Club Members" column never again appeared.[13]

At a stalemate in *Far and Near*, cross-class discussions of workaday life were also deadlocked in club meeting rooms. In some clubs, Grace Dodge later recalled, "industrial topics were . . . not broached or touched upon, as [sponsors] did not understand them and feared results." Thanks to democratization, of course, sponsors' anxieties were not a universally effective barrier to club roundtables on labor issues; and wherever such roundtables took place, they tended, as one lady scornfully put it, to "resolve themselves into the narrow limit of 'How can we get more wages for the labor we are performing, and fewer hours?'" Sponsors very seldom succeeded, that is, in sparking talks on the quality of the performance. Members' efforts to convince sponsors that working girls' clubs should champion labor reform were even more unproductive, however. For both groups, then, dialogues on labor issues came to a dead end.

There they stayed until external developments—new trade-union overtures to working women and the economic crash of 1893—created a different climate for discussion.[14]

TRADE UNIONISM

From the moment of its founding in 1886, the American Federation of Labor (AFL) lent verbal support to the organization of female trades. There were, however, considerable barriers to women's recruitment into the federation. Of the thirteen national unions represented at its inaugural convention, just two—the Cigar Makers' Union and the Typographical Union—admitted female members. Until the spring of 1892, moreover, AFL officials did not as a rule reach out to women workers but waited, rather, for them to come knocking.[15]

Women's ranks within the federation grew nonetheless. One crucial port of entry was special female locals unattached to national unions. Chicago's Ladies' Federal Labor Union No. 2703, chartered in 1888 as a local covering sundry trades, spawned twenty-three single-trade female locals by 1892, for example. In Troy, New York, emissaries from a collar starchers' local chartered in 1891 soon sparked the formation of five more AFL locals of women employed in that city's giant shirt and collar industry. Other women meanwhile entered the federation via new national unions. The Retail Clerks' National Protective Association—based in small midwestern cities where sales clerking was still a predominantly male occupation—was mostly composed of men; but some of its founders, a fair portion of its members, and one of its vice presidents were women. Female minorities could also be found in the Boot and Shoe Workers' International Union and the National Union of Textile Workers, two of the many AFL affiliates that had originally been part of the Knights of Labor. The United Garment Workers, another AFL union established by former Knights, was three-fifths female. Nonetheless, the AFL remained an overwhelmingly male and male-oriented organization. Most of its national unions, which by 1892 numbered forty, included not a single woman; its mixed-sex nationals and locals looked out first and foremost for the men they represented; and its female locals lacked the power to challenge women's exclusion from or second-class status within other AFL quarters.[16]

The expanding female presence made a real difference in some respects, though. It proved not only that women could be organized but also, as events in Chicago and Troy testified, that they were most effectively organized by other women. In light of this evidence, the AFL Executive Council voted in April 1892 to fund the appointment of the federation's first general organizer of women. Assuming the post at the end of May, the Chicago bookbinder Mary Kenney, a veteran of the Ladies' Federal Labor Union, set out immediately for New York City, where she launched a drive to bring northeastern working women into the federation.[17]

Among Kenney's many methods of drumming up support for this drive were talks to working girls' clubs in both New York and Boston. In the late 1880s she had served briefly as the president of a fledgling Chicago club from which she soon resigned. "I was much disgusted with the talk of the group," she later explained. "It was always about outings. I thought that helping to get better wages was much more important." With this thought in mind, she abandoned the club in favor of the Ladies' Federal Labor Union. She kept in touch, however, with some of her old club sisters; and a burgeoning friendship with Jane Addams, whose Hull House settlement provided women's unions with meeting space, eventually drew her back into a form of club activism. On May Day 1892, just weeks before she departed for New York City, Kenney and a half dozen workers she had recruited moved into the Jane Club, a cooperative boardinghouse established at Addams's suggestion and with seed money from Hull House. When Kenney visited northeastern working girls' clubs, therefore, she was greeted not only as an ambassador from the AFL but also as one of the club movement's own—an especially trustworthy promoter of women's unionization.[18]

Hospitable as they were to a visiting club sister, members and sponsors alike put Kenney's powers of persuasion to a hard test. Warmly welcoming her as a "recent addition to New York's bright women," the July 1892 issue of Far and Near also predicted that her progress as a labor organizer would "necessarily be slow" because "New York working-girls seem generally to regard unions as frauds." According to Kenney, the main roadblock she faced was not women workers' distrust for unions but their fear of punishment at the hands of employers. Especially in New York City, she reported, women who joined unions were regularly fired. Far and Near's analysis of the situation was not entirely off the mark, though. Club members furnished incontrovertible proof that at least some working women did indeed equate unions with frauds.[19]

Club members who drew that equation tended to associate unionism with strikes, most of which were union-led in the early 1890s. That might not have disturbed women like Lizzie Burke, whose call for trade clubs was wrapped in rhetoric indicating a readiness to go toe-to-toe with employers; but quite a few club members had clearly decided that strikes cost more than they accomplished. As workers from the Industrial Society of Hoboken explained at the 1890 club convention:

> We do not approve of the principle of strikes. We should prefer to see all matters referring to labor and capital, regulated by law. For this purpose representatives should be sent to Congress who would really represent the wage-earners and their interests. Strikes generally profit no one but the Walking Delegate [union official]. Strikes, in rare instances and in the present state of the laws, are justified, when the employer attempts to bring the wages paid down to starvation rates. They will only succeed if the girls all go out together and if they all remain firm.

Speakers from other clubs echoed this one's call for legislative reform. A member of New York's Endeavor Club, for example, put "better laws" at the top of her list of workers' needs, while a member of that same city's Steadfast Club advised working girls who wanted higher wages to "find time to suggest to . . . fathers and brothers the necessity of better and abler men in public office." No one at the convention put in a good word for strikes; and, as the Industrial Society's swipe at walking delegates suggests, doubts about strikes could easily give rise to suspicious attitudes toward unions.[20]

Such suspicions stemmed, no doubt, not only from the belief that unionism encouraged strikes but also from misgivings about unions' ability or willingness to help women strikers win. The Industrial Society's observation that strikes could succeed only "if the girls all go out together" was right on target; and as some club members had learned firsthand, the presence of a union by no means guaranteed that this "if" would be fulfilled. The odds against united action loomed especially large when there was good reason to worry that strikers would lose their jobs to scabs. In 1889, for example, a union-led walkout at New York City's Higgins and Company carpet mills—which had slashed wages by almost 25 percent and advertised Italian immigrants' readiness to fill the jobs of any employees declining to accept the new rates—temporarily split the 38th Street Society, whose membership included some of the 550 strikers as well as some of the 600 workers crossing picket lines. The walkout ended after three months in utter defeat, and the union quickly fell apart.

A different but no less discouraging tale of division and failure could be told by the Binghamton, New York, Helping Hand Club, whose members spent eight weeks during the summer of 1890 building a wage strike of over two thousand nonunionized women employed in that city's cigar industry. While the women in this case all went out together, the union men whose support they sought lagged behind. Binghamton's all-male Cigar Makers' Union local did not join the walkout until it was well underway and then conducted what amounted to a separate strike-within-a-strike—a work stoppage confined to shops where men's working conditions fell below the best union standards. This gave employers the breathing space to form a strong and eventually victorious united front. The result for the women was tens of thousands in lost earnings, scores of permanently lost jobs, and no change in the wage schedules that had sparked their walkout. Whatever club members thought about "the principle of strikes" or the justice of walkouts in response to "starvation rates," those who had experienced or heard of defeats like those at the Higgins mills and in Binghamton must have wondered whether trade unions possessed enough clout on the one hand and concern for women on the other to make signing up a good idea.[21]

Also militating against Kenney's progress in club circles was the influence there of the AFL's fading rival for the loyalties of American workers: the Order of the Knights of Labor. Most working girls' clubs drew their membership from the same northeastern communities and industries where legions of women had entered the order in the mid-1880s. A sizable portion of the older club members Kenney encountered in 1892 had been among these legions, and some of the younger ones probably had experience in the Knights as well. Though the order was well past its prime in the early 1890s, women's and mixed-sex Knights of Labor assemblies hung on in several factory towns and big-city neighborhoods that were also home to working girls' clubs. The Union Club of Lynn, Massachusetts, for example, operated alongside the Lady Stitchers' Assembly based in that town's shoe factories. The Providence, Rhode Island, North End Working Girls' Association rubbed elbows with the Ladies' Social Assembly 4077. In New York City, the West Side's 38th Street Society met just a few blocks away from the rooms used by the all-female Freedom of Labor Assembly, while the Lower East Side's Endeavor Club was neighbor to the mixed-sex Wendell Phillips Assembly. By 1892, such Knights of Labor locals were so tiny in most cases and so few that active Knights could not have been very numerous in working girls' clubs. Former Knights were fairly plentiful, however; and Knightish thinking was more widespread among club members than the order's fast-declining numbers in the Northeast would suggest.[22]

Outlooks reminiscent of the Knights of Labor bobbed up with particular frequency in club members' thinking about politics. Though the wage earners who flooded into the order during its heyday had usually devoted their best energies to struggles centered in the workplace, they had also embraced political strategies for improving their lives. Sentiments in club circles of the early 1890s suggest that this faith in politics often outlived the enthusiasm for workplace struggles, at least among women wage earners. In addition to arguing that legislation was the best means of improving labor conditions, club members of this era displayed a keen interest in Populism. Farmers' Alliances and the People's Party—both of which were closely connected to the increasingly rural-based Knights—enjoyed considerable sympathy in club meeting rooms. In the January 1891 issue of *Far and Near*, for example, a member of the 38th Street Society attacked the McKinley tariff bill, seconding Knights' and Alliancemen's predictions that it would "raise . . . the cost of everything except labor" and that "the American farmer [would] be the chief sufferer." Readers' complaints about that same month's "World's Events" column, where Alliancemen were dismissed as deadbeats, compelled the journal to adopt a strictly neutral tone in all subsequent reports on Populism. Club members meanwhile began to send in requests for articles on bimetallism, a Populist doctrine that became a favorite topic of club roundtables. Early in 1892, when the People's Party was aborning, some workers running for club offices called themselves the "People's ticket." In step with the Knights, if not directly in touch, the many club members with Populist sympathies were distinctly out of sync with the AFL, whose leaders stood aloof from farmer-labor politics in 1892.[23]

Another Knights of Labor legacy—the hard feelings that some of the club movement's ex-Knights bore their former brothers in the order—simultaneously undermined club members' responsiveness to calls for workplace organizing. Urging a change of heart, the New York City labor activist and sometime club activist Leonora O'Reilly (an ex-Knight herself) argued that most women had entered the Knights with "impossible expectations," chief among them the expectation of "financial support from masses of newly organized men who had nothing to give." That miscalculation, O'Reilly told club members, had led numerous women's assemblies to ruin by way of strikes too poorly funded to be won and squabbles over who deserved the blame for the defeats. These disasters, she observed, had imbued many veterans of such assemblies with a paralyzing despair. They regarded their past losses to employers and disappointments with brother Knights "as proof that nothing can be done"—nothing requiring worker solidarity across gender lines, that is.[24]

The former militants O'Reilly criticized were not the only Knights of Labor veterans to reach this conclusion. As the founders of Baltimore's Myrtle Club could attest, it was possible to travel more cautious routes to much the same sense of betrayal by brother Knights. The Myrtle Club sprang from the ashes of the Knights' Myrtle Assembly, a female local based in a garment factory and guided by officers very wary of workplace conflicts. Their focus on social and educational programs shielded this group from the employer attacks that laid waste to so many other Knights of Labor trade assemblies, but the modest roster of activities did not satisfy the Myrtle Assembly's rank and file for very long. Three hundred strong shortly after its establishment in 1886, the assembly comprised only a dozen members by 1890, when a quarrel broke out over prominent male Knights' disapproval of the group's plan to attract fresh recruits by developing more elaborate recreational programs in cooperation with genteel women outside the order. Charging sabotage, the assembly's members voted to sever ties with the Knights, declared themselves the Myrtle Club, and engaged the Knights' Baltimore executive board in a bitter feud concerning the Myrtle Assembly's assets—a piano the women spirited away and a sick benefit fund in possession of the men, who initially refused to hand it over.[25]

In this case, as in those O'Reilly noted, Knights of Labor men received more censure than they had earned; but no matter how recognizable the exaggerations, tales of male treachery within the order raised questions certain to cool club members' response to a union organizer. The short life span of the typical Knights of Labor women's assembly lent credence to the idea that brother Knights had *somehow* failed their sisters. When the order's history was viewed in this light, its implications regarding unionism were doubly chilling. The fact that most women's assemblies had died within a few months or years suggested that women workers could not build viable, let alone powerful, unions on their own. The fact that Knights of Labor men had not saved these assemblies suggested in addition that women's unions could not count on brotherly assistance in confrontations with employers or in day-to-day efforts merely to stay alive. The despair O'Reilly attributed to working women's experience in the Knights was by no means confined, then, to club members who had passed through the order. The pessimistic conclusions they drew from experience shaped younger club sisters' interpretations of history, constructing a wall of defeatism that any AFL emissary would be hard-pressed to demolish.

Working men were not, of course, the only possible source of support for working women's organization on the job. Genteel women could help as well. Kenney had learned as much in Chicago, where many of the AFL's female locals had received valuable assistance from ladies associated with Hull House or the labor reform campaigns launched by the cross-class Illinois Women's Alliance. As Kenney surely realized, then, club sponsors' recruitment to the cause might convince many an otherwise skeptical club member to give trade unionism a try. Two factors severely limited her power to make headway among sponsors, however. First, summer was not a good time to mobilize genteel women, many of whom left their city homes for various vacation spots as soon as the weather grew hot. Second, what was more important, certain Knights of Labor influences operated no matter what the season to discourage sponsors from setting forth in new directions.[26]

Though leading Knights such as Terence Powderly and his lieutenants had estranged multitudes of wage earners by treating workplace struggles as a sideshow and efforts to uplift minds and morals as the main event, these same priorities had captivated many genteel reformers. By 1890, when the order's membership had fallen from an 1886 high of over 700,000 to no more than 100,000, its leaders' emphasis on uplift had so impressed club sponsors that they invited Leonora Barry, head of the Knights' Women's Department, to address that year's club convention. Barry sent regrets. The address sponsors suggested was scheduled for the same day she married Obadiah Lake, a St. Louis printer, and ended her four-year stint as the Knights' chief organizer of women. Two of her old comrades at the Women's Department showed up in her stead, however, to extend a friendly hand to the club movement. Highlighting similarities between club activities and those of the Knights, Kate Smoot, the department's secretary, described the "literary evenings" organized by Knights' assemblies. Mary O'Reilly, the former secretary, proposed that club sponsors join with the Women's Department to establish educational programs for children whose parents belonged to the order. This proposal generated no action. It might well have borne fruit, however, but for the department's swift collapse following Barry's retirement, for most club sponsors certainly sympathized with the aims articulated by Powderly and other leading Knights advising workers to join with employers for "the mutual development and moral elevation of mankind."[27]

The Knights held other charms, too, for ladies who believed that workers should learn to improve their lot without battling the employing class. Knights of Labor spokesmen issued both repeated advisories against strikes and calls for peaceful, legislative efforts to improve labor conditions. Similar policies and rhetoric prevailed in some AFL unions, especially those open to women. But that fact undoubtedly escaped club sponsors in the summer of 1892, when a bloody, AFL-led strike of steel workers in Homestead, Pennsylvania, made headlines throughout the country, and the AFL Executive Council organized picketing to stop the recruitment of scabs in New York and other northeastern cities. If the Homestead strike made the AFL a band of ruffians in club sponsors' eyes, it made leading Knights' uncombative countenance all the more pleasing. The greater sponsors' certainty that the Knights of Labor was the best labor organization imaginable, the more ready they were to regard its ever-weaker base among working women as proof of unionism's utter irrelevance to club members and their peers.[28]

Club sponsors had been chewing on such ideas for at least several months by the time Mary Kenney appeared on the scene. Consider, for instance, the following item from *Far and Near*'s March 1892 issue: "Mrs. Leonora Barry Lake, who will be remembered as an enthusiastic K of L worker, having an especial interest in factory girls, has recently written of her efforts to organize the working girls of St. Louis. She says she finds it impossible to interest them in labor organizations, so she has tried a social working girls' club for the mutual improvement of the members and it is quite popular." What a flattering testament to the perspicacity of ladies who had surmised much earlier than Mrs. Lake that working girls needed social clubs instead of labor organizations. The self-satisfaction club sponsors derived from that thought would have undermined their receptivity to Kenney's views in any event. Against the backdrop of the Homestead strike, however, the AFL seemed so inferior to the demonstrably outworn Knights that she did not have a prayer of winning sponsors' support. Their commitment to business as usual could only exacerbate the defeatism working against club members' mobilization, and members' hesitancy was certain in turn to harden sponsors' resolve to stand pat.[29]

The impediments to Kenney's progress among working women in general were no less daunting than those she faced in club circles and, given her focus on cities that had once been Knights of Labor strongholds, probably quite similar in kind. Her organizing drive made headway nonetheless, but it did not develop enough momentum to offset the financial pressure to terminate her commission when the AFL Executive Board met in October 1892. By that time, Kenney had established a handful of female locals among garment workers and bookbinders in New

York City, Albany, and Troy, and she had lately made contact with interested women from a variety of trades in the Boston area. Under normal circumstances, the Executive Board might have deemed these results encouraging. In the fall of 1892, however, there were extraordinary demands on AFL unions' treasuries—desperate fund appeals from male unionists under attack from both the militia and the courts amid the Homestead strike and similarly sharp conflicts in Buffalo's railroad yards, eastern Tennessee coal mines, and the silver and lead fields in the Coeur d'Alene region of Idaho. Now that every penny counted in the effort to defend men's unions, a majority of the Executive Board considered appropriations to promote women's unionization expendable. Kenney's post was abolished as of the end of October, just five months after her work began.[30]

No sooner did it end than some club sponsors began to take a friendly interest in trade unionism. Kenney's slow but definite progress had shown that working women were not as uninterested in unions as sponsors had thought. Evidence was accumulating, moreover, that AFL unionism was less combative than the strikes of summer 1892 had suggested. Sponsors in charge of the November 1892 reunion of clubs in Massachusetts—where textile and shoe workers' focus on legislative reform had recently given the AFL a pleasingly peaceable countenance—scheduled two major addresses on working girls' need for labor organizations. One of the two, words from Clare de Graffenried of the U.S. Labor Bureau, was printed the following January in *Far and Near*. A simultaneous report on the AFL's December 1892 convention happily announced that the federation as a whole would henceforth shun battles with employers and embrace legislative action: "One of the most notable things done by the convention was the passage of a resolution declaring that 'the strike and boycott have failed as weapons of organized labor and that a campaign of education should be initiated by the Federation and the irresistible power of the ballot arrayed in the struggle for union supremacy.'" The reporter misread the situation. The declaration she quoted was not a repudiation of militancy but a call for political efforts to stop employers from using courts and troops against strikers, and the convention endorsed strikes in other resolutions. Her word was good enough, though, for the journal's editors, who shortly gave unionism their official stamp of approval. In March 1893, they urged all working girls' societies to study "economic matters" so that members might learn that unions as well as clubs enabled women wage earners to "get by uniting what [they] could never secure single-handed."[31]

There are hints that club members, too, had a growing interest in trade unionism. Lizzie Burke, the trade club advocate, was elected president of New York City's Far and Near Society. Practical talks about unionism multiplied. And *Far and Near's* editorial in behalf of unionism suggests between the lines that a significant portion of club members appeared ripe for unionization—ready enough, at any rate, to make sponsors anxious to inoculate them against labor radicalism. Working girls' societies, the editors argued, should study economics not only to encourage members to organize on the job but also to teach them "that organizations like trades-unions are not for rebellion against employers, but a balance of power, a bulwark for mutual defence rather than a battering-ram. . . . If cool-headed, warm-hearted women . . . do not undertake the training of [working girls], the time may not be far distant when demagogues will seize them and mould them as they have the men in certain localities." Sponsors' jitters notwithstanding, however, club members were not rushing into unions, militant or otherwise. Doubts about women workers' ability to build powerful, lasting unions discouraged efforts to build them at all. When members of the 38th Street Society held a roundtable on women's unions, for example, the main topic of discussion was their tendency to collapse. The explanation most heard was "successful labor unions mean many meetings and much talk; girls have sewing, housework, etc., to do after six o'clock and so have not the spare hours men have." With this problem compounding all the other impediments to success—lack of experience, scarce funds, employers' efforts at sabotage—a great many club members regarded union shops as unattainable, no matter how desirable.[32]

It was easier than ever before, on the other hand, to envision labor reform projects emanating from the clubs, whose sponsors had more spare time than a working woman could ever find. In the fall of 1891, when *Far and Near* ruled discussions of trade clubs out of order, the possibility that sponsors would address labor issues in any helpful way seemed entirely remote. By the spring of 1893, their potential in that regard had expanded significantly to judge from their warming attitudes toward the AFL and unionism in general.[33]

HARD TIMES

The economic crash of May 1893 added a great deal more to labor reform's appeal and sharpened all discussions of labor conditions. By year's end more than fifteen thousand businesses had failed, wages were falling much more steeply than living costs, and nearly three million workers—about 12 percent of the whole labor force and a much higher proportion of its industrial sectors—had no jobs. The results of a survey conducted that fall in New York State provide a microcosm of the national crisis in manufacturing. Of 2,011 factories canvassed, 494 had reduced wages and 1,541 had suspended or significantly curtailed operations. The worst was yet to come. In 1894, the trough of the depression, more than 4.5 million workers were jobless, and average earnings bought less than they had in a decade. Earnings did not return to precrash levels until 1897, and the unemployed numbered over three million until 1899. Overwhelming the clubs' ability to function as usual, hard times created organizational crises that compelled every sponsor to take notice of club members' economic situations; and the calamities evident shook to the core many sponsors' faith that the labor market rewarded virtuous workers.[34]

Though democratization had ended club members' initial silence regarding bad conditions on the job, it had also turned club meeting rooms into recreational centers where workday problems were rather easily put aside. Forgetfulness became impossible, however, when the depression converted these problems into emergencies and deprived club members of the means to finance a diverting associational life. "The working-girls' clubs are experiencing a loss of buoyancy and a sense of discouragement," reported the December 1893 issue of *Far and Near*. Many members were jobless, and many more making do with reduced earnings. Those residing in mill towns, where the collapse of a single industry could throw nearly everyone out of work, were often incapable of paying club dues. An extended shutdown of the silk mills in Canton, Massachusetts, had already destroyed that town's club. Others, like the Havergal Club of Ansonia, Connecticut, where a brass industry slowdown was crippling the local economy, had jettisoned the requirement that members pay dues and started to draw on treasury reserves that could not last much longer. Most clubs—located in cities where working women and their kin labored in a variety of industries and trades—were sure to stay afloat. Their members could usually manage to find the few pennies a week that covered dues, and some found enough to help harder-pressed club sisters stay out of arrears as well. Even under the best of circumstances, however, club members had plenty of reasons to worry about their own and their clubs' futures.[35]

Recreational programs contracted. Special fees for parties, outings, and other extras were increasingly unaffordable. New York City clubs' summer holiday lodges on Long Island received a host of cancellations from workers who could not pay for vacations planned before the crash. Tight budgets compelled Philadelphia clubs to drop plans for the traditional spring reunion. Members of Boston's Friendly Workers, the club movement's most vocal advocates of elaborate recreational programs, dispensed altogether with entertainments. Though few big-city clubs had to go that far, entertainments were less frequent virtually everywhere they still took place. The unprecedented weight of members' economic worries meanwhile guaranteed that, in cities and mill towns alike, talks about the depression's effect on working-class communities would fill much of the time previously devoted to planning and enjoying amusements that cost money.[36]

The talks highlighted facts inconsistent with moral reform's axioms as to both the causes of bad labor conditions and the solutions to such problems. Before the crash, the predominant feeling among sponsors, even those growing friendly toward unionism, had been that workers' personal shortcomings—carelessness, ignorance, disregard for employers' rights and property—explained most of the difficulties they faced in the labor market. That consensus exploded amid the depression. However strong their class prejudices, very few sponsors could believe that the universal suffering they now witnessed had been caused by workers' deficiencies. If millions of wage earners were falling victim to forces beyond their individual control, it was not necessarily true that, as *Far and Near* had confidently announced in an 1891 editorial on work life, "effort" represented "the plain stepping stone to success."[37]

Throughout the year that preceded the club convention of May 1894, then, club sponsors and various guest writers they had recruited presented a welter of thoughts about labor questions in the pages of *Far and Near*. The "World's Events" column for September 1893 expressed sympathy for unemployed workers' mass demonstrations in demand of public relief. "While this may be the very best country there is," the author argued, "it cannot possibly be the best possible form of government when a condition of affairs is possible that makes a month's cessation from labor entail actual suffering to two-thirds of the people." The October issue featured an article in which a home economist recounted problems stemming from workers' tendency to shirk on the job and called upon women workers to spearhead a campaign for greater diligence. Discrepancies of this sort multiplied during the next half year, when the journal published plugs for the idea that hard times were easily weathered by a sufficiently frugal family, laments about the terrible effects of unemployment and wage cuts, a series of reports from genteel women associated with Boston's Denison House settlement (where various labor reform and union organizing projects were afoot), an editorial echoing a charity leader who had advised Boston club sponsors not to squander sympathy on unemployed women unwilling to leave the city for domestic jobs in rural areas, and many similarly contradictory articles.[38]

Most contentious of all was the question of what the club movement should do to ameliorate the hardships facing its membership and other working women. Mounting rank-and-file pressures for some sort of action made this an increasingly hot topic of discussion among club sponsors. Many, perhaps most, would surely have preferred not to discuss it as much as they did, for the issue set them at odds more than anything they had debated in the past. Given the severity of the depression, however, the controversy simply could not be skirted, and as various opinions contended for support, sponsors divided into three camps.

A small group of diehard moral reformers opposed any action that might discourage club members from pulling themselves up by their own bootstraps. One sponsor wrote anonymously to *Far and Near,* for example, to argue against proposals that the clubs serve unemployed members by establishing additional emergency loan funds and more projects like the Alliance Employment Bureau and Children's Dressmaking Company. She defined loans as "almsgiving" and therefore a detriment to recipients' characters. Employment bureaus, she asserted, would "lessen individual responsibility." Cooperative sewing rooms, which might offer good wages to club members with poor needlework skills, struck her as a bad idea, because "the sooner workers know that only excellent work is well-paid, the better for all."

At the center of the moral reform faction stood Mary Richmond, who belonged to the Myrtle Club in Baltimore and held the salaried position of general secretary to the local Charity Organization Society. Though her deep commitment to the charity movement was anomalous in club circles, most sponsors respected charity leaders enough to entertain their advice; and Richmond made sure that advice regarding hard times reached ladies far beyond Baltimore. It was at her instigation, for instance, that Zilpha Smith of Boston's Associated Charities visited a local meeting of sponsors to lecture on the dangers of cooperative workshops and loan funds and on the wisdom of "wasting no sympathy" on jobless club members who were reluctant to work for rural families seeking live-in servants. That anonymous sponsor's letter, which clearly derived from Smith's lecture, later broadcast the charity movement's criticisms of relief projects to every lady who read *Far and Near.* While the moral reform faction was small, its ideas received wide exposure.[39]

At the other end of the spectrum stood a somewhat larger group of sponsors who pressed hard for the expansion of club relief projects and favored the inauguration of labor reform activities as well. Though it included M. E. J. Kelley in New York and a few Philadelphians, this faction's vital base was Boston, where its two premier spokeswomen—the Shawmut Avenue Club's Edith Howes and O. M. E. Rowe—presided over the Massachusetts Association of Working Girls' Clubs. The labor reformers drew their inspiration from the labor movement, especially events in Boston, where Kenney resumed her organizing early in 1894. A wealthy women's rights activist covered her living expenses; Boston's AFL headquarters and the Denison House settlement supplied funds, meeting rooms, and fellow canvassers; and the vigorous outreach very quickly touched off a flurry of union organizing among factory women. These developments made labor activism a singularly exciting prospect for club sponsors in Boston and combined with pressures from club members to make inaction in regard to work issues exceptionally uncomfortable. In other cities, the labor reform faction was either isolated or entirely unrepresented, but the May 1894 convention, which would meet in Boston, promised to change that. Bostonians lined up most of the speakers, and one of the main topics to be addressed was trade unionism, which Howes had pushed onto the agenda. The convention would give the labor reform faction its best opportunity yet to shape other sponsors' thinking about labor issues and what the club movement should do about them.[40]

The vast majority of club sponsors belonged to a middle camp whose opinions seemed up for grabs. They approved the spread of loan funds, employment bureaus, cooperative workshops, and other relief projects; most of them participated in at least one such experiment; and a few gave this work their all. Not even the dynamos spoke of labor reform as a possible adjunct to relief work, however, and the others were still more conservative to judge from their practice. The best of their energies went to organizing entertainments—a line of activity loudly endorsed by Richmond, Smith, and company. Discouraging as this must have been to the labor reform faction, it boded well in one respect. The more sponsors poured into recreational programs, the more they socialized with club members and learned of deteriorating labor conditions. By the time of the Boston convention, then, the middle camp's conservatism competed with a growing sense of labor issues' urgency.[41]

Club members' thinking on the labor question was in flux, too. In the past they had construed it as a question concerning class relations: the division of power and wealth between workers and employers. At the Boston convention they gendered the question by stressing women's right to economic equality with men and an obligation to help each other toward that end. The new approach made good sense if the object was to push club sponsors into labor reform activism. The minority already moving in that direction endorsed labor reform on distinctly gender-conscious grounds, and those yet to move had more progressive ideas about woman's place than anything else.[42]

If club members' redefinition of the labor question was calculated to galvanize sponsors, however, it also reflected a deep faith in sisterhood's power to move them. Sponsors' reactions to the depression encouraged this assumption. Their support for relief projects despite moral reformers' objections suggested a capacity to look at economic life from working women's standpoint; the emergence of a labor reform camp suggested the potential for bolder action on working women's behalf. At bottom, though, club members' faith in sisterhood seems to have rested on the belief that the labor question and the woman question really were closely related and that most sponsors were certain to take up labor reform once they saw it in the proper, gendered light.

CHAPTER 6

Labor Reform

One of the most remarkable things about sisterly rhetoric in club circles is how quickly it faded after burning so brightly in the mid-1890s. Club sponsors' approaches to labor reform help to explain the puzzle. Between the club conventions of 1894 and 1897, sponsors in charge of interclub associations in Boston, New York, Philadelphia, and Chicago organized efforts to improve working conditions for women in occupational groups well represented in club meeting rooms. These were not militant projects, and some were exceedingly modest; but they all betokened a commitment to the idea that the best way to map out a labor reform agenda was to consult with workers. That principle got lost at the close of the decade, when interclub associations in the Northeast formed an umbrella organization that made labor reform by means of vocational education one of its primary concerns. The resulting projects outstripped those of the mid-nineties. They got more sustained attention from leading bodies, mobilized a larger proportion of club sponsors, and made significant contributions to the expansion of vocational training for working-class women. In some respects, it was an eminently sisterly campaign, but not from club members' vantage point. It promised to bring women's wages nearer to men's by equalizing opportunities to train for skilled work, and its energy suggested club sponsors' strong feeling of solidarity with working women. On the other hand, it did not serve women in the occupations club members generally pursued; and whatever sponsors' *feelings* toward working women, the campaign rested on cooperation not with workers but with employers. Against this backdrop, both club

members and sponsors stopped referring to their movement as a sisterhood either in its publications or at its conventions.

Sponsors' new stance as labor reformers was not the only important
factor at play. In the early twentieth century, they brought virtually all
of their club work into line with "scientific methods" that stressed efficiency over cooperation with the members. Labor reform was the piv-
otal issue, however. Club sponsors' retreat from the membership on this
issue foreshadowed retreats on other fronts; and the alliance with employers in the vocational education campaign prefigured a more general orientation in their direction when scientific reform became sponsors'
watchword. If the sisterhood that club members and sponsors had constructed proved flimsy, this was first and most sharply evident in connection with labor reform.

THE LIMITS OF SISTERLY PRINCIPLES

Circulars announcing the 1894 convention billed it as an effort to clarify the club movement's mission. The main question at hand was, in *Far
and Near*'s words, "whether the time will ever come when we must make
a more formal declaration of principles and take a more aggressive position in matters of every-day life." Everyone knew that the most pressing of these matters were labor issues; and as the journal's euphemistic
language underscores, most sponsors were wary even to ponder such
things, let alone make labor reform a club cause. Two labor issues—trade
unionism and women's right to earn money when they could afford to
stay at home—received pointed and extended treatment at the convention. Both were presented in ways that invited the wary to think of the
labor question as something in which all women had a stake and to regard labor reform as a sisterly duty.[1]

The session on women's right to earn "pin money" was dominated
by club members, nine of whom spoke on the issue. The depression made
it an especially heated topic. Hard times not only worsened chronic overcrowding in the female labor market but also exacerbated a longstand-
ing pattern of public censure for working women who, like most club
members, could afford to spend a portion of their earnings on nonessen-
tials. Throughout the late nineteenth century the popular press often
complained that too many working-class daughters earned money merely to satisfy an "inordinate longing," in the words of one writer, "to dress
better than their parents can afford and to wear trinkets." Some of polite society's most prominent reformers identified working girls who

were not entirely dependent on their own earnings as the worst enemies of those who were. As Jacob Riis declared in his famous *How the Other Half Lives* (1890), "The very fact that some need not starve on their wages condemns the rest to that fate. The wages they are willing to accept all have to take." That argument gained momentum amid the starvation wages and critical job shortages that prevailed following the crash of 1893. Both were supposedly the fault of girls working "to decorate themselves beyond their need and station," as state officials in Massachusetts put it. Unsurprisingly, then, club members who addressed the pin money question at the convention took pains for the most part to defend every working girl's right to a job. What is extraordinary given their keen awareness of the mounting competition for work is that the majority granted that right to all women, irrespective of social class.[2]

Class lines were drawn in just two of the four statements against pin money workers. Both described such workers as genteel women stealing jobs from working girls. "If ordinary working girls do not understand the work, let these women spend their time and money in teaching them," argued a member of Boston's Shawmut Avenue Club. Better still, said a Cincinnati club member, women of means should teach themselves how to cook, clean, and such, for "the difficulty in keeping servant girls sometimes arises from the mistress's being uninformed in general housekeeping." Genteel women very seldom if ever competed for working girls' jobs, of course; they were charged, rather, with reducing the aggregate demand for female labor, which struck both speakers as a serious enough crime during the depression. The other two condemnations of pin money work zeroed in on targets much closer to home. Another Cincinnatian contended that working girls earning "dress and candy money" should be barred by law from job competition with those whose wages paid for necessities. A Bostonian from the Jamaica Plain Club complained that working-class housewives stole jobs from needier factory girls by taking in industrial homework. Though all of these speakers defined pin money work as a crime against working girls, there was no consensus as to the class identity of the culprits.[3]

The five club members who spoke in defense of pin money workers were unanimous, on the other hand, in extending the defense to cover women of all classes. There were strings attached. As a Shawmut Avenue Club member explained, "To my way of thinking, any woman has a perfect right to earn money, no matter if she lives on Beacon Street and belongs to the four hundred. . . . But when the woman who need not work goes into the shop, store, or factory, to earn money, and works for less than the standard wages, that I say she has no moral right to do." As this speaker and others emphasized, a pin money worker's entitlement to her job hinged on her willingness to practice solidarity with less affluent sisters. The blanket vindications of her right to work suggest a strong faith, then, in privileged women's capacity for sisterly approaches to workplace issues.[4]

Drawing on another sisterly principle, two speakers from Boston clubs also defended pin money work on the grounds that it promoted gender equality. More women with the means to train for professions ought to do so, declared a Dorchester Club member, because "business life . . . brings women to look upon men as equals, rather than superior beings, and to look upon marriage not as a necessity." A member of the Boylston Club applied a similar lens to the popular notion that a working girl whose job provided money for small luxuries was "usurping the position": "If men have enough to live on they never think of being looked upon as usurping another's place, and told to remain at home. . . . They try to lay aside the surplus. Why should not women? The average girl has just as much cause to look out for the future as a man, since there are not enough of the latter for each to have one to look out for her." As suggested by the parallel statements regarding professional women and working girls, optimism about the potential for female solidarity with respect to labor questions sprang in part from the belief that women of different classes had common interests in challenging male supremacy. To judge from the majority position on pin money work, an issue that usually pitted women against one another, sisterly ideals played a central role in club members' thinking about labor issues.[5]

The same ideals took center stage when the one club member who spoke at the convention's session on trade unionism said her piece. The Jamaica Plain Club's Mary Buckley based her argument in behalf of unionism on the proposition that women's entry into the labor market was an unalloyed good—a cause for "joy and satisfaction" among all in favor of female independence. The problem was that working women were not justly compensated for their labor; the proof of that, Buckley contended, lay in the differential between women's and men's wages in similar jobs. The only promising solution she saw was for women to band together in trade unions.[6]

She had in mind unions like her own, an independent female local whose 130 members included every fur hat trimmer in Boston. The Trimmers' Association was born in 1886, when male hatters, who had been organized for some years, adopted a union-label agreement as a means of regulating their relations with employers. The male hatters received a closed shop, a no-lockout pledge, and the promise that working conditions would henceforth be determined by negotiation. Employers received a no-strike pledge and the right to market hats bearing a label that would attract working-class shoppers. And, since only union members could legitimately take part in the production of union-label goods, the female trimmers received an ultimatum: join the newly formed women's local or find other jobs. Though many trimmers "at first disliked the idea of joining," Buckley reported, their local was now packed with loyal members who had turned it into much more than a justification for men's use of the union label. Operating within the no-strike, no-lockout framework the hatters had constructed, the Trimmers' Association cooperated closely with male unionists yet maintained its autonomy as an organization run by and for women.[7]

"We have become accustomed to . . . conducting the business of our society," Buckley explained; and her description of that business was sure to catch the ear of anybody concerned with falling wages and job shortages. The local's "bill of prices" for various types of work was reviewed, revised, and resubmitted to employers every six months. The negotiations that followed had nudged piece rates up on several occasions and, more immediately significant, had kept the rates steady following the economic crash. The local also prevented overcrowding in the trade by negotiating limitations on the number of apprentice trimmers that employers could hire. The result, even amid hard times, was that everyone had plenty of work most months of the year and enough to earn decent pay during the usual dull months. As her local demonstrated, Buckley concluded, a union was "an agency which unites women in an organization for mutual protection and sympathy" and thus deserved the full support of "all humanitarians."[8]

Each of the other pro-union speakers—a club sponsor, a settlement leader, and two labor activists—echoed Buckley in some fashion. Rejoicing on the one hand that women had "entered the industrial field as competitors with men," M. E. J. Kelley argued on the other that they could not possibly compete successfully until they stopped "trying to be twins"—stopped, that is, devoting so many hours to domestic duties that they lacked time for labor organizations. Ellen Gates Starr, cofounder with Jane Addams of Hull House, noted that wages in well-organized male trades far surpassed those in unorganized female trades and urged the club movement to help close the gap by becoming an "organ of propaganda" in unionism's behalf. Boston's E. Frances Pitts, a Typograph-

ical Union member recently hired by the local AFL as a general organizer of women in that city, invited club sponsors to help trade unions eliminate "the gulf that divides our society into rich and poor" and usher in
"the true sisterhood of woman." Leonora O'Reilly advised club members to abandon the "sweet domestic virtues" that militated against
union activism and admonished sponsors for failing to lead working
women out of "their narrow, customary sphere" into labor organizations.
Club members were not the only proponents of the idea that sisterly
principles contained answers to labor questions.[9]

Sisterhood could have slippery implications with regard to unionism,
however, as the two antiunion speakers made clear. Invited in the interests of fairness to present employers' viewpoint, Boston print shop owner
George Ellis announced that he was "thoroughly in favor" of paying men
and women equal wages for equal work and warned against trusting
unions to promote gender equity. Mary Richmond of Baltimore's Myrtle Club, the premier mouthpiece for the sponsors' moral reform faction,
argued that advocates of female solidarity would be foolish to endorse
a form of organization that excluded all but working women and divided them according to trade.[10]

Ellis related an anecdote concerning the Typographical Union, which
had recently launched a campaign to enlist women employed in Boston's
print shops and raise the new recruits' piece rates to 95 percent of union
men's. At a meeting with master printers, he confided, union spokesmen
inadvertently revealed that the campaign's real purpose had nothing to
do with women's interests. When employers threatened to dismiss wom-
en rather than give them the pay demanded, one unionist allegedly blurt-
ed out: "That is what we are after." While it lured women in with promises of equality, the labor movement's real aim, according to Ellis, was
to reserve the most lucrative trades for men. The story he told to illustrate this point may well have been fictitious, but it resonated with some
undeniable facts. Though the Typographical Union was one of the first
U.S. craft organizations to admit women, it had a history of trying to
exclude them from the print shops, even women who were its members.
In this trade and others, moreover, demands for equal pay for women
were sometimes used by union men as tools of exclusion. Given these
patterns, a commitment to gender equality could just as easily discourage a sympathy for unionism as foster it.[11]

To illustrate her point regarding female solidarity, Richmond presented a novel explanation for the old Myrtle Assembly's break with the
Knights of Labor, to which she had never belonged. The quarrel with

brother Knights played only a minor role, she contended. Far more important was the fact that the assembly's members, who "looked at life from much the same point of view" because they were all garment workers, coveted "that wholesome friction of varying points of view which we all find so educational." The enlightenment they sought and every working woman needed could be achieved, Richmond argued, only in organizations where women united across class and occupational lines: it was "impossible in the trades-union, which is, in its very nature, exclusive." Workers might find that contention insulting to their intelligence and ingenuity; but it gave club sponsors, most of whom were leery of labor activism in any event, a very appealing rationale for keeping their distance.[12]

The 1894 convention reshaped sponsors' attitude toward labor issues and labor reform in one respect. Immediately following that gathering they were noticeably less reluctant to discuss such things in *Far and Near*, at club roundtables, and at meetings where the directors of interclub associations laid plans. Talk did not generate much action outside of Boston, though; and only the Massachusetts Association of Working Girls' Clubs developed cooperative relations with labor organizations. A number of factors contributed to the sluggishness in other club strongholds. New York, Philadelphia, and Chicago did not see anything like the vigorous union activity among Boston's working women in the mid-1890s. The labor reform faction lost its main vehicle for influencing the mass of club sponsors when *Far and Near*, which many club members could no longer afford to purchase, went bankrupt in November 1894. The growing talk about labor reform so dismayed some sponsors—Grace Dodge, for instance—that they cut back considerably on their work for interclub associations. The dawdling with regard to action so disappointed others, such as M. E. J. Kelley, that they dropped out of the club movement entirely. Those who remained fully active now agreed for the most part that every woman had a stake in labor issues, but only a small minority treated labor reform as a crucial sisterly duty.[13]

AN "EMINENTLY PRACTICAL" PROJECT

By April 1897, when the third movement-wide convention of working girls' clubs met in Philadelphia, interclub associations had taken up several labor reform experiments. Sponsors in Philadelphia were polling club members as to labor conditions in department stores that barred investigators from the local Consumers' League and passing the information on to league officials. Similar activity was afoot in New York, another city where many club members worked as salesclerks or cash girls. Just weeks before the convention, the Chicago Association of Young Women's Clubs, which included several giant clubs of office workers, had opened a nonprofit clerical employment agency that broke the monopoly formerly enjoyed by commercial agencies whose services cost up to two weeks' pay. And the Bostonians could point to accomplishments that dwarfed all of the others combined.[14]

Within months of the 1894 convention, Edith Howes, O. M. E. Rowe, and other directors of the Massachusetts Association of Working Girls' Clubs (MAWGC) were helping trade unionists drum up audiences for the "social talks" held by Industrial Education for Women, a group Mary Kenney had formed to acquaint women wage earners in Boston with the labor movement's policies and aims. This enterprise combined with club members' complaints about labor conditions to inspire a concerted effort by MAWGC leaders to improve conditions in department stores, where a great many Boston club members worked. At the request of the Dry Goods Clerks' Benefit Society, an all-male union that had been trying in vain to win shoppers' support for earlier store closing hours, Howes and company took up the cause in December 1895. The men supplied petitions carrying the MAWGC's endorsement of a five o'clock closing, and club sponsors took them door to door, collecting thousands of signatures in the fancy residential districts of Boston and its suburbs. By winter's end, workers in all of the city's department stores enjoyed an eight-hour day![15]

The MAWGC then helped the women workers build their own labor organization. That assistance was something of a hindrance at first. Born in the spring of 1896, the Women Clerks' Benefit Association of Boston recruited just eighty-five members by summer, for many saleswomen feared it might have connections to a charity. Its connections to club sponsors, who had prodded other prominent Bostonians to pledge support as well, surely fed that suspicion. Ties to high society proved useful in the fall, however, when the association entertained fashionable guests at a fund-raising ball whose elegance made association members the envy of their workmates. Within weeks of that event, five hundred new members signed up. By spring 1897 the expanded organization was using information gathered by club sponsors to map out a citywide campaign to eliminate the fines levied against saleswomen by floorwalkers.[16]

The news from Boston sparked a lot of excitement at the 1897 club convention, especially among the hundreds of club members in attendance. Some undoubtedly expected that sponsors in other cities, too, would soon be petitioning for the eight-hour day, building labor organizations, campaigning against fines, or otherwise intervening in the workplace. The convention's program committee had stoked such expectations by appointing Boston's Edith Howes to draw up plans for an umbrella federation that would standardize interclub associations' priorities and "stand for something eminently practical" in the way of labor reform. And the workers enlisted to address the convention's session on industrial life had no shortage of ideas as to what needed reforming and what methods looked promising. Philadelphia club members enumerated a host of complaints about labor conditions for carpet weavers, dressmakers, and office workers. The carpet weavers' spokeswoman reported that their 1895 strike against wage cuts had been partially victorious and their union successful in pressuring employers to rescind three subsequent cuts. A former Knights of Labor organizer praised the labor movement for teaching women how to stick together. A speaker from the Philadelphia AFL championed the eight-hour day. The president of the Women Clerks' Benefit Association outlined its history and called for similar initiatives in other cities. As it turned out, however, club sponsors' alliances with labor activists were not about to expand; the umbrella federation born at the Philadelphia convention would instead bring these alliances to an end.[17]

The federation's central purpose was to shore up interclub associations in the Northeast, whose combined membership had fallen steadily as the depression dragged on. The Brooklyn Association of Working Girls' Club—1,600 strong in 1894—had disbanded by 1897. The Connecticut Association had shrunk from well over 1,000 on the eve of the depression to no more than 500. The New Century Guild's 1895 defection to the General Federation of Women's Clubs had reduced the Pennsylvania Association's membership by more than 600, and some of the oldest clubs in the New York Association had fallen apart. These losses brought the total number of club members in the Northeast from about 11,000 in 1894 to no more than 6,000 in 1897. Howes's challenge, then, was to design an umbrella federation that would reverse the shrinkage by stimulating club sponsors to go out and organize new clubs, recruit new sponsors, and raise money for the establishment of a central office and new monthly journal. The only suitable labor reform campaign in this context was one that would appeal to sponsors of all ideological stripes—the labor reform faction, the moral reform faction, and everyone in between.[18]

O. M. E. Rowe captured the spirit of the moment beautifully in her convention speech entitled "The Shorter Workday." Describing the MAWGC's early closing campaign, she invited other interclub associations to consider similar projects. She also argued, however, that the club movement could best serve the eight-hour cause by increasing club members' *"personal efficiency"* so that employers would realize that reductions in the workday need not reduce workers' productivity. "Never forget for an instant," she added, "that the industrial problem is solved only in the life of the individual worker. Every instance of tardiness or negligence, every shiftless hour, every piece of 'scampwork' hinders the advance of labor." This coda, which replicated arguments formerly used to fend off club members' calls for labor reform, announced that sponsors who had lately heeded those calls would now try to reconcile with moral reform stalwarts.[19]

By the end of the 1897 convention, this conciliatory spirit was well on its way to becoming flesh. Howes had presented a plan for the creation of a National League of Working Women's Clubs that would try in a yet undetermined way to improve women's labor conditions. Directors of interclub associations based in Massachusetts, Connecticut, New York, and eastern Pennsylvania had appointed a joint organizing committee. Mary Richmond had given the project her wholehearted endorsement. Moreover, Richmond and Howes had each made it clear that workers, who'd had a fairly strong voice in every labor reform project launched thus far, would not significantly influence the new league's agenda.[20]

Both women's speeches at the convention's closing session identified sponsors as the club movement's rightful leaders. Richmond delivered the message in the form of a scolding to club members:

> I regret very much that there is a certain *attitude* on the part of some workers here, of arrogance about being workers. . . . It is possible for persons to know a great deal about working people, have a generous sympathy with them, and the power of helping them, without being wage-earners themselves. . . . There are so many women who work hard and get no wages, and these are some of the best laborers in our Working Girls' Clubs. If they are any use in the clubs, they are the last people to assume, as of their natural right, any particular position in the club whatever; they earn their position or else they do not get it.

Workaday experience did not, that is, entitle wage earners to deference from the league's organizing committee. Appointed in recognition of their past service to the clubs, committee members had by Richmond's standards earned the right to hammer out a program on their own. According to Howes, programmatic decisions were also club sponsors' duty. "Most of the mental obligations of club work," she argued, "have to be borne by those whose shoulders are not so heavily burdened outside, and then the work is equalized." It would be unfair, in other words, to ask wage earners to participate in the deliberations sponsors were about to undertake. Though Howes's ideas about leadership differed somewhat from Richmond's, their practical implications were identical.[21]

The National League's organizers proceeded, then, without input from club members or from labor activists with friendly ties to the clubs. The isolation fostered internal unity. Indeed, all votes seem to have been unanimous when the organizing committee met in November 1897 to turn itself into the executive board of the National League of Working Women's Clubs (soon renamed the National League of Women Workers). Under the joint leadership of the newly elected President Howes and Vice President Richmond, the board made the expansion and consolidation of the club movement the league's first priority. A campaign to expand women's access to vocational education became the whole of its labor reform agenda.[22]

Sponsors' broader commitments to labor reform did not disappear, but those commitments now resided for the most part in Consumers' Leagues instead of the club movement. Edith Howes and O. M. E. Rowe became tireless organizers for the Massachusetts Consumers' League, which they helped to found in 1898 and to build into a 1,400-member network within two years. Club sponsors' names meanwhile began to dot the lists of Consumers' League officers and committee members in New York and Pennsylvania. After the turn of the century, state branches of the National League of Women Workers (NLWW) took up a variety of projects in cooperation with Consumers' Leagues, helping them lobby for protective labor laws, petition for the early closing of department stores, and prepare "White Lists" of merchants and garment manufacturers whose wares could be purchased in good conscience. Just a handful of club sponsors participated in such projects, however. The rest paid little if any attention to labor problems that could not be remedied with vocational education.[23]

Ladies operating under NLWW auspices accomplished a great deal on that front—quite enough in their opinion to vindicate the one-note approach to labor reform. In 1902, leaders of the New York Association of Working Girls' Societies oversaw the establishment of the tuition-free Manhattan Trade School, whose student body numbered several hundred within a few years. This was the first school in the United States to train teenaged girls for industrial trades: dressmaking, millinery, pasting and gluing, many varieties of machine sewing, and a few artistic crafts such as fashion sketching and photo retouching. A board of trustees composed of genteel reformers and dominated by club sponsors governed the school until 1910, when New York City's Board of Education took over. By that time, the Boston Trade School for Girls, brainchild of the NLWW's Massachusetts branch, was celebrating its fifth birthday, club sponsors in Philadelphia had opened a summer school in professional dressmaking and millinery, NLWW spokeswomen throughout the Northeast had served in successful drives to interest public school officials in training girls for wage work, and the Boston-based Girls' Trade Education League, an NLWW offshoot, was preparing bulletins that would provide public schoolgirls and guidance counselors with information about labor conditions and skill requirements in various female trades. Measured by the sheer quantity of achievements, the vocational education campaign far outshone club sponsors' earlier, piecemeal experiments with labor reform. From some perspectives, however, this advance looked like a fallback: the campaign alienated the NLWW from the labor movement and did more harm than good to many in the club movement's rank and file.[24]

As champions of vocational education, club sponsors climbed aboard a bandwagon that had been rolling for some time and colliding with trade unionism all the while. During the labor upsurges of the 1880s, businessmen in midwestern and northeastern cities funded the establishment of several private trade schools that trained boys in crafts traditionally learned through union apprenticeships. Responding to pressures from local employers and ignoring objections from many unions, municipal boards of education also founded similar schools and made manual training part of grammar and high schools' curricula in dozens of cities in industrial states. By 1890, the vocational education movement had caught the eye of monopolists such as J. P. Morgan and John D. Rockefeller, who were soon pouring millions of dollars into the cause. The 1895 formation of the National Association of Manufacturers, which promoted trade schools almost as vigorously as it attacked trade unionism, gave the movement another financial boost and an even more distinctly antilabor flavor. Objectively, then, sponsors' vocational education campaign aligned them with some of the labor movement's worst enemies.[25]

It is quite likely, moreover, that the campaign's architects made a conscious decision to distance the NLWW from trade unionists. As at least some of the NLWW's founders surely remembered, George Ellis—the master printer who vilified unions at the 1894 club convention—had urged club sponsors to promote women workers' trade training instead. Unlike him, NLWW spokeswomen did not explicitly label vocational education a substitute for unionism, but they certainly treated it as such, on paper and in practice. When the NLWW's journal, the *Club Worker*, ran an article by the Massachusetts labor commissioner on methods of raising women's wages, for instance, an accompanying editorial ignored his plug for "industrial organization" while expanding at length on his call for "efficient training." In contrast to *Far and Near*, moreover, the *Club Worker* never opened its pages to labor activists. Nor were they invited to address club conventions. The NLWW's brand of vocational education did nothing to encourage organization in the workplace. In 1908 Leonora O'Reilly, who had been teaching machine sewing at the Manhattan Trade School for five years, quit her job. What drove her out the door was the school's steadfast refusal to implement her suggestions for "intellectual" courses promoting worker solidarity. There and elsewhere, the NLWW placed an overweening emphasis on manual training, ignoring advice from old friends in the labor movement and eventually estranging them altogether.[26]

Club members got short shrift, too—shortest of all in New York City and Boston, where the vocational education campaign was most energetic. Work in connection with the new cause prompted club sponsors in both cities to abandon old projects. The Bostonians lost touch with the Women Clerks' Benefit Association and its drive to stop department stores from fining saleswomen. The Children's Dressmaking Company—the sewing and retail cooperative established by New York's Far and Near Society in 1890—collapsed in 1898, when the ladies who had managed that enterprise turned instead to groundwork for the Manhattan Trade School. Clearing the decks for similar activities, the New York Association of Working Girls' Societies handed the Alliance Employment Bureau over to a new administrative committee whose members came mostly from settlement houses and assorted charities. Each of these shifts in sponsors' commitments carried certain costs for club members. Those working in Boston's department stores lost allies in the effort to eradicate fines; those employed by the Children's Dressmaking Company lost their jobs; and once the Alliance Employment Bureau was associated with charities, club members almost never used its services.[27]

The vocational education campaign did precious little, moreover, to offset these losses with benefits to club members in either city. Early hints that the campaign would be tailored to meet their needs proved misleading. In 1901, workers throughout the NLWW were asked to report their occupations, earnings, and schooling in order to help sponsors decide what kind of trade training should be promoted. The survey revealed that about two-thirds of club members in New York and Boston were salesclerks or office workers: women who could have made good use of courses in bookkeeping, stenography, and other commercial subjects but had nothing to gain from the two industrial trade schools the NLWW soon founded. Nor were such women likely to appreciate the schools' efforts to arm students bound for factory jobs with a smattering of clerical skills, so they could tide themselves over slack seasons by switching temporarily to retail or office work. Both fields were already overcrowded, and big-city office workers in particular often complained that their wages were dragged down by barely competent competitors willing to work for a pittance. The most elaborate and, by club sponsors' lights, fruitful components of the vocational education campaign offered club members less than they had derived from the projects discarded when the campaign got rolling.[28]

Distancing sponsors from working-class influences, the vocational education campaign also drew them closer than ever before to employers. Nowhere was this more evident than at the Manhattan Trade School. As the *New York Herald* reported in 1902, New York City's manufacturers immediately "hailed the [school] as though it were designed primarily for their interest," pledging to support it in every possible way as long as it supplied them with large numbers of appropriately skilled workers. Three years later the school's supervisor announced that "large employers . . . not only give money to help it but visit it in person and suggest means for rendering its work more serviceable to trade." While the money that accompanied these suggestions undoubtedly added to their allure, employers did not have to buy their way in. Thanks to generous contributions from donors such as Mrs. Benjamin Guggenheim and Mrs. Andrew Carnegie, the school did not need local employers' financial backing. Its administrators' determination to equip students with marketable skills prompted very close attention to the fluctuating needs of those who did the hiring, however. The same was true of the NLWW's trade school in Boston, the summer school in Philadelphia, and the various committees where club sponsors devised proposals for trade training in public schools. In all quarters, then, the vocational education campaign necessitated constant consultation with employers and encouraged NLWW activists to look at the labor market from a boss's vantage point.[29]

This outlook bore a remarkable resemblance to the one embraced by sponsors before the depression of the 1890s had shaken their faith that labor conditions would improve if workers would only work harder. In addition to campaigning for vocational education, therefore, NLWW spokeswomen were soon treating the *Club Worker*'s readers and the students in NLWW-sponsored trade schools to sermons on the rewards of being a "prompt, punctual and faithful" employee. Though club sponsors no longer rejected labor reform, their zeal for reforming laborers was once again ascendant. That this should be the outcome of sponsors' turn in the mid-1890s toward "a more aggressive position in matters of every-day life" was most ironic, but the new alliances with employers made it just as inevitable.[30]

"SCIENTIFIC METHODS"

As an official NLWW history notes, the early twentieth century saw a widespread change in club sponsors' understanding of their social mission as working women's allies. The old tendency "to take the shorter view of immediate relief rather than permanent change of conditions" went by the boards. Taking its place was an enthusiasm for "scientific methods" that promised to generate sweeping reforms by bringing detailed information on working women's needs to the attention of the bourgeois public. This strategy was not entirely new to club sponsors; painstaking research and publicity directed at the elite had been part of the vocational education campaign from its inception in the late 1890s. The notion that such methods were "scientific" and ought to be more broadly applied was new, however, and its spread vastly increased sponsors' distance from club members.[31]

Sponsors' new interest in science reflected a more general trend spearheaded by social workers, reform-minded intellectuals, and research foundations. In every big city of the Northeast and Midwest, settlement and charity leaders united in the early twentieth century to found schools of social work whose curricula stressed social research. Reform movements of all stripes meanwhile attracted increasing numbers of college graduates, social science Ph.D.s, and others anxious to apply academic expertise to real-life problems. Richly endowed philanthropies, most notably the Russell Sage Foundation, began to fund elaborate studies of working-class life in various cities and extensive campaigns to publicize the findings. While these developments combined to make scientific methods the hallmark of genteel reform in the Progressive Era, a small group of highly educated newcomers to the club movement pushed sponsors to think more scientifically about their purposes.[32]

The push came from administrative secretaries hired by the National League of Women Workers and its state branches to organize new clubs and coordinate club sponsors' work. The first post, funded by the NLWW's executive board in 1898, went to Charlotte Wilkinson, a Smith College graduate with a bachelor's degree in economics and a year's experience at the Hartley House Settlement in New York City, where the league's central office was located. In 1901 she was replaced by Jean Hamilton, who held both bachelor's and master's degrees in sociology from Vassar College. Between 1906 and 1913, similarly credentialed women went to work for all of the NLWW branches—its founding associations in Massachusetts, Connecticut, New York, and eastern Pennsylvania and two new groupings in Rhode Island and the Pittsburgh area. The secretaries' reports on what other reformers were doing and suggestions as to what club sponsors should do generated a surge of "scientific activity." By the mid-1910s sponsors throughout the movement had conducted surveys of conditions in public parks and playgrounds, field studies of commercial amusements and lodging houses patronized by working women, and publicity blitzes designed to get private donors and public agencies to fund the establishment of chaperoned dance halls and residential hotels for women workers. Training sessions led by experts in social work meanwhile encouraged more "scientific" relations with club members. Thanks to a new stress on meticulous record keeping as to club members' personal circumstances, for example, information sponsors had once acquired over time by befriending new members was now collected at the door in a thoroughly businesslike manner. The external research projects militated against intimacy with club members, too, by reducing the amount of time that sponsors' spent in club meeting rooms.[33]

Underlying all of this and Progressive reform as a whole was an orientation toward top-down solutions to social problems. Despite numerous disputes as to the relative importance of improving working-class environments and working-class morals, genteel reformers of the late nineteenth century had operated on the assumption that the major task was to get working people to set things right. From the charity movement's friendly visitors at one end of the spectrum to the most radical settlement activists on the other, reformers of that period had given their best energies to cultivating relations with the same people they aimed to help. A maxim coined by Grace Dodge in the late 1880s—that club sponsors were "working *with* not *for*" club members—captures the prevailing reform spirit of the age. Progressive reformers, on the other hand, focused on getting society's more privileged sectors to look out for the welfare of the "other half." Social research was a means to that end. The data amassed became the stuff of publicity initiatives and lobbying campaigns designed to mobilize public officials, businessmen, civic and religious leaders, and other people of influence.[34]

As sponsors' research projects distanced them from club members, NLWW leaders drew even closer to employers, especially those experimenting with welfare capitalism, and became utterly oblivious to women's labor activism. Welfare capitalists had had a foot in the NLWW's door since 1897, when the National Cash Register Company (NCR) in Dayton, Ohio, sent emissaries to tell the clubs' convention in Philadelphia about the company's new employee welfare program. Under that regime, women worked a bit less than eight hours a day, got free lunches in the company dining room, and enjoyed the use of lavish recreational facilities, including lounges set aside for the company-sponsored Women's Century Club. By 1903, NCR was in the vanguard of a national crusade to inaugurate similar policies and services at all woman-employing firms. *Woman's Welfare,* a quarterly journal subsidized by the company, edited by its welfare secretary, and widely distributed to employers and genteel reformers, broadcast women's rights rhetoric along with calls for "industrial betterment" projects aimed at female employees. One typical issue featured an essay by the prominent feminist Charlotte Perkins Gilman, who hailed events at NCR as an example of "women . . . sweeping upward in ever-growing numbers and velocity"; a damning report on labor conditions in New York City's garment shops; a glowing description of welfare measures at the Heinz pickle factory in Pittsburgh; and a reverential obituary for the pioneer woman suffragist Elizabeth Cady Stanton. As this journal's contents suggest, the employer-led welfare movement made a strong bid for the sympathetic attention of genteel reformers with a dual commitment to workplace reforms and women's rights.[35]

NLWW leaders responded so positively that they barely noticed when the Women's Trade Union League, founded in 1903, launched an organizing drive that dwarfed all previous efforts to bring women wage earners into the AFL. The only kind of workplace organizing that attracted the NLWW's attention fell under the heading of welfare capitalism. The club movement's administrative secretaries organized at least eleven employer-backed factory clubs in New Jersey and Massachusetts between 1906 and 1912. Several NLWW officials meanwhile found a comfortable second home in the National Civic Federation (NCF), the welfare capitalists' main headquarters and—following the 1908 formation of the NCF Woman's Department—a gathering place for employing-class women interested in the welfare movement.[36]

Club sponsors' embrace of welfare capitalism subtracted no troops from frontline efforts to unionize women workers, but it was part of a larger phenomenon that left many women's unions in the lurch. Action in the trenches, where sponsors had never served, picked up after the birth of the Women's Trade Union League (WTUL), whose membership included a small cadre of middle- and upper-class women—mostly settlement residents—as well as working-class activists. By 1914 the WTUL had helped women workers build a fair number of new unions in northeastern and midwestern cities; but outside the garment industry, where working men provided crucial assistance, the vast majority of these unions had died in infancy. One reason was the ascendancy in the AFL of craft unionism, which combined with a sex-segregated labor market to ensure that most of the WTUL's organizing campaigns focused on the construction of female locals. Given their low wages and domestic responsibilities, the members of these locals very rarely had sufficient money and time to maintain a solid organization in one shop, let alone reach out to women in unorganized workplaces. In order to withstand hostility from employers, gather enough strength in numbers to win significant improvements in working conditions, and avoid the erosion sure to follow failures on that front, most women's unions needed help from outside their own ranks. In the absence of strong backing from union men, they especially needed help from the legions of genteel women endeavoring in the Progressive Era to improve the working woman's lot through protective legislation, ethical shopping, vocational education, and employers' welfare programs. With precious few exceptions, however, such women—members of Consumers' Leagues, Women's Educational and Industrial Unions, the Industrial Committee of the General Federation of Women's Clubs, and many other organizations in addition to the NLWW—did nothing to assist the establishment or maintenance of unions.[37]

This state of affairs derived in some measure from the antiunion propaganda that poured out of the National Association of Manufacturers and kindred organizations in the early twentieth century; but the employers who most influenced club sponsors and their like soft-pedaled antiunionism and wore a more amiable, pro-woman face. National Cash

Register's president, John Patterson, and his colleagues at the helm of the welfare movement worked the hardest to endear themselves to advocates of women's rights. The welfare movement was not, however, the only arena where employers stole a march on trade unionists by collaborating with genteel women interested in labor reform. As developments at the Manhattan Trade School demonstrate, the vocational education movement became another important site for such collaboration. Garment manufacturers meanwhile used cooperation with Consumers' Leagues to undermine the power of the union label, regaling conscientious shoppers with goods that carried the leagues' "White Label," a rival seal of approval. And when some large employers, leaders of the National Civic Federation in particular, started in the 1910s to endorse protective labor laws for women, legislative campaigns achieved a success rate high enough to draw numerous reformers away from the usually slower-going drives to organize unions. These partnerships with labor reformers gave capital many opportunities to shape their agenda. The proliferation of such partnerships probably accounts more than any other factor for union women's crippling isolation from the vast majority of working women's middle- and upper-class sympathizers.[38]

This isolation had a considerable ripple effect. It not only weakened female unions but also undercut union organizers' power to mobilize working women, whose reputed indifference to rallying cries was not simply a figment of AFL men's imaginations. Women workers, like their male counterparts, were hardly anxious to hazard the risks involved in organizing unless there seemed good reason to hope that a strong, viable union would be the result. In light of their slim chances of achieving that outcome on their own, the women counted the number of allies on the horizon with particular care. As the WTUL concluded in a 1929 booklet summarizing the lessons of a quarter century's efforts to establish new unions, the need for public support was "especially great as a background for organizing women." The greater the genteel public's tendency to ignore unions in favor of other remedies for women workers' problems, the more reluctant these workers were to give unionism a try. That reluctance increased AFL leaders' already sizable doubts about the value of organizing drives aimed at women. Though the intention was to serve working women, club sponsors and like-minded reformers made a significant, albeit indirect, contribution to their disfranchisement on the job.[39]

Working women's power within the club movement meanwhile diminished as sponsors withdrew from cross-class sociability, which had been club members' central means of influencing sponsors' thinking. The democratization of interclub governance might have assuaged the loss, giving workers a modicum of formal control over sponsors' activities outside club meeting rooms. As long as "scientific methods" were in command, however, the NLWW and its state branches tended to operate along strictly undemocratic lines. Their executive boards were not elected by the rank and file but appointed by prominent sponsors, who never chose working women. State boards usually convened on workday afternoons, preventing club members from even observing the proceedings. Though the NLWW board met on weekends, club members were uninvited and sometimes explicitly urged to stay home. By scientific standards, club members' ideas as to how the NLWW could best be of service were scarcely worth hearing, let alone soliciting.[40]

Sponsors displayed a similar attitude in individual clubs, where their failure to let members decide what kind of help they needed constantly irritated the rank and file. Shortly after the turn of the century, club members began to complain in some quarters that the "ladies . . . leave too much to the girls to do and plan." In others, they complained that overbearing ladies made workers serving on club committees feel like "an ornamental appendage." As such dissatisfactions multiplied, club members grew increasingly cold, if not downright hostile, toward new recruits to sponsors' ranks. Old hands meanwhile got the silent treatment as many clubs' monthly business meetings degenerated into what Jean Hamilton termed "Quaker Business Meetings," where sponsors waited in vain for "the spirit to move *somebody* to get up and make a motion." There was no dialogue about the deterioration in cross-class cooperation. Sponsors preferred to ignore that problem, even when club members made unvarnished attempts to bring it to their attention. In 1909, for example, one member sent the *Club Worker*'s editors the following plea, addressed in effect to all sponsors: "I have yet to see a club where the class distinction did not stick out conspicuously, and I should like to know if our attitude toward it is quite consistent or disingenuous. . . . Of course, I know that we must always compromise between the ideal and the possible, but I should like the compromise to be a bit clearer." Neither the editors nor any other lady replied. Club members ignored the letter as well. By 1909 they were as detached from club sponsors as sponsors were from them.[41]

As relations deteriorated, cross-class discussions of labor issues and all other social questions grew exceedingly rare. Sponsors very seldom tried to draw out rank-and-file opinion on such things. There is no evidence that club members attempted to initiate dialogue, and their responses to the occasional request for an opinion on work life displayed nothing of the feministic spirit evident at the 1894 convention. When women's right to hold paying jobs came up at club roundtables, for instance, pin money work was now almost universally condemned. Nor did club sponsors articulate the slightest faith that sisterhood across class lines contained solutions to labor problems. Within a few years of the NLWW's birth, in fact, no one talked of sisterhood at all. NLWW spokeswomen described club work in businesslike terms—"a good 'investment in futures,'" as one put it. In the *Club Worker* and at NLWW conventions, club members and sponsors described their activity without reference to "oneness," "common ground," or even plain friendliness between the two groups. Working women came to the clubs to socialize with one another; club sponsors came to collect data, tend to administrative tasks, and serve as chaperones; and interclub officials oversaw reform projects designed to benefit working women but never to activate them. By the mid-1910s, when NLWW leaders developed second thoughts about scientific methods, the breakdown in club members' and sponsors' cooperation had extended so far beyond the vocational education campaign that oneness could not be restored.[42]

CHAPTER 7

Disintegration

Though the National League of Women Workers fared well by numeric measures for more than twenty years, the club movement never regained the cohesion and dynamism it had possessed before the league's birth. Expanding recreational programs gave NLWW clubs a wonderfully effective drawing card. As the amusements they offered proliferated, so did the NLWW's membership, which rose from about 7,000 in 1900 to 15,000 in the mid-1910s and peaked at 30,000 in 1920. In contrast to earlier times, however, sociability did not generate a strong sense of common cause. The Philadelphia club officer who lamented in 1916 that "lots of girls come to the club merely for the good times" described a trend ascendant throughout the NLWW from the turn of the century onward. Governance, educational projects, community service, and social reform all got far less attention than they had received from the first generation of club members.[1]

If the emphasis on recreation marginalized other concerns, it did not erase their significance. That was especially evident in the mid-1910s, which saw a short-lived surge in members' involvement in club governance, a spate of patriotic projects in connection with World War I, and scattered expressions of rank-and-file support for labor reform and woman suffrage. The aspirations behind these initiatives are matters of conjecture, for twentieth-century club members lacked their predecessors' opportunities for discourse on whys and wherefores. NLWW publications and conventions were forums for factual reports on club activities, not for the exchange of ideas. Despite the silences, however, two things

seem quite clear. First, club members' disproportionate emphasis on recreation was not a straightforward reflection of their preferences; it also
reflected sponsors' dominance of all other components of club life. Second, the more members' loyalties to a club rested on its recreational program, the more perishable that club was over the long haul. Less than a
decade after its membership reached thirty thousand, the NLWW lay in
ruins, undone both by financial crises that decimated its recreational
programs and by members' and sponsors' inability to find other grounds
for cooperation.

DEMOCRACY NLWW-STYLE

In the spring of 1914, when a short economic downturn was sapping
the clubs' capacity to fund all the entertainments that members had come
to expect, NLWW leaders launched a multifaceted effort to beef up what
they called the "thoughtful" side of club life. Phase one was a campaign
to democratize the movement's governance. The league's central office
in New York City replaced its endorsements of "scientific methods" with
criticisms of "scientific detachment from the human elements" of club
work and warnings that reformers "working for, but never with, those
whom they would aid, are necessarily guiding through a fog." By year's
end, democracy was every sponsor's watchword, and NLWW headquarters was overseeing a movement-wide drive both to revive self-government in individual clubs and to involve working women in the administration of interclub affairs.[2]

Changes in interclub governance were essentially cosmetic. The *Club
Worker* captured their drift when it ushered in the democratization campaign with an editorial advising the membership to "Strive for leadership, that is your right; indeed it is *the* right democracy gives you, but
strive by having noble enthusiasms and upholding the policies of those
whose strength can carry these enthusiasms further than you can as yet.
No one ever was a victorious general who had not first learned to *obey
commands.* Democracy means a striving upward to a higher level for all,
not a pulling back of the best to the lower level of the majority." Club
members were invited, in other words, to share the chores of interclub
governance but very few of the prerogatives. Under a new constitution
drafted at NLWW headquarters, the central executive board became an
elective body chosen on a one-club, one-vote basis at the league's biennial conventions. The board also began to consult with workers serving
on newly formed advisory bodies—"auxiliary boards" to which each

club could send two delegates. The NLWW's state branches meanwhile amended their constitutions to provide for the popular election of governing councils, resolved to hold council meetings at times when working women could attend, and created cross-class committees to handle administrative tasks formerly monopolized by sponsors. None of these new avenues for self-assertion took club members very far.[3]

There were too many roadblocks, most of them erected by NLWW leaders, who had no intention of making interclub bureaucracy an instrument of majority rule. Though the executive board no longer elected itself, nominations remained its prerogative. Because board members received no compensation for what amounted to full-time jobs, they had to be wealthy women. For similar reasons, working women who stepped forward to meet the lighter demands of service on a state council could not become its officers. Nor did election to a council guarantee workers a voice in all its proceedings. Several councils that resolved in 1914 to meet at times when club members could attend were soon holding some meetings on workday afternoons—the most convenient time for club sponsors. Service on the cross-class committees organized by state councils gave club members a voice only to the extent that they said things sponsors wished to hear. Council officers had the authority to override a committee's decisions and rule its proposals inappropriate for submission to the membership. The NLWW's auxiliary boards—nominally free to publicize any proposal they pleased—issued few suggestions other than those as to how club members could implement directives from league executives, whose secretaries set the agenda for auxiliary board meetings and chaired them as well. All in all, the reforms in interclub governance had a miniscule effect on the distribution of power. Club members' response, following a surge of exploratory activity, was almost wholly apathetic.[4]

In individual clubs, power shifted in more meaningful ways, but here, too, democratization had a downside. It revived sponsors' didacticism, which burst forward after many years in the closet and clashed with members' enthusiasm for recreation, not to mention their pride. With recruitment utmost in mind, ladies throughout the NLWW had committed themselves for over a decade to making club life lots of fun. Emissaries from NLWW headquarters had overseen the establishment of a host of new clubs where educational activities were few and amusements plentiful. In long-standing clubs, sponsors formerly full of suggestions for lectures, classes, and roundtables had become tireless organizers of fun and games—including mixed-sex parties, which were now part of nearly every club's weekly calendar. Sponsors' commitments to making club life fun had competed all along, though, with a desire to teach instead of entertain. By the early 1910s, more than one lady was complaining to NLWW headquarters that "the club doesn't seem to be accomplishing very much" due to a scarcity of "thoughtful" members. The democratization campaign promised to remedy that shortfall. Members were not only urged to participate in club governance but also instructed as to proper methods of participation. The main lesson sponsors tried to convey was that self-government required solemnity—that it was not, as many club members seemed to think, a task that could be handled in a jolly, catch-as-catch-can manner.[5]

There was no denying that self-government had been a sham in most clubs for some years and that this problem had something to do with members' taste for recreation, romantic pastimes in particular. The root of the problem, however, was sponsors' interventions into situations like those portrayed in a play entitled "A Club Comedy," written by members of Boston's Wiltse Literary Club in 1909. The play depicts the unceremonious adjournment of a club business meeting when its participants learn that a dance is about to begin at a local men's club, a picnic where club members muse about their future husbands instead of laying plans to fill an empty treasury, and the club's decision, after a failed attempt to produce *Macbeth*, to raise money by performing a play with a "love plot."[6]

When "A Club Comedy" appeared in the *Club Worker*, the editors dubbed it an "excellent parody of many club efforts," and it probably gave most sponsors a chuckle; but they were not at all amused by the realities the play burlesqued. Most clubs in operation since before the NLWW's birth ran like well-oiled machines, thanks to the presence of veteran members who recalled the democratization drive of the early 1890s, aimed to preserve its results, and had passed the age when romance was likely to distract them from other concerns. Clubs of this sort were ever fewer in number, however. Dominated by aging members whose preferred pastimes did not especially appeal to youth, they regularly disintegrated when the old-timers grew too old to carry on. The NLWW was increasingly composed, then, of newer clubs where youth predominated, romantic preoccupations abounded, and sponsors, certain that they alone could avert chaos, appropriated numerous responsibilities that belonged by rights to the rank and file or to the mostly working-class officers they elected.[7]

Democracy's failures were much discussed by club sponsors, but only rarely did they consider that their constant circumventions of democratic structures made it rather pointless for the membership to keep those structures in good working order. As one unusually perceptive speaker remarked at a 1907 meeting where sponsors gathered to review their problems as "club leaders": "Some leaders may say that their girls will not govern themselves, that they are not interested. No sensible girl will be interested if she feels that the leaders will decide, and do decide every question or any question which is presented to her, even though she never formulates this feeling." In general, sponsors preferred to think that their undemocratic practices merely compensated for shortcomings on the part of "their girls." Doubts about members' readiness for genuine self-government weighed most heavily on club sponsors in big cities, where competition from commercial amusements was so great by 1910 that club meeting rooms once abuzz six nights a week stood empty on many evenings and the falloff in attendance suggested that members were unwilling, if not unfit, to run the show. Even in booming clubs, however, sponsors could find reasons to believe that they simply had to take charge. Though they worried a great deal about the state of club governance, therefore, sponsors very seldom took remedial action until NLWW leaders virtually ordered them to follow democratic procedures to the letter.[8]

Picking up on leaders' cues in more ways than one, the meddlers mended their ways in an obnoxiously preachy manner. Pamphlets issued by NLWW headquarters described the self-governing club as a "school of character" and a means to "teach citizenship." The idea that club members needed instruction figured even more prominently in sponsors' efforts to promote democracy. Club members were admonished for skipping business meetings, for talking too little or too much when they did attend, for ignorance of parliamentary procedure, for lackadaisical or peremptory behavior as club officers—the list went on and on. Some of this rhetoric featured oblique references to the woman suffrage movement and faint suggestions that self-government's primary aim was to get working women into the habit of exercising voting rights. But rights were never mentioned in connection with workers' role in club governance, which the NLWW's president Sarah Ollesheimer summarized in three constantly heard words: "obligations, duties and responsibilities." For the most part, club members' response to all of this was quite cold: the majority continued to show up at their meeting rooms for the good times alone.[9]

126 THE COMMON GROUND OF WOMANHOOD

Good times were also on the minds of the minority of club members who allied with the democratization campaign—and defeated its architects' purpose. They attended club business meetings on a regular basis; took the lion's share of responsibility for recruitment, fund-raising, publicity, dues collection, and so on; handled their assignments with dispatch; and managed in the process to make fun and romance even larger components of club life. Bigger crowds at business meetings meant a broader array of recreational proposals. The greater the members' participation in a club's recruitment efforts, the greater the number of lavish recruitment parties, especially events to which men were invited. Fund-raising, too, entailed more mixed-sex entertainments when members took charge, and their publicity schemes sometimes had a romantic flavor as well. A club in Winsted, Connecticut, for example, "gained much good advertising" by setting up a correspondence bureau that put members in touch with state militiamen called to the Mexican border in 1916. On balance, the democratization of club governance did more to bolster the supremacy of recreation than to extend members' involvement in endeavors that club sponsors deemed "thoughtful."[10]

Members' priorities go a long way to account for that irony, but so does sponsors' enduring command of interclub bodies, the NLWW's executive board in particular. In the early 1890s, when interclub bureaucracy was in its infancy, democratic reforms in club governance had not only mobilized a larger proportion of the membership but had also generated a wider range of initiatives on their part. In addition to turning their meeting rooms into livelier recreational centers, club members of that era had inaugurated polemics against proposals for abandoning self-support as a club principle, challenges to sponsors' attempts to domesticate working girls, discussions of labor problems and their solutions, and other efforts to bring the club movement's policies into closer line with rank-and-file concerns. Once the NLWW was established, however, its executives claimed exclusive jurisdiction over all policy issues. Any club member who imagined that the democratization campaign would alter this fact was soon set straight.

There were constant reminders that self-government in individual clubs did not increase members' control of the club movement. NLWW headquarters regularly issued communiqués like the following from June 1915: "Club members should remember that the Executive Board which determines League policies and [a]ffects the life of each club, is a representative body *for whom they are responsible,* and should demand a *detailed* report twice a year." The board's reports contained quite a few surprises, moreover, for the fact that it was now a titularly elective body certainly did not make it representative of the NLWW's membership. While club members pondered the ins and outs of fund-raising and dues collection, for instance, the executive board reopened the question of self-support and declared in 1918 that the NLWW would henceforth admit clubs dependent on endowments. Nor did rank-and-file opinion have any discernible influence on the executive board's decisions as to which social causes would be discussed at club conventions, covered in the *Club Worker,* or stamped with NLWW endorsements. As club members could not help but realize, their thinking about the club movement's principles and social purposes carried so little weight that more elaborate recreational programs were about the best they could hope to gain from the democratization campaign.[11]

"ONENESS" REVISITED

If phase one of club sponsors' push for thoughtfulness came to nothing, so in the end did phase two: a concerted effort from 1914–20 to engage club members in talks designed to "throw a different light on . . . important social questions and prepare us for practical co-operation and action." After years of treating social reform as the province of privileged classes, club sponsors and NLWW officials now invited club members to unite with them in behalf of "civic good." Here, as in the democratization campaign, rank-and-file enthusiasm for good times combined with sponsors' control of interclub affairs to militate against a sweeping change in the movement's tenor. But there were also more fundamental obstacles to members' cooperation with sponsors in support of social causes. Club members' status in society at large robbed cross-class alliances of the allure they had enjoyed in the late nineteenth century. Members' desire to distance themselves from working women of lower status limited the range of causes that could win rank-and-file support. And most important of all perhaps, sponsors' commitment to cooperative civic action proved less durable than their wariness of labor militancy and desire to endear the NLWW to the employing class.[12]

In October 1916, the *Club Worker* reported that members' and sponsors' discussions of civic affairs and responsibilities were "awakening us to a sense of our *oneness*." That word, used in the 1890s as a synonym for sisterhood, had not been part of club rhetoric for many years. Its reappearance reflected NLWW leaders' optimism in response to hints that the present generation of club members might eventually be as eager as their late nineteenth-century predecessors to become sponsors' partners in social reform. If oneness was on the rise, however, the word no longer referred to a feeling of common cause rooted in shared definitions of woman's proper place, for that issue was not very important in clubs of the 1910s.[13]

Oneness had been a burning question twenty years earlier, when club members had reason to worry about their image in the public eye. Concerns evident at the club movement's inception (the 1884 meeting where charter members of the 38th Street Society voted to "show New York that we are not ashamed of *work*") shaped workers' agenda throughout the movement for more than a decade to come and provided the glue for their sisterly relations with sponsors. The democratization of club life in the early 1890s emboldened members' challenges to the idea that working women lacked respectability. Conspicuous compliance with gender orthodoxy—rhetorical endorsements of "true, noble womanliness," for example—gave way to rejections of orthodox thinking about woman's place. Yet anxieties about public opinion remained a guiding force, as observers noted as late as 1897. The idea that a respectable woman devoted herself to domestic concerns drew especially heavy fire, for polite society's claims to that effect lay at the heart of most public aspersions on working women's character. Another demeaning doctrine—the popular notion that, for women of small means, any husband was better than none—came under attack in club talks about marriage and spinsterhood. The demand that men mind their manners at mixed-sex club sociables asserted members' right to respect from the general public as well as gracious treatment from male guests. Club sponsors allied with all of these projects. Indeed, their most valuable trait as allies was an impeccable respectability, which lent a reputable air to everything in which they were involved. Their sympathy for rank-and-file attitudes toward domesticity, marriage, and men supplied the raw material for oneness, but it was club members' anxieties about their public image that made this material significant.[14]

In 1916 such things were scarcely significant, for polite society had revised its standards for deciding women's face value as respectables or moral suspects. The old axiom that working women were suspects until proved otherwise now yielded to the assumption that some of them were respectables. This shift was partly a function of new trends in the occupational and class composition of the female labor force. Professional, managerial, and clerical jobs proliferated during the long economic upswing that began at the end of the 1890s and continued through World

War I. Many of the new positions—mainly those in the clerical field and relatively humble professions like teaching, social work, and librarianship—were filled by women, including genteel women, whose rate of gainful employment between schooling and marriage reached unprecedented heights. The greater that rate, the less genteel culture's arbiters stigmatized female participation in the labor market and the more they praised what one termed "the courage, cheerfulness, [and] pluck of women with careers." By the mid-1910s, advice manuals addressed to middle-class women warmly endorsed employment before marriage and in some cases added that wives were justified in taking jobs once their children had grown. Refined journals like the *Century* saluted the fact that some women from extremely wealthy families "not only earned their own living outside the home, but . . . earned it with conspicuous success." Polite society believed, of course, that working women from the working class were inferior to those from privileged backgrounds, and writers hailing genteel women's employment sometimes took pains to distinguish them from the "usually vulgar, sometimes immoral factory girl." But the days were gone when work sufficed in and of itself to mark women as disreputable.[15]

Employment served, in fact, as a badge of good character for the expanding ranks of club members and other working-class women in clerical jobs, which employed less than 4 percent of the female labor force in 1900 and 16 percent in 1920. Polite society was especially quick to assume the respectability of occupational groups that included significant numbers of its own daughters. The clerical group amply filled that bill, despite the predominance of working-class women. The Intercollegiate Bureau of Occupations—an employment agency for college women—placed numerous clients in stenographic positions; and secretarial jobs were regularly mentioned when the genteel press delineated fields where women with college degrees had built successful careers. Genteel women in office work did their best to distinguish themselves from working-class wage earners. When middle-class office women formed the National Federation of Business and Professional Women in 1918, for instance, one of their objectives was to speed "woman's progress in business" by making a high-school diploma—something many working-class clericals lacked—a requirement for office work. Employers did not comply, however, and, to genteel women's dismay, casual observers could not tell the difference between office women from "good families" and those from the working class. In popular parlance, the term "businesswoman" covered everyone from file clerks to executives. If this lowered middle-class office women, it also elevated their working-class counterparts. Club members' public image as working women was especially respectable, then, in commercial centers such as New York City and Boston, where clerks, stenographers, and bookkeepers made up about half of the NLWW's membership in 1901 and a steadily larger proportion thereafter.[16]

Genteel culture's racial hierarchies also enhanced the ascriptive status of the vast majority of NLWW members, from the clerical and sales workers who predominated in big-city clubs to the factory workers who packed club meeting rooms in smaller cities and mill towns. Whatever the locale, most club members belonged to what was often called the "American race": they were native-born women of northern and western European ancestry. The same had been true of nineteenth-century club members and had placed them, according to dominant standards, a cut or two above people of other races. But the stigma attached to the fact that they were "daughters of labor" had overshadowed the prestige they enjoyed on the basis of racial identity. By the mid-1910s, however, race had a more potent cultural meaning than it had a generation earlier, and the fact that club members belonged to the "American race" was enough to give them a prima facie claim to respectability.[17]

This development reflected changes in the makeup of the working class in the northeastern states where the NLWW was based. Beginning in 1896, the streams of "new immigrants" from southern and eastern Europe exceeded the inflow of northwestern Europeans. Toward the end of the peak immigration period of 1902–14, when Italians, Slavs, and Jews from the Russian-Polish Pale arrived in especially gigantic numbers, the gender composition of the Italian and Slavic streams—overwhelmingly male in earlier times—assumed the more balanced proportions long typical of Jewish immigrants. There was a smaller but significant influx of African Americans: a steady trickle of southern migrants, more than half of them women, before World War I and a veritable river during the war years, when about 5 percent of black southerners moved north. Within this context, class hostilities often assumed a racial character, and so did upper-class social thought. Employers' associations, professors, prominent clergymen, and journalists made race an increasingly central theme in their discourses on all manner of issues, from strikes to world history. Polite society's aspersions on working women's character were now aimed for the most part at race-specific targets without much representation in the NLWW.[18]

Nowhere was this trend more evident than in elite discourses on prostitution. In the 1880s and nineties, northeastern moral reformers had associated commercial sex with working girls, whose class identity had supposedly made them exceptionally prone to vice. Progressive Era reformers sounded a very different theme: they identified vice-prone women by race. Muckrakers such as George Kibbe Turner won journalistic fame by churning out images of brothels packed with "little Italian peasant girls" sold into prostitution by their fiancés, Slavic women lured in by men they had met at dance halls, and "ignorant immigrant girls" from Russian Jewish enclaves like New York City's Lower East Side, which Turner deemed "the chief recruiting-ground for the so-called white slave trade in the United States, and probably in the world." Reports issued by the municipal vice commissions that proliferated after 1900 added another racial stereotype to popular images of the brothel: "colored maids trim and smart in white aprons." Genteel reformers involved in protective work on behalf of new immigrants or African American migrants from the South regularly broadcast warnings that women from these groups were apt to wind up in houses of sin if left to their own devices. By the mid-1910s, the notion that brothels were haunts for new-immigrant and African American women prevailed throughout the Northeast—despite the fact that white, native-born women of the "American race" outnumbered all others arrested during police sweeps of red-light districts.[19]

At the same time, popular culture abounded with imagery suggesting that new-immigrant and African American women did not measure up to "American" moral standards even if they never set foot in a brothel. Black temptresses caused no end of trouble, for example, in best-selling romance novels like Thomas Dixon's *Clansman* (1905), which also enjoyed a long run as a stage play and reached gigantic audiences when it came to movie screens as *The Birth of a Nation* in 1915. Reformers' exposés of factory women's labor conditions remarked on the "boisterousness and slatternliness" of the foreigners. Professors of sociology, eugenics, and related subjects showered lay readers with treatises claiming that, as one book put it, a "low type of group morals" obtained among all descendants of Africa while the new European immigrants included "altogether too large a proportion of the 'three D's'—defectives, delinquents and dependents." Endorsing those propositions, advice manuals addressed to working women of the "self-respecting American" sort warned against mixing with women on a "lower plane." Though class hierarchies still entered the picture, a woman's race now loomed larger than any other factor in shaping the dominant culture's assumptions as to her character. The average NLWW member was not only immune to the race-specific mainstream of aspersions on working women's morals;

she also enjoyed a mantle of respectability thanks to her racial difference from the targets of these aspersions.[20]

The prestige that club members of the mid-1910s derived from their racial identities, from their jobs in the case of clerical workers, and from elites' disinclination to stigmatize unmarried women's work outside the home precluded a revival of the old oneness with club sponsors. Cross-class discussions of domesticity and marriage had all but disappeared. Sponsors' thought on both subjects was probably quite agreeable on the whole to the membership, but it was also irrelevant. Its significance had receded along with club members' need to persuade a doubtful public that they qualified as respectables.

Cross-class discussions of men still took place, but they hardly promoted oneness, for members' and sponsors' rules of sexual decorum were now worlds apart. Consider, for example, the controversy behind the NLWW Executive Board's decision in the winter of 1913–14 to hand down "Rules for Correct Dancing" at club parties attended by men. Though these gatherings were quite tame by rank-and-file standards, club sponsors had been trying for some years to make them tamer still by taking up cudgels against the modern—and, in sponsors' opinion, lewd—dances that came into fashion among working-class youth around 1905. Unhappy with the meager results of sponsors' efforts to eradicate modern dancing club by club, the executive board proposed a general ban on close embraces, "deep dips," "conspicuous movements of the hips or shoulders," and the "undue display of hosiery." There is no record of club members' response to this proposal, but it is doubtful that the executive board's action subtracted anything from modern dances' popularity in club meeting rooms.[21]

The controversy would never have mushroomed to the point where it commanded the board's attention if most club members had thought it important that their etiquette win sponsors' approval. Class tensions on that front were not a novelty in club circles; they had been evident more than twenty years earlier in members' readiness outside club meeting rooms to defy the high-toned behavioral code sponsors recommended for everyday use. Club members were now so confident of their claims to respectability, however, that they also felt free to defy that code in sponsors' presence. Initially confined to the margins of club life, class tensions surrounding questions of etiquette had moved to the center by the mid-1910s and overshadowed the remnants of members' and sponsors' "common ground of womanhood."

NLWW leaders' civic action campaign, which began when such tensions were reaching a crescendo, helped to diffuse them by giving club members and sponsors an alternate basis for cooperation. There lay the kernel of truth in the *Club Worker*'s announcement that a new sense of oneness was on the rise. Activities embodying that feeling were mighty few, however, until the United States entered the world war, and never assumed much momentum overall. In the summer of 1914, Philadelphia's Lighthouse Club founded a woman suffrage society that agitated among textile workers in the Kensington district. A year later, five hundred women from New York City clubs marched in a local suffrage parade. In the winter of 1915–16, a petition drive organized by a pair of clubs in Pittsfield, Massachusetts, persuaded local retail establishments to close early on Tuesday evenings. News of the war in Europe meanwhile inspired several clubs to start rolling bandages for civilian relief organizations. A few months after the United States joined the combatants, most NLWW clubs were "doing their bit" in one way or another—buying or selling Liberty Bonds, for instance, cultivating war gardens, promoting food conservation, or working with the Red Cross. Some clubs and several of the NLWW's state councils also agitated for strict enforcement of labor laws during the military mobilization, when employers with government contracts went unpunished for numerous violations of statutes protecting workers. Though each of these projects mobilized women across class lines, a durable platform for cooperative civic action did not materialize. In the end, club members' and sponsors' opinions as to which causes merited action proved more discordant than compatible.[22]

Their most widespread form of cooperation on behalf of "civic good"—service to the U.S. war effort—was not nearly as unifying as the large amount of activity would suggest. While sponsors were foursquare behind war service from the moment the United States went to war in April 1917, the *Club Worker* reported in June that only half of club members were interested in taking up service projects, and once such projects were underway, the level of rank-and-file participation fell short of NLWW leaders' expectations. While nearly every club did something, lots of members—the majority in quite a few clubs—left that something to others, and many more were only sporadically active. By the spring of 1918, NLWW headquarters was relatively happy with the total volume of service but worried that too few club members had "waked up to the fact that these times demand something of *them*,—and that they are not 'good Americans' until they have done their share."[23]

In clubs where war service caught on like wildfire, moreover, it revolved around an activity that NLWW officials did not promote: outreach to men in uniform. In some cases this meant writing to the troops. Wherever local conditions permitted, however, club members made face-to-face contact by organizing dances and other entertainments for enlisted men. Those events were legion in Boston, New York City, and Philadelphia, all of which were packed with soldiers and sailors for the duration of the war and for nearly a year after the armistice of November 1918. Club members in smaller cities and towns close to military installations got in on the act, too. The Girls' Club of York, Pennsylvania, for example, held dances for tank engineers at Gettysburg's Camp Holt, and the Unity Club of White Plains, New York, did the same for infantrymen encamped in that city. Servicemen's integration into club social life attracted multitudes of new members. The Unity Club's dances brought its active membership from 12 to 150; the word from York was that "crowds of girls joined in order to attend the dances." Several big-city clubs reached sizes never before seen. New York's United Club acquired a membership of 900, thanks to "Army and Navy dances," which also helped the Girls' City Club of Boston grow from 200 at the time of its founding in October 1918 to 1,000 by April 1919. The newcomers added to the already large proportion of NLWW members who viewed good times as their clubs' only raison d'être. War service, which dwarfed all other civic action projects, did more on the whole to reinforce the rank-and-file emphasis on recreation and romance than to foster the "thoughtful" activity NLWW leaders had envisioned when they pushed for such projects.[24]

The military demobilization did not dent the festive atmosphere, moreover, for as the servicemen went home the employing class began to shower the NLWW with extraordinarily generous gifts that expanded the recreational opportunities available to club members. NLWW leaders had paved the way for these donations by issuing wartime publicity pamphlets that described the club movement in terms guaranteed to please the upper crust. One typical pamphlet outlined the league's aims as follows:

> *Teaching loyalty*, to nation, community and employer. . . .
> *Developing dependability and leadership*. A good officer in a club becomes a good boss in a factory.
> *Reducing unrest*, by furnishing outlet for surplus energy and creative instinct and providing a community interest.

The main payoff from such publicity came during the giant strike wave of 1919 and for a half year or so after that upheaval, which mobilized multitudes of women workers and coincided with vigorous drives to unionize women in white-collar occupations as well as those in industrial jobs. Chapters of the Women's Trade Union League reported many victories for strikers and numerous advances by union organizers. Against this backdrop the well-to-do regarded the National League of Women Workers, with its promises of "reducing unrest," as an extremely worthy cause. New sympathizers stepped forward to help the NLWW establish outposts in Ohio, and its clubs in the Northeast were literally showered with gifts. Local corporations presented various mill town clubs with large clubhouses—complete with fancy furniture, pianos, and Victrolas—and hired "club secretaries" to organize jam-packed recreational programs. Other clubs in small and big cities alike acquired similar accommodations and personnel, thanks to donations or loans from upper-class individuals and civic groups. Fund-raising drives conducted by the NLWW's state branches raked in well over $100,000, providing money for the purchase or rental of still more clubhouses and the hiring of more club secretaries. The proliferation of lavish recreational facilities and programs drew thousands of fresh recruits into NLWW clubs.[25]

Members' and sponsors' cooperation on behalf of civic causes meanwhile dissolved. Woman suffrage—endorsed by an overwhelming majority at the 1918 club convention—was a dead issue by fall 1919, when the Nineteenth Amendment had been passed by Congress and ratified by the legislature of nearly every state where the NLWW operated. Club sponsors' interest in labor reform disappeared during the 1919 strike wave, giving way to calls for cooperation with employers. Club members did not support the causes that sponsors embraced in the postwar era, when NLWW headquarters proposed movement-wide efforts to uplift African American women and "Americanize" new immigrants by recruiting both into the NLWW.[26]

The reigning assumption in all club quarters was that people of purely European ancestry were inherently superior to those of African descent. Club spokeswomen had never issued formal decrees to this effect, but club activities and publications had made it apparent for many years that both members and sponsors held African Americans in contempt. Minstrels and skits performed in blackface were incorporated into recreational programs in the early 1890s and grew especially common after 1900. The *Club Worker* encouraged their spread by printing vivid descriptions of entertainments like "The Darkey Wedding," a "side-splitting" burlesque staged by Baltimore's Myrtle Club in 1907. NLWW secretaries organized a similar performance at the 1914 club convention, which featured an "historical" pageant in which club members portrayed slaves dancing in "the care-free, buoyant spirit of the South." Minstrel shows held in public halls were key components of a fund-raising campaign launched by the NLWW's New York branch in 1918. And in May 1920, just months after the *Club Worker* had endorsed African American women's recruitment into the NLWW, the editors broadcast their version of minstrel humor by printing a joke that began with the line, "He was a little pickaninny," and degenerated from there. Club members' and sponsors' only noticeable difference with respect to color prejudice was that sponsors' sense of superiority to African Americans was laced with feelings of noblesse oblige while members' was of the purely phobic variety. This one difference was enough, however, to place club members sharply at odds with NLWW officials' call for outreach to the legions of African American women who had migrated northward during the war.[27]

The call for outreach appeared in the *Club Worker* in the fall of 1919, shortly after a group of African American working women confronted a league organizer soliciting funds for the establishment of a club that would serve "the girls of the community." Did the community she had in mind include them? The answer was no. Interclub associations in Pennsylvania and Massachusetts had each admitted one African American club in the 1890s; the Massachusetts club, Boston's Phillis Wheatley Union, had stayed long enough to become part of the NLWW; and the trade schools founded by the league in New York City and Boston had always admitted African American students. Black and white women had never joined the same clubs, however. By 1919, when the Phillis Wheatley Union was long gone and the NLWW's trade schools had been absorbed into public school systems, the league's membership was entirely white, and none of its projects served African Americans.

Criticism from African American women—workers like those mentioned above and, NLWW headquarters reported, a number of middle-class reformers as well—combined with news of the race riots sweeping northern cities to persuade club sponsors that it was time for a change. Not a revolutionary change: no sponsor suggested that existing clubs recruit women of color. According to the *Club Worker*'s October 1919 editorial, however, it was imperative that club members and sponsors find a mutually agreeable method of bringing African American clubs into the NLWW. "As a democratic organization," the editors declared, "we must find some way to make our experience of service to colored girls. . . . *As practical club girls we must make a wise plan that will work!*" Club members were urged to discuss the matter thoroughly so that their delegates to the upcoming auxiliary board meetings would be ready to help NLWW executives hammer out a suitable program. To get the discussions rolling in profitable directions, the *Club Worker* also printed an article in which a National Urban League official described the hardships and achievements of "The Negro in the North."[28]

Club members did indeed talk things over, but their conclusions were not at all like those of club sponsors. The auxiliary board meetings in November 1919 were unique in two respects. They were the only board meetings to which each and every club sent a delegate, and they were the only meetings where board members refused to rubber-stamp a proposal presented by NLWW executives. Some delegates were willing to consider a plan under which African American clubs would join the NLWW on a Jim Crow basis, forfeiting the right to send representatives to the NLWW's state councils, to use the vacation lodges run by the councils, and to participate in social activities organized by white clubs. The rest of the delegates wanted African American women to stay out altogether, and they expressed this opinion with such vehemence that NLWW executives decided in December 1919 to table the issue for twelve months. As club members mulled things over, the NLWW's central office hired Sarah Collins Fernandis—an African American social worker and veteran organizer of interracial civic projects among genteel women in Baltimore—to tour the various clubs and tell the membership about "the need of recreational clubs for the girls of her race." Club members greeted her cordially but did not change their minds about African American women's recruitment, and league executives did not fulfill their promise to reopen the question. Though clubs for African American working women proliferated in northern cities in the postwar era, they never forged ties with the NLWW.[29]

When NLWW headquarters proposed a recruitment drive aimed at immigrants from eastern and southern Europe, club members were not so much contentious as indifferent. New immigrants, Italians in particular, had been targets of hostility and derision in club circles of the 1880s and nineties. From the turn of the century onward, however, the prevailing rules of club etiquette prohibited displays of contempt for any European race, mainly because women from new-immigrant communities—an infinitesimal part of nineteenth-century clubs—were trickling into the NLWW at a fairly steady rate. The cumulative influx by the end of World War I was widespread but small and almost wholly composed of women who had been born in the United States or arrived so long ago that they were indistinguishable from natives. The scarcity of more recent arrivals among club members reflected the movement's shady reputation in new-immigrant communities, where most of the older generation thought it scandalous for a young woman to socialize with men unless family members were present. Club sponsors could not solve this problem on their own; and though club members had no particular objection to socializing with assimilated immigrants, they did not intend to help sponsors reach the "foreigners." Rank-and-file indifference toward NLWW leaders' call for a campaign to "attract more foreign-born girls" amounted, then, to a very effective form of resistance.[30]

Barely a year after the call was first issued, league headquarters declared the campaign a surefire success. In March 1919, the *Club Worker* featured a front-page article in which Frances Kellor, a social worker prominent in upper-class efforts to crush immigrant radicalism during the war, urged club members to "help the immigrant woman keep her faith in America" by bringing her into their midst. In June 1920 the journal reported that club members throughout the NLWW had decided that "the *good* club is the high school of Americanization" and that those in mill towns were already experimenting with methods of "attracting the pupil to the school." The testimony of a participant from outside the NLWW indicates, however, that the campaign to recruit new immigrants did not in reality go well at all.[31]

That participant was Arous Azadian, whose graduate thesis for Columbia University's Teachers College describes her fieldwork with a club that league headquarters hailed as a pacesetter where immigrants' recruitment was concerned. Though her thesis identifies the club by pseudonym ("Merrytown Girls' Centre"), the data provided leave no doubt that she worked with the Valley Girls' Club in Arctic, Rhode Island—one of a string of textile villages in the Pawtuxet Valley, where immigrants made up 80 percent of the population. When Azadian arrived on the scene in early 1920, the "Girls' Centre," which had a clubhouse and secretary paid for by mill owners, comprised seventy-five members, nearly all of them native born. The secretary had tried to arouse an interest in reaching immigrants but found that the "American women were self contained and indifferent." Azadian's assignment was to supply the "Girls' Centre" with an immigrant base by traveling to nearby towns and organizing satellite clubs for the foreign born.[32]

It proved a tremendously difficult and largely futile task. Few foreign-born parents would allow their daughters to have any connection to the central club, whose program featured numerous "dances of cabaret style" and whose consequent reputation in immigrant enclaves was best summarized by a Polish mother who declared, "My daughters not go . . . ; too rough, no good for ladies." By promising wary parents that the satellites would focus exclusively on educational activities, Azadian managed by summer 1920 to establish four small clubs composed mainly of Polish and Portuguese women. In August, however, the central club dealt the satellites a crushing blow by holding a lawn party where games of chance were played, lewd wrestling matches took place, and couples danced late into the evening. As word of those doings spread, many parents pulled their daughters out of the satellites, which never recovered from the loss.

In spring 1921, when the *Club Worker* hailed the Valley Girls' Club and its outlying units as the sterling example of native- and foreign-born women's unity under the NLWW umbrella, Azadian's thesis reported that three of the four satellites she had founded were practically extinct while the lone survivor maintained only nominal ties to the central club. If events in the Pawtuxet Valley gave the *Club Worker* cause to cheer, the drive to unite the clubs' "American girls" with immigrants must have made neglible headway before it petered out in mid-1921.[33]

Club members' noncooperation with that drive and outright opposition to African American women's recruitment embodied a lot of home-grown bigotry, but polite society's racialism played an important role as well. Though it gave working-class women of the "American race" far more prestige than they had enjoyed when the club movement was born, it did not by any means close the gap between their status and that of upper-class women. This gap was apparently much on the minds of the hundreds of workers who attended the NLWW's June 1920 convention, which voted to change the league's name from National League of Women Workers to National League of Girls' Clubs (NLGC). Club members instigated the change because, as a reporter noted, "they wished to assert their title to wide and beautiful living such as any girl might enjoy, to a horizon not limited by their jobs." The "any girl" in question came, of course, from an upper-class family—the kind that might send a girl to Bryn Mawr College, where the convention met. And the racial exclusivity that characterized not only Bryn Mawr but virtually every upper-class institution and organization made exclusivity all the more attractive to club members. In addition to reflecting their own racial phobias, exclusivity enhanced their claims to equality with the daughters of an ever more consciously white and "American" bourgeoisie.[34]

While NLWW leaders' appeals for interracialism set them apart from the mainstream of bourgeois culture, moreover, their postwar civic action platform most certainly did not suggest a strong identification with working-class daughters of any race. To put the best construction on things, one might surmise that the league's executive board intended to chip away at club members' bigotry so that the NLWW could draw working women of all races into an alliance for self-advancement. If the board was genuinely committed to challenging bigotry, however, why did it table the question of African Americans' recruitment as soon as the auxiliary boards balked? And why did the *Club Worker* pretend that club members' indifference toward new immigrants' recruitment constituted warm support? As NLWW leaders had shown many times in the past, they were scarcely shy about badgering recalcitrant rank and filers to change their ways. If the executive board's fondest wish was to unite working women across racial lines, why did it abandon agitation in behalf of labor reform? Though racial stratification in the labor market imbued African American women, new immigrants, and members of the "American race" with disparate grievances and aspirations with respect to work life, the universal discontent they evinced amid the labor upheavals of the late 1910s was the closest thing they had to common ground. NLWW leaders' awareness of that fact stands out quite clearly in the wartime publicity pamphlets that identified unrest among working women as the order of the day. All things considered, it seems that mobilizing workers was the last thing on the executive board's mind as it designed an postwar civic action platform. Given the absence of a labor reform plank, it is impossible to escape the conclusion that the primary goal was to devise a platform acceptable to the wealthy donors who stepped forward in 1919 to help the NLWW combat labor militancy.

Conservatism suffused the club movement, then, during the postwar era. Club members elected to safeguard their respectable image as "American girls" by keeping their distance from working women of subordinate races. NLWW leaders' hands-off attitude toward labor issues outrivaled whatever remained of their commitment to social reform in partnership with workers. Club sponsors stopped pushing for such partnerships once the appeals for outreach to African American and new-immigrant women fell flat. For all of these reasons, the cross-class oneness aborning during the war utterly disintegrated. As phase two of the drive to beef up club life's "thoughtful" side drew to a close, a few clubs organized classes in civics, but civic action was a thing of the past. An all-consuming focus on amusements once again became the rule.

CRISIS AND COLLAPSE

The emphasis on recreation did not undermine the club movement's stability as long as its coffers remained full; but the flush times immediately following the war paved the way for disaster during the hard times that soon arrived. Employers and other wealthy donors provided money for the employment of more and more club secretaries—one for every 160 club members in Massachusetts, for example—and the college women who served in that capacity took over numerous governance chores and prerogatives that had been assigned to the membership during the democratization campaign of the mid-1910s. Many clubs' facilities and programs grew so elaborate that members could not possibly keep them intact without financial assistance. By spring 1920 at least half of the league's clubs needed help with their monthly expenses, despite the fact that interclub bodies or local benefactors paid for club secretaries. The increasingly lavish clubhouses and entertainments vastly accelerated the movement's growth. In June 1920, when the NLWW became the NLGC, its members numbered 17,000; by November it had added another 13,000 to the rolls! As events were about to reveal, however, trends in club governance and funding made the movement considerably less sturdy than the NLGC's elated leaders assumed.[35]

The crunch came in the winter of 1920–21, with the onset of a two-year depression that drastically reduced the inflow of aid from the employing class, tossed many club members out of work and into arrears in their dues, and triggered cutbacks in recreational programs from one end of the NLGC to the other. Though the club movement had lost legions of members amid similar cutbacks during the depression of 1893–97, roughly equal numbers of loyalists had taken a proprietary interest in seeing their clubs through hard times. When the 1921–22 depression hit, on the other hand, the widespread presence of salaried club secretaries and extensive financial dependence on wealthy outsiders precluded a strong sense of proprietorship among club members—especially the thousands who had signed on during the postwar boom.

If patterns in governance and funding exacerbated the effects of recreational retrenchment, moreover, so did NLGC officials' response to deteriorating labor conditions. Following the executive board's lead, club sponsors and secretaries steered entirely clear of labor reform experiments, which had added to the movement's momentum in the 1890s. A visitor to the 1922 club convention "noticed in the discussions of economic subjects . . . a slackness of grip, as if the speakers were not altogether sure that these problems were theirs." Genteel women throughout the NLGC were no more ready to address such problems in practice than they were to speak of them. Their only acknowledgment of club members' economic difficulties came in the form of vocational guidance and assurances that the labor market ultimately rewarded diligence. This time around, then, cutbacks in recreation dealt the club movement an eventually fatal blow.[36]

From early 1921 onward, the National League of Girls' Clubs was in a state of decay. Its membership, still 30,000 strong in January 1921, had shrunk to 25,000 by June, when the *Club Worker* folded for lack of funds. The record of the movement's fortunes beyond that date is sketchy but points unmistakably to a steady decline. The NLGC's membership stood at 14,500 in June 1922, when league executives inaugurated a campaign to enhance the clubs' appeal to the presumably "thoughtful" members who had stuck around despite recreational cutbacks. Club sponsors began to pour their best energies into organizing classes in the liberal arts, and league headquarters covered all costs for teachers and supplies. This slowed the movement's contraction but by no means stopped it. Though the classes held in club meeting rooms usually filled and a summer school later established at a club vacation lodge on Long Island had many more applicants than the forty-bed dormitory could accommodate, rank-and-file enthusiasm for the educational campaign was too thin to save the movement from extinction. In 1924, the NLGC's branch in western Pennsylvania dissolved, reporting that all but three of its nineteen clubs had fallen apart. NLGC clubs had disbanded elsewhere, too: their total number was now 87, as opposed to 150 in 1920. Fewer than 50 clubs—from New York, New Jersey, and New England only—sent representatives to the league's 1928 convention, where the committee appointed to choose a slate of nominees for the executive board announced that it could not find enough willing candidates. By the convention's end, delegates had voted to declare the NLGC defunct, and its state branches dissolved over the next two years.[37]

Though some clubs endured long after the national league's death, they did not remain gathering places for youth. As an observer noted in the mid-1940s, they became havens for "older women who were members as girls." Surviving clubs had probably entered the 1920s with a good many older members, too. Postmortems by former NLGC leaders blamed its demise on working women's waning interest in single-sex leisure activities, on increased competition from commercial amusements, and on a proliferation of endowed institutions—such as YWCAs and publicly funded community centers—with fancier recreational facilities than the clubs could offer. None of this was likely to undercut the loyalty of longtime members, who came to club meeting rooms mainly to chat with old friends.[38]

Young members, who defected in droves, could care about things other than men and amusements, too, of course, as they demonstrated on many occasions during the club movement's early years. Once the National League of Women Workers was established, however, club life tended to discourage attention to "thoughtful" concerns. That pattern altered little amid sponsors' campaigns in behalf of democracy, civic action, and liberal arts education, for none of the campaigns added much practical weight to rank-and-file opinions about the league's internal policies or social purposes. The less those opinions mattered, the greater members' tendency to disappear, rather than push for revisions, when club programs failed to please. The club movement died out not only because it no longer met young working women's demands for fun and romance but also because twentieth-century club life gave members of all ages so few reasons to regard the movement as theirs to mold and preserve.

Conclusion

Working women used the club movement in three abiding ways—to demonstrate their respectability by bourgeois standards, to assert themselves on their own terms, and to have fun after a hard day's work. Practice on each of these fronts altered considerably over time. In the 1880s, for example, bourgeois respectability required homage to the "true woman" ideal; by the 1920s, it demanded little more than racial exclusivity, which tightened club members' grip on the prestige they enjoyed as daughters of the "American race." Opposition to judgments from above took a series of forms: early efforts to disprove the notion that working girls could not be true women, subsequent challenges to conservative wisdom on the woman question and labor issues, and, a generation later, noncompliance with NLWW leaders' wishes to make club life more "thoughtful" and racially diverse. An initial emphasis on fun in the form of "parties of the sisterhood" gave way to a growing and eventually overweening stress on entertaining men. As the recipes for respectability, self-assertion, and recreation changed, moreover, so did their relative importance to club members. Claiming true womanhood topped their agenda in the 1880s; asserting working women's rights held first place from the democratization drive of the early 1890s to the founding of the National League of Women Workers in 1897; recreation took precedence thereafter.

These priorities derived in each instance from club members' relationship with sponsors and their estimate of its possibilities. Club life wasn't the only significant factor here. In all three periods, genteel women marching to the same beat as club sponsors were so plentiful outside the clubs that virtually every member must have encountered or heard of them. This reinforced club life's lessons as to sponsors' potential as allies and how to make the best of it. The fundamental issue, however, was the distribution of organizational power, whose shifts propelled club members from one priority to the next.

The movement was born in an era when legions of upper-class women were reaching out to less privileged members of their sex for didactic and disciplinary purposes. Housewives in tenement districts faced an expanding cadre of "friendly visitors" who went forth from Charity Organization Societies (COS) to dispense moral advice and determine whether families applying for material aid belonged to the "worthy" or "unworthy" poor. Similar encounters took place in working girls' clubs, YWCAs, Girls' Friendly Societies, and kindred groups, where upper-class women claimed the moral authority to instruct wage earners in right living and to monopolize organizational governance. Democracy was little more than a slogan in club circles of the 1880s and not even that in other arenas where ladies ministered to working girls. Here, as in the tenements visited by COS agents, working- and upper-class women met under circumstances that replicated the class hierarchy in society at large and furnished constant reminders of the elite's sense of innate superiority to people below.[1]

Club members reacted with a vigorous effort to show the world, and club sponsors in particular, that daughters of labor had as much womanly virtue as ladies bountiful. This project originated in the class consciousness workers brought to the clubs—the pride in family and labor evident at the 38th Street Society's inaugural meeting. What kept the ball rolling, though, were club members' dealings with club sponsors, whose control of the movement and lectures on the ways of true womanhood sharpened members' awareness of class stratification.

Gender consciousness permeated the more boldly self-assertive agenda that took shape in the early 1890s, when reforms in club governance tipped the balance of power toward workers and transformed club meeting rooms from lecture halls into social centers. Sponsors, who now had many more opportunities to learn than to preach, traded efforts to domesticate working girls for projects that addressed needs defined by club members. Comradeship across class lines flourished, and patron-client relations withered. Working girls' clubs were not the only place working- and upper-class women became comrades during this period. Cooperation also thrived in the mushrooming settlement movement, whose democratic tenets laid the groundwork for genuine helpfulness on ladies' part. During the depression of 1893–97, moreover, labor reform attracted unprecedented sympathy from ladies in both cross-class movements and genteel venues such as the General Federation of Women's Clubs and Woman's Christian Temperance Union. Though friendly visitors still made rounds in working-class communities, they were now outnumbered by women offering more respectful and valuable assistance. Against this backdrop, club members concentrated on asserting their rights to a better lot in relation to the opposite sex.[2]

That concern with women's rights was most conspicuous in their critiques of housework, their reach for control over mixed-sex recreation, and their arguments for egalitarian marriage—projects that enjoyed broad support from club sponsors. Following the economic crash of 1893, however, club members applied similar perspectives to the far more divisive labor question. Whereas previous discussions of this issue had focused for the most part on workers' rights and duties vis-à-vis employers, the central themes now were women's right to gender equality and duty to advance their sex. This approach clearly had an instrumental side: it encouraged club sponsors to become labor reformers for sisterhood's sake. The fact that some sponsors were already moving in that direction gave gender analysis a deeper logic too, though, and so did labor reform's growing appeal to ladies in other movements. If cross-class women's alliances offered solutions to labor problems, then gender mattered just as much as club members said, for genteel women's commitment to labor reform typically rested on sympathy for workers of their own sex, not on concern for the working class. Here and across the board, club members' stress on the woman question testified to optimism about sponsors' potential in addition to discontents with the gender system.

Sisterly rhetoric and practice disappeared under the NLWW, whose establishment reversed democratization. This did not recreate the 1880s, though. In the club movement and virtually every place genteel women gathered to help the woman worker in the Progressive Era, reform on the old charity organization model was a dead letter. Progressive women specialized in material assistance, not moral tutoring. They entered social realms that the friendly visitor had left to men, lobbying legislatures, negotiating with employers and city officials, overseeing employee welfare programs, and otherwise intervening in politics and the workplace. They ushered in a host of reforms that made positive, practical differences in working women's lives, and they provided an unprecedented array of recreational, educational, and other services. For all these reasons, women's historians have identified the Progressive Era as the heyday of "class-bridging" women's movements. If we look at the movements' governance, however, the bridge seems undeniably tenuous. Only in the Women's Trade Union League did workers hold executive positions. None of the other organizations, from the National Consumers' League to the YWCA to the Girl Scouts, made its executives formally accountable to the working women for whom they spoke. And the daily round of executive business—bureaucratic chores, research projects, special task forces, and such—grew so large as to make close contact with the rank and file impossible just about everywhere. The club movement's structure epitomized the age, in other words, and so did the NLWW distribution of power along class lines. This did not preclude reform agendas of benefit to working women, but it militated against their mobilization as reformers in their own right.[3]

Within this context, club members—once their movement's proprietors, now merely its customers—focused almost exclusively on recreation, which had a more conservative flavor than in the past. In the nineteenth century, they had organized entertainments that attacked social hierarchies. The kitchen bazaars, mothers' nights, and other home-oriented events popular in the 1880s had "elevated the working class in the minds of the world" by displaying working girls' domesticity. Challenges to male supremacy had influenced recreational programs in the 1890s, when mixed-sex parties demanding Sunday-best manners fostered the "training of our future men." The old connections between good times and social change disintegrated in the NLWW, however. Instead of elevating the working class or training men, club members now had fun in ways that replicated racial cleavages in an increasingly race-conscious society. Skits and minstrels performed in blackface proliferated; rollicking parties brought men and women together in a fashion that distanced the clubs from new-immigrant communities; and club members resisted proposals that they share the movement's recreational services with working women who did not belong to the white "American race." At bottom, though, recreation under NLWW auspices had to do with fun, not politics, and NLWW members' racialism was a politically passive stance—more a confirmation of their place in the social order than a strategy for getting ahead. Optimism about the club movement's potential to change the world had clearly died away.

There are lessons here about the dynamism and interdependence of class, gender, and racial identities—all often mistaken for fixed constructs in competition with one another. In the 1880s, when club life was highly class stratified, commonalities that would later bring members and sponsors together as sisters were virtually meaningless to both groups. Ladies were ladies and working girls were working girls—defined by class as much as by gender and divided on both counts so long as sponsors championed a true woman ideal that put them on a pedestal and club members on the defensive. Then, in the 1890s, democratic reforms in club governance and a concomitant surge in cross-class sociability made gender the stuff of unity. Ladies and working girls were still present to some degree; that is clear in sponsors' exhortations on the subject of etiquette and members' when-in-Rome capitulations, not to mention the various stalemates and controversies regarding labor issues. The dominant pattern, however, was cooperation on the "common ground of womanhood," where club members and sponsors constructed a new, mutual gender identity rooted in the proposition that their sex deserved the same rights as men. Democracy and sociability gave class differences new significance, too; members and sponsors both pointed to their comradeship across class lines as proof of sisterhood's power to transform the social order. Their oneness did not signal a triumph of gender consciousness over class consciousness. Gender and class both took on fresh meanings, rather, when working- and upper-class women allied in ways that defied their stratification in society at large.

Once democracy collapsed under the NLWW, club life again fortified identities congruent with the wider society. But twentieth-century club members were not working girls in the old sense and seldom referred to themselves by that term. Racism's mounting influence on the national culture gave them unprecedented prestige as part of the "American race," a neologism their nineteenth-century predecessors had never heard, let alone embraced. Whereas club members of the 1880s and nineties had not explicitly made an issue of their racial identity, the new generation declared itself "American girls." If race had new meanings, so did gender and class. A genteel public that used to worry loud and long that wage labor corrupted women's morals changed its tune once its own daughters poured into the labor market in the early twentieth century. Conventional wisdom now held that women who worked could belong to the same, respectable gender as ladies, and that shift in gender ideology made club members' class status less stigmatic than in the past. The term "American girls" was as telling in its silence about work as in its emphasis on race.

Club sponsors' self-descriptions changed as well. In the nineteenth century, they had called themselves ladies or leisured women; now they preferred to be known as "club workers." While this connoted kinship with working women, workers of club members' class were not the kin sponsors had utmost in mind. Their new title—which they also applied to the NLWW's salaried, college-educated administrative secretaries but never to its membership—asserted rather that sponsors' volunteer activities were the equivalent of professional social work, whose "scientific methods" they were busily applying to their work as recreational directors and NLWW bureaucrats. Professionalism promised to replenish sponsors' aging ranks by making club sponsorship more attractive to genteel women of the younger, increasingly career-oriented set. It also promised to boost the NLWW's sagging cachet in the larger world of social welfare projects, whose movers and shakers belonged to a new generation of reformers with college degrees, graduate training, and other professional credentials that club sponsors lacked. Neither promise panned out, though, and sponsors' desire for recognition as social workers' equals persisted nonetheless, for professionalism was more than a recruitment or face-saving device. Its deepest meanings had to do with sponsors' identity in relation to club members when the neat, nineteenth-century dichotomy between ladies and working girls fell apart.[4]

The class hierarchy emblematized by that dichotomy remained intact, despite the growing significance of race and despite the fact that many genteel women were going to work. Nowhere was this clearer than in the NLWW, whose multilayered bureaucracy made the club movement more steeply hierarchical than ever before. Sponsors' rationale for taking charge had an entirely different logic than in the 1880s. Back then they had deemed themselves club leaders by birthright—the "true" femininity supposedly inherent to daughters of the leisure class and foreign to daughters of labor. To "club workers," on the other hand, leadership was a profession, a personal achievement instead of a class inheritance. This mindset was in some respects an improvement over the old elitism: the professionalized, "scientific" sponsor did not insult club members by putting on aristocratic airs or prying into their private lives, and the services she offered were certainly more useful than sermons in behalf of true womanhood. But if sponsors were less blatantly snobbish than in the 1880s, they were also more firmly and complacently ensconced as the club movement's sovereigns. Bureaucracy elaborated their power. The theory that they had earned instead of inherited leadership gave their prerogatives a comfortingly democratic stamp; and their "scientific" distance from club members provided insulation against criticism from below. In the NLWW, then, class stratification was as durable as it was steep.[5]

A generation earlier, democratization had transformed working girls and ladies into sisters in support of women's rights. Whether "American girls" and "club workers" could have allied on similar grounds is a matter of conjecture, for the structural conditions for cooperation never materialized under NLWW auspices. Both groups had ample cause to care about women's rights, however; though the gender system was less demeaning and restrictive than in the age of true womanhood, male supremacy remained quite alive and well. So the raw material for a feminist alliance of one sort or another certainly seems to have been present. That nothing came of it is tragic but more than that instructive. The absence of sisterhood in the NLWW underscores the same lesson as its presence in the 1890s: women cannot find common ground across class lines unless they combine as equals.

Partnerships of this sort have been discouragingly rare, and the clubs' history helps to explain why. It also tells us that they are possible, however, and suggests some preconditions for their construction. If middle- and upper-class women can recognize their class privileges as just that instead of as inherent gifts or individual attainments, if working-class women can resist subordination without despising or dismissing more advantaged women, if women from different classes can build movements where they genuinely share power, then they just might be able to fulfill the vision of the club member who predicted in 1891 that "woman's feeling toward her fellow-woman" was going to become "a new force in the world." Here's to that possibility.[6]

APPENDIX 1

New York Association of Working Girls' Societies: Programs of Selected Member Clubs for the Year Ending April 1890

38th Street Working Girls' Society, New York City (262 members)

Practical talks (weekly); relief work; Three P's Circle; occasional lectures; classes in dressmaking, sewing and fancy work, cooking, first aid, singing, musical drill (calisthenics to music), and literature; a reception for visiting club members; a Christmas entertainment.

Ivy Club, New York City (90 members)

Practical talks (weekly); relief work; a junior club; classes in dressmaking, plain sewing, singing, musical drill, stenography and typewriting, German, and "night-school" (academic) subjects; a club fair.

Prospect Heights Club for Working Girls, Brooklyn (50 members)

Practical talks (weekly); relief work; classes in dressmaking, plain sewing, embroidery, cooking, music, and calisthenics; an entertainment.

Industrial Society, Hoboken, New Jersey (159 members)

Practical talks (weekly); relief work; monthly lectures; classes in dressmaking, millinery, embroidery, cooking, candymaking, music, singing, calisthenics, musical drill, and "night-school" (academic) subjects; two receptions; an entertainment.

Helping Hand Society, Allegheny, Pennsylvania (191 members)

Practical talks (monthly); relief work; classes in millinery, plain and machine sewing, garment cutting and fitting, cooking, singing, gymnastics, and English; an excursion; an entertainment.

Perseverance Club, New Haven, Connecticut (40 members)

Practical talks (weekly); classes in dressmaking, plain sewing, crocheting, singing, and travel; monthly entertainments; a Christmas party.

Help Each Other Club, Danielsonville, Connecticut (51 members)

Practical talks (weekly); classes in dressmaking, sewing, cooking, gymnastics, reading, writing, and English; several entertainments; a party.

Young Women's Guild, Springfield, Massachusetts (70 members)

Classes in dressmaking, embroidery, calisthenics, German, and painting; parties and sociables (number unreported).

Source: AWGS Convention 1890, Appendix 2, unnumbered pages.

Practical Talks at the 38th Street Society:
Three Essays Presented by Club Members, 1890–92

M.J. on "Women as Moral Reformers"

It is not so many years since the direct and personal participation of a woman in any public enterprise was looked upon as unseemly or as unsexing her, according to the spirit of the times. The great temperance and other moral reforms of the first part of this century proceeded without the help of women as active agents. Women, as a rule, contributed their prayers and their influence in domestic life, but they were listeners and not speakers. In the churches women constitute two-thirds of the membership, but the organization of the church is in the hands of men. In the early centuries it was considered disgraceful for a woman to assume to meddle in such matters. It was considered her duty to stay indoors, except where duty absolutely called her abroad; to hold her peace in the house of God, and to cover her head even when she prayed.

When women first began to appear on public platforms, people shook their heads and prophesied degradation for society as the inevitable consequences. Women would unsex themselves, said the critics; they would lose their feminine charms, homes would be neglected, and manners would be roughened. A favorite picture of those days was of the distracted husband tending the baby while the wife was off battling for her rights. Good and conservative people really thought that the disposition of women to exercise their full powers in society, and to attain the fullest intellectual development, was the sign of untold evils to come on the race.

A generation ago it was a rare and brave girl who ventured beyond the narrow sphere within which conventionality confined feminine activity. Now all that has changed, and the change has come with surprising rapidity.

The appearance of women as speakers on public platforms, and as organizers and directors of public enterprises, is taken as a matter of course. Women of social distinction will serve on committees of the World's Fair at Chicago. Women commissioners to that exhibition will be appointed by the Governors of the States. Clubs and societies of women discuss questions of public reform in all parts of the Union. The present temperance movement is largely, if not chiefly, in the hands of women, the Women's Christian Temperance Union being foremost in the good work. At political meetings seats are set apart for women concerned as to public questions, and there is hardly a movement, secular or religious, which starts or proceeds without calling in the aid of feminine energy.

This introduction of the feminine element into the work of the world, and more especially the work of moral reform, involves a new phase of civilization. It means that the forces of reform are to be strengthened and enlarged to an enormous extent. The half of the race which of old was counted out of such movements, is now to be counted in. Women have thrown off the shackles with which long time customs, conventionalities, and prejudice bound them. They have found out their strength, and they will exert it for the benefit of society. Social opinion and public sentiment do not now stand in the way of their progress, and hence the occasion for their former timidity about taking part in public enterprises has passed away. It looks, therefore, as if we [are] entering upon a new phase of civilization in which the feminine influence will be powerful everywhere, and with it will come a higher moral tone, a keener and more sensitive moral sentiment, and a profounder sense of moral obligation.

In quiet and unobtrusive ways, in the home and in society, women have always been doing their best to reform individual men. Now, they are extending the sphere of their exertions and seeking to reform all men. They are also working with a tenacity of purpose so great, and with so much intelligent zeal, that they are moving the world by their concerted efforts. Whether the duty of suffrage is imposed upon them or not, sooner or later they are destined to be the chief agents in bringing about the reformation of society, its elevation, and its purification. They have taken the forward steps, and they will not go back. They will move ahead steadily and irresistibly. The "Woman's Age," as a well known writer calls it, is in its beginning only.

M.G. on "Factory Life"

Factory life brings up the old question, Why do people as a rule look down on factory girls?

I will say that from my own experience in the factory, I have met with as lovely girls as I would care to know—girls who have made their lives one sacrifice that would in a measure be a lesson for some of our more fortunate sisters to learn.

Their good influence in this workroom has been felt by both young and old. When I have heard people speak disrespectfully of the factory girl, one cannot imagine my feelings, particularly when I have these bright, self-sacrificing creatures before me; yet I had to keep still instead of defending them, which I could do if the conversation was directed to me.

This is a very deep subject, and I cannot treat it as I should. If people would only look at this subject as they ought, and put themselves in our position, and see if they would make their lives as great a success as we factory girls have, I think that circumstances would alter the case very much. When one thinks of the long hours in a confined, crowded factory, with the din of machinery constantly grinding on our ears all day long, is it a wonder that girls who talk loudly on the streets are classed as factory girls? They are so used to shouting when they do talk in order to be heard above the noise of the machinery, and as it takes time to effect a change, the time between their leaving the factory and appearance on the street is so short, the only way to avoid this will be shorter hours for work and more time for improvement.

I have known girls from twelve years up, who have worked in the factory for ten hours and a half per day, rush home in the evening, eat a hurried supper, and then go to night school. This same thing for six days in the week, and then Sunday comes, the only day of rest. Off to church in the morning— Sunday school in the afternoon, and at this point let me ask what time have these girls for improvement? I am not upholding factory girls simply because I work there, for if I could better my condition I would willingly do so, and I believe that every other factory girl would do the same.

The question arises, Can a conversation such as is intended to elevate be carried on in the factory for any length of time? I say that it is next to an impossibility, as you would have to speak so loud that you would get hoarse in a very short time. The factory girl is considered by some as rude and vulgar, yet when it comes down to practical charity you will find them more than willing to help anyone in need or distress as much as they possibly can. I have met many people outside of a factory, yet when they come to know you are a factory girl it seems to condemn you. Why do these feelings exist? But at any rate they do. Why don't these people who talk about the factory girls so much use a little of their spare time to bring about a change instead of talking about it? Then I think there would be a great many more happy homes as well as work-rooms, as the girls would have more time to brighten their lives as well as their homes.

One of the greatest advantages of the day for the bettering of working girls, has been the formation of clubs where factory girls meet the teachers, etc., on an equal standing, uniting and bringing their ideas and interests more closely together, cultivating good-fellowship, and meeting people better educated and more fortunate than themselves.

I.T. [Irene Tracy] on "Club Life—Its Power"

It seems a little thing to say that the Club has taught one to think, has roused one to thought. In our busy lives, we say we have so little time to think, but after we have belonged to a club a while, it is astonishing to find how much time we have to think, and how much we can think of in a very short time; also that it is the busiest people who think most, and are the people whom you can rely on when anything is to be done.

Thoughts are like pebbles thrown into the river; just how deep they go or just where they strike we do not know; all we can follow are the ever widening circles, and even they are lost to view in a little while. No one but the Supreme Being is able to tell how small or how great an influence they carry with them, or how far the influence will extend. When we are at work and happen to look up with a sudden smile and catch a neighbor's eye, and they ask, What means the smile they caught, we say, Well, you see, I was feeling rather low in my mind last night and thought I would go to the Club, which I did. I can hardly explain just what it is that makes me feel better: sometimes I think it is in the atmosphere of the rooms; again, it seems the pleasant smile or jolly word or two; then again we have our "Practical Talks," which give me food for days sometimes, but above all, I think, is the oneness, if I may put it so. There's almost every kind of work represented at the Club, and some of our members don't have to go out and earn their daily bread; we all meet on the common ground of womanhood and sisterhood; we mutually bridge over a chasm which many people smiled on incredulously some time ago, and some even said it could not be done without injury to one or the other. Happily for us we proved that it could be done, and it has been working successfully now for some years, and the injury has not appeared; the Club working girl does not feel that she is looked down on, but feels she has gained the respect, love, sympathy, and loyalty of a stanch friend, while the woman of leisure feels she has gained a true friend in the girl who has to go out in the world alone, who has learned so well how to help herself, and is such a true, womanly woman; for there is something strong and self-reliant about her; she is to be trusted.

If ever I feel blue, let me go to the Club, if only for a half hour, and I will feel differently when I come out. It wakes me up, puts new life in me, and gives me pleasant thoughts for the morrow, and what seems a trouble before melts into nothing, and you wonder at yourself for having thought that it did.

In our "Talks," we exchange thought and opinions, thereby gaining help and hints that prove invaluable.

Do you wonder, then, at my smiling to myself when I have such pleasant things to think of—why it makes me feel light, and my work seem easier? Then, too, I have so much to tell those at home that we don't have a chance to get rusty or fall behind the times; meeting so many different girls, you learn something new almost every time you meet them, and that creates such an interest that your folks look for it almost as much as you do.

It is wonderful how your little store of knowledge increases—you learn so much more than you are conscious of at the time.

Yes, the dear old Club, I fear I couldn't do without it; it does me so much good and gives me such strength and courage that to lose it would seem as if half the light of my life were gone; the Club is so necessary to me that I must make myself necessary to the Club. God bless and prosper our dear old Club always.

Source: G. Dodge, *Thoughts of Busy Girls,* pp. 89–93, 101–5, 131–35. This volume identifies the essays' authors by initials.

APPENDIX 3

Club Members' Writing in *Far and Near:* Selected Articles, 1891–94

Lucy A. Warner (Help Each Other Club, Danielsonville, Conn.),
"Why Do People Look Down on Working Girls? How It Looks
from a Working Girl's Standpoint," no. 3 (Jan. 1891): 37

Why do people look down on Working Girls? This is the question that we girls ask each other over and over again. It is not a hard question, but it has never yet been answered to our satisfaction.

Is it because we lack natural ability? Do working girls lack natural ability? Go into the places where we work and see the delicate and difficult work that we are doing—work that requires the help of eye and hand and brain, and, when you have gone the rounds, if you should give us your candid opinion, would not that opinion be that working girls are not deficient in natural ability? Are working men and the sons of working men lacking in natural ability? For answer, we point you to the men prominent in scientific, literary, religious, and business circles. No, working men are not lacking in natural ability. Neither are working women. There is no copyright on brains. God is no respecter of persons, and so, to us working girls, he has entrusted one, two, and, to some, even five talents.

Is it because we lack education? That we do lack education, we admit. We have the brains. Give us the time and opportunity to use them. We are hungering and thirsting for knowledge. Make it easier for us to satisfy that thirst and hunger. It is true that there are some among us who would not improve the opportunity to obtain a higher education and greater culture if such opportunity were ours. But is that not also true of those in a higher station than we? A man now prominent in literary circles once said of his wife: "My wife has had time since her marriage to have obtained a higher education."

My cultured friend, you who have just received your well earned diploma at Wellesley or Vassar, are there not ladies in "your set" who have had equal opportunities with yourself and yet have not improved those opportunities? There are many working girls who are spending every leisure moment in study, not because they think others will respect them more, but because such study is to them a delight.

Is it because we lack virtue? Are working girls, as a class, virtuous? Years ago, a man who knew whereof he affirmed, wrote: "Not even the famed Hebrew maiden as she stood on the giddy turret, more sacredly guarded her honor than does many a half-starved sewing woman in the streets of New York." And we who have comfortable homes and receive fair wages, can the same be said of us? Yes, we are as proud of our honor, we are as careful of our reputation as our sisters who dress in "purple and fine linen and fare sumptuously every day." It is true, there are exceptions, but has not the immoral working girl her rivals among a class of women who should be her teachers in all pure and noble living?

Is it because we work? What an absurd idea! People look down on us because we work? Why, the lawyer and the doctor and the clergyman and the professor and the merchant all work, and work hard, too, and every one looks *up* to them. "Of course," says a bright, young lady, "we expect men to work and support their families, but ladies do not work." Don't they? We have lady artists and musicians, lady doct[o]rs, lawyers and lecturers, trained nurses and teachers. If it isn't *work* that they are doing, what is it? "But," says the same young lady, "have you never discovered that there is a difference between brain work and manual labor?" Yes, we have discovered it, to our sorrow. The teacher considers herself superior to the sewing girl, and the sewing girl thinks herself above the mill girl, and the mill girl thinks the girl who does general housework a little beneath her, and Miss Flora McFlimsy, "who toils not, neither does she spin," thinks herself superior to them all. Is one kind of work more honorable than another? Is any honest work degrading?

My friend, have you ever considered that "brain work" enters into every department of manual labor? An intelligent girl will do better work anywhere than an ignorant one. Isn't it a work of art to make a dress? It is just as necessary that a cook should mix her bread with "brains" as it is that an artist should mix her colors with the same material.

Dear sister workers, we who work in shop and store and factory, and in countless homes all over the United States, if it is because we work that people look down on us, then let us pray that the Lord will change their opinion, and go quietly about our business, for, among the "nobility of labor" there is an illustrious company, at whose head stands the Carpenter of Nazareth, by Whom labor was forever glorified.

Lizzie Burke (Far and Near Society, New York City), letter
to the "Correspondence Column," no. 13 (Nov. 1891): 16

For the past two years I have looked upon the Working Girls' Club as a valuable auxiliary to the formation of Trade Unions among women. For the reason that while it affords a great source of enjoyment to the members and friends after weary hours of toil, it is also instructive in detail. Its tendency is to teach woman to be independent in her sphere in life by exacting a trifling amount for dues, for which she obtains in return the advantage of becoming acquainted with matters in this life which are of material benefit to her in her present condition, and of much greater interest when she assumes the responsibility of a home.

But why dilate on this subject which is well known to all members of such clubs, when there is a question of paramount importance to all girls who earn their bread by the sweat of their brows? It is an undisputed fact that women in most industries are very poorly paid, while the grasping employers are hoarding their ill-gotten wealth with perfect adoration to the "Golden Calf," striving to accumulate millions at the expense of their "industrial slaves." Now, this is an extraordinary evil and one that we can best combat by thorough organization of our trades. As the Working Girls' Clubs are organized for independent action they must certainly rely each member on another to offer and accept what is most beneficial to all.

Therefore, to be consistent, they might go a step farther and say, Girls, your labor belongs to you, and justice demands that you should receive the highest possible wage in return therefor. And add that while we strive to teach and inculcate these maxims the lesson to be derived from such teachings is one that would encourage girls to organize "Trade Clubs" of their respective calling, which would be of lasting benefit in aiding to ameliorate the condition of girls poorly paid and help release them from the grasp of the grinding "capitalists" whose object is almost to own them body and soul.

In conclusion I hold that it is in strict compliance with the rules and usages of the W.G.C.s to foster such organization and assist in promoting the same, as I am quite certain they would prove necessary adjuncts, as one aids the intellect by education and harmless amusements, the other would be a means to obtain the desired end with a better view of the relations that should exist between employers and employees.

Therefore, to my way of reasoning, it is not a misnomer, I think, to say that the Working Girls' Clubs and Women's Trade Clubs are sister organizations, this the relation that should exit.

Mary Lonergan (Hope Club, Rockville, Conn.), "True Womanhood,"
no. 18 (Apr. 1892): 113–14

This is a very broad subject to discuss but I will confine myself to this one point: Are not factory girls capable of reaching the goal of true womanhood?

I maintain that *they are,* although the mill girl is looked down on by the majority of our more favored sisters, the college girls.

And why is this? Indeed I may say that shop girls, saleswomen and all wage-earning women outside the mill, have opinions of their own about the mill girls. Whether we deserve this is for us to consider how we conduct ourselves. Unfortunately the mill girls at times do act in such a boisterous way that we cannot blame people who think the way they do.

I do not mean to say that every girl who works in the mill acts rudely, for there are many lady-like mill girls with whom we are all acquainted.

The majority of girls employed in the mills have been taken away from school at a very early age,—I regret to say that I was counted a mill girl before I reached my twelfth birthday. And what can a child know at such an age? If there is even one boisterous girl in a room with such girls she is enough to lower their tone.

I have often wondered why shop girls feel above mill girls; we don't realize this feeling until we hear a shop girl express her opinion. I overheard two such girls talking in a city where there is just one mill. One girl was seeking a place to work and this friend told her that some girls were needed down at the mill. She appeared to feel insulted, and said "she had not become so low as to go to work in a mill."

Well, perhaps you can better imagine my feelings than I can describe them now, after I heard such a remark. I began to think then, are we girls in the mill so very bad? If we are not, then why do people have such a poor opinion of us?

We must admit that there is a carelessness of speech and manner used in the mill which should *not* be tolerated.

In saying this I am not blaming the girls, I am simply trying to give my opinion how we can best change this state of affairs.

And in going to and from work some of those girls carry with them this same freedom of speech and manner. They mean no harm at first, but in a very short time it becomes habitual with them, and then they are held up as typical mill girls.

Take a girl of rough nature and she will be rough in her fun, and then some girls will think they must imitate that smart girl who is noticed so much by her male friends.

Such a girl thinks of nothing else only rough fun, and how soon she can get married. Instead of making herself useful and calmly resting in her maidenly dignity she rushes on, forgetting the proverb—"The more haste the less speed."

This sort of girl not unfrequently assumes a "fast" style of talk, manner and dress, in order to make herself attractive to the male sex.

They may nibble at her bait but they *will not* allow themselves to be caught. This loud girl may have a time of popularity, and attract attention, but we should not endeavor to follow her. Men of the baser sort may amuse them-

selves with her but no man worth having would think of marrying her. There
is a liberty that makes us free and a liberty that makes us slaves, and the girls
who take liberties with modesty of speech and manner, and who cross over
the boundary into masculine territory, are not more free but more enslaved
than before. And the approbation of man, which is the end in view, is lost
by the means used to gain it. Whatever men may be themselves, they like
gentleness, modesty and purity in act and thought in women. They want
their wives to be better than themselves; they think that women should be
the conservators of all that is restrained, chivalrous and gentle.

And no matter *how much* we may deny it, the fact remains that all girls, or
rather women, I should say, are happy in the thought that their friends, particularly their male friends, admire their way of conducting themselves.

If this be true, then we mill girls should act in such a way that we may feel
that we are bringing credit to ourselves and to all girls employed in the mills;
then we are able to *hurl back* the oft repeated remark that we are rough.

Each one of us has in mind, no doubt, an ideal woman, and if we haven't
let us try to have, and then see how near we can follow her.

We will not dare to pretend that we are anything else than just what we
are—working girls. But we will try to be so careful to defend the fair name
of *woman* that the public in general will cease thinking that the factory girls
are unladylike.

It is certain that our grammar is doubtful, and I am sorry to admit that we
use slang. Slang always disfigures the speech, and we should avoid it as something *utterly hateful*. Young girls, and women, I might add, are apt to pick it
up in the mill, on the street, and elsewhere; and use it unconsciously. If we
would consider how offensive some of those slang expressions are, we would
be more careful to avoid repeating them. In such cases they would receive so
little encouragement that such phrases would not travel so rapidly.

Slang always indicates a want of taste, and is too suggestive of low-com-
pany to be used by any lady. Unfortunately the practice has become prevalent, and I have known even some educated ladies who pride themselves on
the saucy slang phrases that they adopt. Such habits lower the tone of society and the standard of thought.

Instead of falling into the habit of using slang, we girls who have been
deprived of an education should try to improve [our speech].

We need it more than we imagine. It would be time spent that we would
never regret, and we have it in our power to improve our education. With
such an excellent corps of teachers as we have in our club rooms generally
it is a pity the girls do not take the opportunity to study. This should be the
most popular class.

Next to studying comes reading, not the sensational stories so common now,
but something more wholesome. The autobiographies of noted women would
help to quicken our perceptions and broaden our ideas and lead us on to true

womanhood; not so with cheap literature, its influence is corrupting, it teaches us false views of society, of life, of ambition, and of destiny.

And another characteristic of true womanhood is *truthfulness*. It seems a very simple thing to tell the truth, but, beyond all question, there is nothing so easy as lying. There are women in all communities who are believed to be honest, yet whose word is never taken as authority on any subject. They do not utter a lie consciously, perhaps, but really their language fails to present truth and state facts correctly. Much of this is owing to carelessness and much to habit. We should always be careful not to fall into such an evil habit, for a habit once formed is very hard to break.

Since the future of a nation is shaped by no other element so important as the development of its budding womanhood, it is our duty to try to reach the standard of true womanhood, and we can do it if we will.

Resolve to be ladies in thought, word and deed, remembering that gentle breeding is not a thing easily acquired. Take all the chances for education and refinement that the clubs give.

There never has been a time when the working girl had such a chance for self-improvement as we girls of to-day. We should not waste this opportunity but rather grasp it, and make the most of it, and always remember that if we respect ourselves all others are bound to respect us.

Anonymous (Girls' Union, Ithaca, N.Y.), "Working Girls," no. 22 (Aug. 1892): 209 [The author was a domestic worker.]

There are a great many strange people in the world, and I think no one could tell more about them than the working girls, for the girl who works out [as a live-in household servant] has to put up with a great many hardships. There are many people who do not use their girls as they should; they seem to think, "well, she is nothing but a working girl," so they give her the worst room in the house; for instance, where she has to go up the back stairs, over a coal bin, through an attic, and at last to a little room off at the side, where the only thing she has to feast her eyes upon when she goes to her room to rest her tired bones is some one's back yard. Then they tell her she can have a couple of hours [free] on a certain afternoon, and she *must* be in at half-past eight; she must not have any gentleman callers and they scold her if she has too many lady callers. This is discouraging to any girl; soon she is seen meeting her companions around on the different street corners. Next behold her eating at the kitchen table where she eats her scanty meal, after it has been slid through the dumb waiter with a "Now *you* can eat your dinner." What if the potatoes are cold, or the turkey all eaten from the bones? What if only a spoonful of pudding remains? Warm potatoes, turkey and pudding weren't meant for servant-girls' mouths anyway. No doubt anything will digest in a working girl's stomach. After all, how could people get along without us, for are we not "the ones who move the world"?

Mary W. Jordan (Working Girls' Club of Lawrence, Mass.),
"Would the Ideal Working Girls' Club Be Composed Entirely
of Wage-Earners?" no. 36 (Oct. 1893): 237

A club founded of course on the basis of co-operation and organization, firmly built upon the rock of self-support and independence, each of its members a wage-earner, filled with longing to overcome all "barriers built by circumstance perverse" and armed with an earnest resolution to climb the hill of knowledge, through co-operation would, it seems to me, be an ideal working girls' club. But I have read that

> In this world each ideal,
> That shines like a star on life's wave,
> Is tossed on the shore of the real,
> And sleeps like a dream in a grave.

So, if this is true of all other things, why may it not be so of a working girls' club?

Because, where will we find the girls, who, no matter how earnest their desires for improvement, have not, after years of wage-earning, had their ambition chilled, seen their lofty dreams dissolve, for want of time or money or lack of some advantage?

For the fight against circumstances is a hard one, and many grow weary and give it up. I do not mean to imply that the general wage-earner has no ambition or no desire to rise from the position where circumstances have placed her. No, indeed. But I do mean to say that, having worked all day long, every day, she is not nearly as ambitious at the end of the week as she would be if she hadn't; and one of her greatest desires is, naturally, recreation, which in our real clubs, if composed of both classes, we can combine with mutual improvement. For those who are not wage-earners, with all the advantages of wealth, culture and leisure on their side, can, from their experience and example, bring into the club many edifying ideas that the working girl would not have. As for the wage-earners, who will say that the example of self-supporting girls and women is not a noble one? And it is right that each should know the other, else how could we obey that greatest command, to love our neighbors as ourselves? Then, if our ideal club is to be "tossed on the shore" of the real club, let us work together, heart and hand, and make the real a success far beyond the ideal.

Miriam Dudley (club unidentified), "City vs. Country," no. 43
(May 1894): 99 [This article was written in response to charity
officials' suggestion that jobless working girls look for live-in
domestic employment in rural communities.]

If one has a handsome house in the country, with all city conveniences, gas, bath, steam heat and such important trifles; if one can surround one's self there with books and pictures and landscape gardening; if one can afford to entertain lavishly; if one can take a trip to the city whenever one wants to hear Melba or Irving [Dame Nellie Melba, an Australian soprano, and Sir Henry Irving, an English actor] or otherwise enjoy one's self, why, then the country would be very delightful indeed. But very few people are rich. The ordinary individual who lives in the country has to submit to sponge baths and kerosene lamps, and to getting his ideas of plays and operas mainly from the newspapers. For such unfortunates, the city is the only place to be considered, even though they have to stay there the year round without even two weeks' vacation in August—poets and philosophers to the contrary notwithstanding. Poverty is bad enough under any circumstances, but if we must be poor, let us be poor in the city, where we can have gas and steam heat and hot and cold water; where we can sit on the steps of the gallery . . . and see Irving for fifty cents; where we can read all the leading periodicals and get almost any book we may happen to want for nothing; where we can wander at will through art galleries and museums; where on Sundays, instead of being bored to death by a prosy sermon and tortured by an untrained choir, we can listen to the sublimest music and the divinest eloquence, with no outlay but car-fare and collection; and where we can pick up dry goods at a bargain for next to nothing and make it up in the latest style after the models seen in shop windows and church pews. *Vive la ville!* And yet there *are* people who wonder why women who are obliged to support themselves *will* stay in New York and starve when they might have "good homes," etc. in the country.

My friends, it is by no means proved that we could have good homes in the country. It is just as hard to earn a living in the country as in the city, and when it is done life is not worth living.

APPENDIX 4

Interclub Organizations and Projects: Chronology, 1885–1920

1885 — est., New York Association of Working Girls' Societies
1888 — est., Brooklyn Association of Working Girls' Societies
1889 — est., Massachusetts Association of Working Girls' Clubs
1890 — AWGS convention in New York City
— New York association opens a vacation house at Miller's Place, Long Island; by 1914 the association operates five such facilities.
— est., *Far and Near* (Nov. 1890–Oct. 1894)
1891 — est., Connecticut Association of Working Girls' Societies
— est., Pennsylvania Association of Working Women's Guilds
— New York association opens the Alliance Employment Bureau and inaugurates a sick benefit fund for club members.
1892 — Connecticut association opens a vacation house at Madison.
1894 — AWGS convention in Boston
1895 — est., Chicago (later Illinois) Association of Young Women's Clubs
— Massachusetts association launches petition drive for the early closing of Boston department stores.
1896 — Massachusetts association assists the establishment of the Women Clerks' Benefit Association of Boston.
1897 — AWGS convention in Philadelphia
— Illinois association opens a nonprofit clerical employment agency.
— est., National League of Women Workers, comprising interclub associations of New York, Brooklyn, Massachusetts, Connecticut, and Pennsylvania (Following the NLWW's establishment, these associations called themselves "Associations of Women Workers.")
1899 — est., the *Club Worker* (Mar. 1899–May/June 1921)

— Pennsylvania association opens a vacation house at Whitford.

— Brooklyn Association reorganizes as the Long Island Association.

1901 — NLWW convention in Buffalo

1902 — NLWW completes a sample survey of club members' occupations, work histories, educational backgrounds, countries of origin, and living arrangements. The survey's results, covering 982 individuals, are published by the Massachusetts Bureau of Statistics of Labor in 1906.

— New York association engineers the establishment of the Manhattan Trade School (taken over by the New York City Board of Education in 1910).

1904 — NLWW convention in New York City

— Massachusetts association assists the establishment of the Boston Trade School for Girls.

— est., Rhode Island Association of Women Workers

— est., Baltimore Council of the Pennsylvania Association

— Massachusetts association opens a vacation house at Bayside (replaced in 1907 by a facility at Rockport).

— Long Island Association disbands and its three remaining clubs join the New York association.

1905 — NLWW convention in Providence

— New York, Massachusetts, and Pennsylvania associations investigate lodging house conditions in larger cities.

1906 — NLWW convention in Philadelphia

— NLWW forms an Extension Committee to organize new clubs.

— Rhode Island association opens a vacation house at Oakland Beach.

1908 — NLWW convention in Washington, D.C.

— est., Brooklyn Council of the New York association

1909 — All NLWW associations form Extension Committees.

1910 — NLWW convention in Gloucester, Mass.

— New York association establishes a chaperoned dance hall open to the general public for a small fee.

— NLWW organizes clubs in Pittsburgh's public playground buildings, in cooperation with the Playground Association.

1911 — NLWW opens a vacation house at Scottdale, Pa., later operated by the Western Pennsylvania Association of Women Workers.

— Pennsylvania association investigates the moral tone of commercial amusements in Philadelphia.

— NLWW inaugurates a group life insurance plan for club members.

1912 — NLWW convention in Montreal and Quebec City

— est., Western Pennsylvania Association of Women Workers

1913 — Massachusetts association sponsors a course on club principles
       and methods at the Boston School for Social Workers.
1914 — NLWW convention in New York City
     — NLWW Executive Board votes to establish "auxiliary boards"
       composed of club members.
     — NLWW associations take steps to democratize their governance.
1915 — first semiannual meetings of NLWW auxiliary boards (There are
       five regional boards, comprising two representatives from each
       club in the designated regions. The boards are chaired by NLWW
       officials.)
     — New York association launches mass recruitment campaign,
       publicizing the club movement through large employers of
       women workers.
1916 — NLWW convention in Pittsfield, Mass.
     — Auxiliary boards expand to include three representatives from
       each club in the designated regions.
1917 — Following U.S. entry into World War I, the NLWW Executive
       Board and directors of state associations organize war service
       activities in cooperation with the Red Cross, the Women's
       Patriotic League, the Girls' Work Division of the National Service
       Commission, and kindred groups.
1918 — NLWW convention at Wellesley College
     — NLWW conducts two Training Courses for Girls' Workers at
       Columbia University's Extension Teaching Department.
     — Active NLWW staff expands to include women representing the
       National Consumers' League, settlement houses, the Commission
       on Training Camp Activities, and the Intercollegiate Community
       Services Association. The NLWW also works with an advisory
       staff including both women and men from the Chicago School of
       Civics and Philanthropy, the New York Training School for
       Community Center Workers, Bryn Mawr College's Graduate
       Department of Social Economics, the National Child Labor
       Committee, the National Girl Scouts, the Russell Sage Founda-
       tion, and the National Federation of Settlements.
1919 — NLWW associations change their names to "Leagues of Women
       Workers."
     — est., Maryland League of Women Workers
     — Eastern Pennsylvania league joins with the Association of
       Collegiate Alumnae and the Women's Trade Union League to
       mobilize mass support for the League of Nations.
     — New York league lobbies in Albany for protective labor laws and
       organizes a New York City rally for such reforms.

— NLWW Executive Board begins short-lived investigation of possibilities for building clubs among African American working women and launches a brief campaign to recruit daughters of new-immigrant communities into existing NLWW clubs.

— NLWW conducts a third Training Course for Girls' Workers at Columbia University.

1920 — NLWW Executive Board establishes an Ohio Division overseeing clubs in Cleveland, Columbus, Dayton, and three other cities.

— NLWW convention at Bryn Mawr College (Convention votes to change the NLWW's name to National League of Girls' Clubs; state leagues follow suit.)

— NLGC holds training courses for club secretaries.

Sources: AWGS Convention 1894; AWGS Convention 1897; NLWW, *History; Club Worker,* 1914–20.

APPENDIX 5

The NLWW Bureaucracy, 1900 and 1918

1900

(7,000 NLWW members; 80 clubs; interclub associations in New York, Brooklyn, Connecticut, Massachusetts, and Pennsylvania, each with a council of directors)

NLWW Executive Board:

    Edith M. Howes (Boston), President

    Mary Richmond (Baltimore), Vice President

    Sarah Ollesheimer (New York City), Treasurer

    Plus five board members

Salaried staff:

    Charlotte Wilkinson, NLWW Secretary

1918

(15,000 NLWW members; 125 clubs; interclub associations in New York, Connecticut, Massachusetts, Rhode Island, eastern Pennsylvania, and western Pennsylvania, each with a council of directors and at least one salaried secretary)

NLWW Executive Board:

    Fannie Pollak (New York City), President

    Sarah Ollesheimer (New York City), First Vice President

    Jessie H. Hunt (Providence), Vice President

    Edith M. Howes (Boston), Vice President

    Marion H. Niles (Wellesley Farms, Mass.), Vice President

    Virginia Potter (New York City), Vice President

Jessie V. Budlong (Providence), Treasurer
Plus eighteen board members
Salaried staff:
Jean Hamilton, General Secretary
Ruth C. Reed, Assistant Secretary
Alma Nilsen, Corresponding Secretary
Grace Johnston, Publicity Secretary
Ida Levoff, Office Secretary

Sources: Club Worker 2, no. 1, suppl. (Jan. 1900): 3–4; NLWW, *History,* p. 4; NLWW
Convention 1918, unnumbered page and p. 3.

APPENDIX 6

Sample Calendars of NLWW Clubs, Fall 1919

North Adams Girls' Club, North Adams, Massachusetts (membership 750)

Calendar for September:
Thursday, 9/11—Business Meeting, followed by music and dancing
Saturday, 9/13—Corn Roast at Windsor Lake
Monday, 9/15—Masquerade Party
Thursday, 9/18—Supper for Captains of Fundraising Drive
Sunday, 9/21—Hike to Cascade
Monday, 9/22—Club Sing
Thursday, 9/25—Fundraising Entertainment
Monday, 9/29—Club Supper

Girls' City Club, Boston (membership 1,200)

Calendar for October:
Wednesday, 10/1—Preview of Winter Classes
Saturday, 10/4—Canoe Trip
Sunday, 10/5—Hike
Monday, 10/6—Business Meeting
Saturday, 10/11—"See-Saw" Party
Saturday-Sunday, 10/18–19—Camping Expedition
Monday, 10/20—Stunt Party
Sunday, 10/26—Tea and Musical
Monday 10/27—Rally for Old and New Members
Friday, 10/31—Masquerade and Dance

United Club, New York City (membership 1,000)

Calendar for October:
Thursday, 10/2—Business Meeting
Tuesday, 10/7—Committee Meetings
Thursday, 10/9—Dance for Club Members and Servicemen
Sunday, 10/12—Fundraising Event
Tuesday, 10/14—Roundtable: "The Coming Election"; Supper for Captains of Fundraising Drive
Thursday, 10/16—Game Evening
Saturday, 10/18—Fundraising Carnival
Tuesday, 10/21—Supper for Captains of Fundraising Drive
Thursday, 10/23—Musical Evening
Saturday, 10/25—Fundraising Entertainment
Tuesday, 10/28—Roundtable: "Cooperation between Employer and Employee"
Thursday, 10/30—Halloween Party

Girls' Community Club, College Point, New York (258 members)

Calendar for October:
Friday, 10/3—Meeting of the Club Council
Monday, 10/6—Business Meeting
Thursday, 10/9—Hayride
Friday, 10/17—Hobo Party
Tuesday, 10/22—Roundtable: "What Makes a Girl Attractive?"
Saturday, 10/25—Hike
Friday, 10/31—Halloween Party

Huntington Club, Syracuse, New York (375 members) [This club was in the process of joining the NLWW.]

Calendar for October:
Sunday, 10/5—Inaugural Meeting of Musicale Club
Tuesday, 10/7—Business meeting followed by refreshments and dancing
Monday, 10/13—Fundraising Block Party (concert and dance)
Thursday, 10/16—Roundtable: "Should Girls Remain in Industry after They Marry?"
Sunday, 10/19—Hike
Wednesday, 10/22—Meeting for Club Leaders
Thursday, 10/23—Home-Making Class
Friday, 10/24—Supper for the Club Council
Friday, 10/31—Halloween Party

Myrtle Club, Baltimore (120 members)

Calendar for October 10–November 7:
Friday, 10/10—Discussion of the *Club Worker* [NLWW journal]
Friday 10/17—Travel Lecture
Sunday 10/19—Excursion to Great Falls
Friday, 10/24—Club Dance
Friday, 10/31—Halloween Party
Saturday, 11/1—Rummage Sale
Sunday, 11/2—Tea Reception
Friday, 11/7—Business Meeting

Progress Club, Spring Grove, Pennsylvania (40 members)

Calendar for October 9–November 6:
Thursday, 10/9—Crocheting
Thursday, 10/16—Sewing Dolls' Dresses for "Empty Stocking Club"
Thursday, 10/23—Entertainment
Thursday, 10/30—Musicale
Thursday, 11/6—Business Meeting

Source: Club Worker 19, no. 2 (Oct. 1919): 3.

Notes

Introduction

1. Graham, *Grace H. Dodge,* p. 85.

2. Ibid., pp. 65–72; AWGS, *Discussions of the Convention . . . 1890,* p. 29 (hereafter cited as AWGS Convention 1890); G. Dodge, *Paper on the Association of Working Girls' Societies,* p. 3. Dodge's long career in the working girls' club movement is examined in Kriegel, "Daughter of Privilege and the Daughters of Labor"; Katz, "Grace Hoadley Dodge."

3. [NYAWGS], *Association of Working Girls' Societies* [annual report for the year ending March 1886], p. 2; NLWW, *History,* pp. 23–24; AWGS Convention 1890, pp. 125–26 and Appendix 2; "Women Who Work and Their Clubs," *Chicago Tribune,* Nov. 24, 1895, p. 45; *Far and Near,* no. 7 (May 1891): 129–30; no. 8 (June 1891): 150; no. 11 (Sept. 1891): 212; no. 15 (Jan. 1892): 63; Board of Lady Managers, Reports on American and Foreign Exhibitors, World's Columbian Exposition, Chicago, 1893, Collected Papers, vol. 41, unnumbered pages, Chicago Historical Society; [AWGS], *Report of Proceedings of the Second National Convention . . . 1894,* pp. 198–99 (hereafter cited as AWGS Convention 1894).

4. Wilson, *Religious and Educational Philosophy of the YWCA,* pp. 4–14; "Agency History," introduction to the Records of the Girls' Friendly Society, p. 1; U.S. Congress, *Report of the Secretary of the Interior,* pp. 31–57; Ferguson, *Boarding Homes and Clubs;* Henrotin, *Attitude of Women's Clubs;* Girod, "Catholic Women's Association"; *Mission of Our Lady of the Rosary;* Toomy, "Some Noble Work of Catholic Women"; Willard, *Occupations for Women.* See also A. Scott, *Natural Allies,* pp. 85–174; Pascoe, *Relations of Rescue,* pp. 3–173; Conzen, "Ethnicity as Festive Culture"; Diner, *Erin's Daughters,* pp. 120–38; Abell, *American Catholicism and Social Action,* pp. 121–23; Dinnerstein, Nichols, and Reimers, *Natives and Strangers,* pp. 163–66.

5. *Far and Near,* no. 1 (Nov. 1890): 15; no. 5 (Mar. 1891): 84–87; no. 8 (June 1891): 149–50; AWGS Convention 1890, p. 126; AWGS Convention 1894, pp. 80–87. See

also *Working Woman's Journal* 5, no. 5 (May 1892): 40; [MAWW], *MAWW: The Work, the Method, the Result,* p. 39.

6. As my approach to the club movement's history suggests, I believe there are valuable things to be learned from poststructural theory's challenges to the dichotomization of the material world and social discourse. By repeatedly drawing my attention to discursive elements of "objective reality," club members compelled me to take these challenges seriously—they identified negative stereotypes of working girls as palpably oppressive constructs, for example, and defined sociability, rather than a universal female experience, as the bedrock for cross-class sisterhood in club circles. For these same reasons, however, it seems foolish to trade historical materialism's tendency to neglect discourse for poststructuralism's tendency to extract it from social contexts. My studies of working girls' clubs have time and again confirmed the wisdom of Ava Baron's advice that women's labor historians combine materialist and poststructural analysis; see her "Gender and Labor History," pp. 16–17.

Provocative arguments for and against poststructuralism's application to social history can be found in J. Scott, *Gender and the Politics of History;* Palmer, *Descent into Discourse.* Some especially interesting amalgamations of Marxist and poststructural theories appear in Berlanstein, *Rethinking Labor History;* see in particular Johnson, "Lifeworld, System, and Communicative Action."

7. Kessler-Harris, "'Where Are the Organized Women Workers?'"; Wertheimer, *We Were There;* Tentler, *Wage-Earning Women.* An excellent summary of recent scholarship in women's labor history appears in Baron, "Gender and Labor History," pp. 2–16; the other essays in Baron, *Work Engendered,* provide outstanding examples of research that genders labor history as a whole. For provocative discussions of gender as an analytic category in labor history, see Buhle, "Gender and Labor History"; Kessler-Harris, "New Agenda for American Labor History." On the interplay of workers' lives on and off the job, see Pleck, "Two Worlds in One."

8. Stansell, *City of Women;* Eisenstein, *Give Us Bread;* Peiss, *Cheap Amusements;* Cameron, *Radicals of the Worst Sort.* Both Peiss and Eisenstein offer valuable discussions of working girls' clubs, though in neither case are the clubs the main subject at hand. Working girls' clubs are also discussed in Pivar, *Purity Crusade;* Rothman, *Woman's Proper Place;* and Reitano's especially valuable "Working Girls Unite." All of these researchers have influenced my thinking about the club movement, even on the many occasions when I've disagreed with their conclusions.

Chapter 1: Daughters of Labor

1. Ames, *Sex in Industry,* p. 32; Rideing, "Working Women in New York," p. 36; Fawcett, "Woes of the New York Working-Girl," p. 30. See also Powell, *National Purity Congress,* pp. 306–19, 398–405, 427–34.

2. Abbott, *Women in Industry;* Stansell, *City of Women;* Groneman, "'She Earns as a Child.'" Though printers, shoemakers, and tailors fought the feminization of their trades, they also approved women's employment alongside male kin. In all three crafts, mid-nineteenth-century bans on women's work in union shops

specifically exempted union men's daughters and wives; see Commons, Saposs, Sumner, Mittelman, Hoagland, Andrews, Perlman, and Taft, *History of Labour*, vol. 1, p. 596.

3. MBSL, *Twentieth Annual Report, December 1889*, pp. 541–49; Chandler, *Visible Hand*, pp. 245–46; Clark, *History of Manufactures*, vol. 2, pp. 154–59; wage data computed from Lebergott, *Manpower in Economic Growth*, table A-19, p. 528. Quotation is from a speech by William J. Cannon at the convention of the Cigar Makers' Union, Paterson, N.J., Sept. 1875, cited in McNeill, *Labor Movement*, p. 590.

4. Edwards, *Comparative Occupation Statistics*, tables 8 and 10, pp. 104–12, 122–29; U.S. Bureau of Labor, *Work and Wages*, pp. 583–638; Gordon, Edwards, and Reich, *Segmented Work, Divided Workers*, pp. 96, 112–21.

5. Chandler, *Visible Hand*, pp. 224–29. Statistics are computed from Edwards, *Comparative Occupation Statistics*, tables 8 and 10, pp. 104–12, 122–29. Quotation is from Hower, *History of Macy's*, p. 65.

6. Statistics are computed from U.S. Congress, *Report of the Secretary of the Interior*, table 2, pp. 118–19; table 4, pp. 174–79; table 9, pp. 248–49; table 11, pp. 300–303; table 13, p. 325; table 15, p. 350.

7. Hillel, "Working-Girls," p. 329.

8. DeVault, "Work and Honor," pp. 2–5. Quotation is from *National Labor Tribune*, Oct. 11, 1879, cited in DeVault, p. 4.

9. Fink, *Workingmen's Democracy*, pp. 13–14; Foner, *History of the Labor Movement*, vol. 1, pp. 433, 509; vol. 2, pp. 61–62; Levine, *Labor's True Woman*, pp. 104–5.

10. Commons et al., *History of Labour*, vol. 2, pp. 114, 127. Quotation is from Knights of Labor General Assembly, *Proceedings* [1888], p. 13, cited in Levine, *Labor's True Woman*, p. 135. McEnnis, *White Slaves of Free America*, is a sterling example of Knights' denunciations of female "wage slavery." The best analyses of the Knights' position on the "woman question" can be found in Levine, *Labor's True Woman*, pp. 103–53; Schofield, "Rise of the Pig-Headed Girl," pp. 83–119.

11. U.S. Congress, *Report of the Secretary of the Interior*, pp. 15–18, 25; statistics computed from table 13, p. 325; table 15, p. 350.

12. See, for example, Maine, *Annual Report*, pp. 94–112; Kansas, *Annual Report*, pp. 322–26; Rhode Island, *Annual Report*, pp. 149–55; Pennsylvania, *Annual Report*, pp. A25–A63. Quotation is from Rhode Island report, p. 150.

13. Campbell, *Prisoners of Poverty*, pp. 221–43; Salmon, *Domestic Service*, pp. 140–66; Katzman, *Seven Days a Week*, pp. 146–83. Quotation is from Mrs. John Sherwood, *Manners and Social Usages* (New York, 1884), pp. 270–71, cited in Katzman, p. 226.

14. Wright, *Working Girls of Boston*, pp. 5, 118–26; U.S. Congress, *Report of the Secretary of the Interior*, pp. 73–77; NYBSL, *[Third] Annual Report for the Year 1885*, pp. 172–79. Quotations are from Wright, p. 5; U.S. Congress, pp. 76–77; NYBSL, pp. 174–75. For a more extensive discussion of state and federal investigators' concerns with working women's morality, see Kessler-Harris, *Out to Work*, pp. 97–105.

15. Wharton, *House of Mirth*; "Women Who Work," *Chicago Tribune*; *Far and*

Near, no. 15 (Jan. 1892): 62; New Century Guild, *100th Anniversary*, p. 29; "A Good Life Work Ended," *New York Times*, Feb. 10, 1883, p. 8; May, *Protestant Churches*, pp. 178–79, 184–85, 239, 241; Baltzell, *Protestant Establishment*, p. 161. Quotation is from Wharton, p. 9.

16. "Wendell Phillips," *Woman's Journal*, p. 84; James, *Notable American Women*, vol. 3, p. 485; AWGS Convention 1890, pp. 93–95.

17. Scudder, *Letters to the Companions*, pp. 1–34; *Far and Near*, no. 8 (June 1891): 149–50; [Civic Club, Philadelphia], *Directory*, pp. 174–87. Quotation is from Howells, *Hazard of New Fortunes*, p. 432.

18. For sterling examples of sponsors' perceptions of their role in the clubs, see AWGS Convention 1890, pp. 16–20; Lockwood, "Women Who Do the Work"; AWGS Convention 1894, pp. 7–10, 23–25. Quotation is from G. Dodge, *Moral Elevation of Girls*, p. 12.

19. There is no occupational census of club members in the 1880s or nineties, but club documents frequently mention members' jobs. See, for example, NYAWGS, *How to Start a Working Girls' Society*, p. 5; *Working Woman's Journal* 4, no. 5 (May 1891): 41–42. Wage data are drawn from U.S. Congress, *Report of the Secretary of the Interior*, pp. 520–29. A description of the Fall River club appears in [MAWW], *MAWW: The Work, the Method, the Result*, pp. 26–27. Quotation is from *Far and Near*, no. 6 (Apr. 1891): 98.

20. A 1901–2 sample survey of nearly a thousand club members found that about 85 percent resided with their families. There is every reason to assume that this pattern also held in the nineteenth century, when family life was a regular topic of club discussions. The 1901–2 survey results appear in MBSL, *Thirty-Sixth Annual Report, March 1906*, pp. 1–37, esp. 33–34. Quotations are from *Far and Near*, no. 15 (Jan. 1892): 57; no. 32 (June 1893): 168. See also *Far and Near*, no. 6 (Apr. 1891): 108.

21. AWGS Convention 1890, pp. 65–68; AWGS Convention 1894, pp. 161–64. Quotations are from AWGS Convention 1890, p. 68; *Far and Near*, no. 13 (Nov. 1891): 15.

22. de Graffenried, "Condition of Wage-Earning Women," p. 71; "New Field for Catholic Women," *Pilot*; *Far and Near*, no. 9 (July 1891): 151; no. 13 (Nov. 1891): 19; no. 16 (Feb. 1892): 84; no. 27 (Jan. 1893): 59; no. 31 (May 1893): 147; no. 32 (June 1893): 171.

23. Henrotin, *Attitude of Women's Clubs*, p. 515; E. Turner, "Report of the New Century Guild," p. 9; *Far and Near*, no. 25 (Nov. 1892): 2; Betts, *Leaven in a Great City*, pp. 147–49.

24. Addams, *Twenty Years at Hull-House*, pp. 239–41, quotation is from p. 240. On the respectable/rough dichotomy in working-class culture, see Broder, "Informing the 'Cruelty'"; Fones-Wolf, *Trade Union Gospel*, pp. 20–36.

Chapter 2: Quests for Respectability, Demands for Respect

1. *Working Woman's Journal* 3, no. 8 (Oct. 1890): 6; AWGS Convention 1890, p. 70.

2. AWGS Convention 1890, pp. 20–23; G. Dodge, *Thoughts of Busy Girls*, pp. 135–37; Davidge, "Working-Girls' Clubs," p. 620; AWGS Convention 1894, pp.

5, 10–11, 14–16, 110. Quotations are from AWGS Convention 1894, p. 110; AWGS Convention 1890, p. 20; AWGS Convention 1894, p. 5.

3. AWGS Convention 1890, pp. 32–37, 57; *Far and Near*, no. 13 (Nov. 1891): 15; no. 18 (Apr. 1892): 113–14; no. 30 (Apr. 1893): 125; no. 36 (Oct. 1893): 254. Quotations are from AWGS Convention 1890, pp. 57, 35, 32–33. The most extensive reports on club activities can be found in *Far and Near*'s monthly column entitled "Club Notes."

4. *Far and Near*, no. 3 (Jan. 1891): 37. This article's entire text is reprinted in Appendix 3. For other expressions of Warner's views on self-improvement, see AWGS Convention 1890, p. 107; *Far and Near*, no. 5 (Mar. 1891): 78. Denning observes similar challenges to elite values in dime novels about working girls, especially those by the incomparably popular Laura Jean Libbey; see his *Mechanic Accents*, pp. 185–200.

5. AWGS Convention 1890, pp. 79–86, quotations are from pp. 81, 86, 84.

6. AWGS Convention 1890, pp. 42, 71–74; *Far and Near*, no. 3 (Jan. 1891): 47; no. 4 (Feb. 1891): 65; no. 8 (June 1891): 141–42; no. 14 (Dec. 1891): 40; no. 16 (Feb. 1892): 83; no. 22 (Aug. 1892): 202; no. 29 (Mar. 1893): 103; no. 42 (Apr. 1894): 90. Quotation is from AWGS Convention 1890, p. 73.

7. *Working Woman's Journal* 2, no. 2 (Feb. 1889): 3; AWGS Convention 1890, pp. 56–58; *Lend a Hand* 5, no. 12 (Dec. 1890): 878; *Far and Near*, no. 3 (Jan. 1891): 48; no. 12 (Oct. 1891): 230; no. 15 (Jan. 1892): 19; no. 16 (Feb. 1892): 82–83; no. 25 (Nov. 1892): 19; no. 28 (Feb. 1893): 82–83; no. 41 (Mar. 1894): 75. Quotations are from *Far and Near*, no. 16 (Feb. 1892): 82, 83.

8. AWGS Convention 1890, p. 57. A good summary of the activities and outlooks of Charity Organization Societies in the late nineteenth century can be found in Boyer, *Urban Masses and Moral Order*, pp. 142–61.

9. Kaplan, "Female Consciousness and Collective Action," pp. 545–51.

10. Campbell, "Association in Clubs," p. 65; AWGS Convention 1894, p. 15. Quotation is from G. Dodge, *Thoughts of Busy Girls*, pp. 6–7.

11. NLWW, *History*, p. 10; *Far and Near*, no. 9 (July 1891): 157–58. Quotation is from *Far and Near*, no. 2 (Dec. 1890): 18.

12. *Far and Near*, no. 2 (Dec. 1890): 18, 25, 26; no. 7 (May 1891): 127; no. 17 (Mar. 1892): 102; no. 18 (Apr. 1892): 126. Quotation is from *Far and Near*, no. 1 (Nov. 1890): 9.

13. AWGS Convention 1890, pp. 27, 10, 22.

14. New York *Evening Post*, Apr. 15, 1890, cited in Davidge, "Working-Girls' Clubs," pp. 626–27.

15. Allen, "Must Working Girls' Clubs Be Self Sustaining?" pp. 278–79; *Far and Near*, no. 6 (Apr. 1891): 97–99; no. 7 (May 1891): 117–20; no. 33 (July 1893): 190. Quotations are from *Far and Near*, no. 6, p. 98; no. 7, p. 120. See also NYAWGS, *Reasons for Advancing the Principle of Self-Support*; Coleman, "Model Working Girls' Clubs."

16. Quotations are from G. Dodge, "Newark, N.J.[,] Address before Charitable Society, Nov. 30, 1891," bound in "Personal Work, Papers and Addresses," pp. 100–107, Grace Hoadley Dodge Papers, Milbank Memorial Library, Teachers College, Columbia University.

17. AWGS Convention 1894, pp. 121–25; G. Dodge, *Paper on the Association of*

Working Girls' Societies, p. 5; NYAWGS, *Suggestions for Club Work*, p. 4; *Far and Near*, no. 4 (Feb. 1891): 66; no. 9 (July 1891): 167; no. 16 (Feb. 1892): 83. Quotations are from AWGS Convention 1894, pp. 121, 122. For an example of the argument that working girls' clubs should, like colleges, be endowed, see "Which Is the More Important?" *Outlook*.

18. AWGS Convention 1890, pp. 58–59, 111; "The Three P's Circle," 3 vols., unnumbered pages, Dodge Papers. Quotations are from AWGS Convention 1890, p. 58.

19. Graham, *Grace H. Dodge*, pp. 94–95.

20. G. Dodge, "Glimpses into the Lives of Working-Women," pt. 2. Quotations are from Dodge, p. 67; *Far and Near*, no. 31 (May 1893): 147.

21. G. Dodge, "Association of Working Girls' Societies," p. 18, and "Glimpses into the Lives of Working-Women," pt. 2; AWGS Convention 1890, pp. 79–86, 113–14.

22. AWGS Convention 1890, pp. 95–98, quotations are from pp. 95, 97, 97.

23. G. Dodge, *Thoughts of Busy Girls*, p. 137.

Chapter 3: Patrons and Friends

1. Tracy's essay appears in G. Dodge, *Thoughts of Busy Girls*, pp. 131–35, quotations are from pp. 132–33. This essay's entire text is reprinted in Appendix 2.

2. AWGS Convention 1894, pp. 18–19; [Wedding announcement], *New York Times*, Mar. 31, 1891, p. 8; Addams, *Democracy and Social Ethics*, p. 36; Betts, *Leaven in a Great City*, pp. 234, 240. Quotation is from AWGS Convention 1894, p. 18.

3. *Far and Near*, no. 18 (Apr. 1892): 117.

4. *Far and Near*, no. 1 (Dec. 1890): 2, 4–6; no. 4 (Feb. 1891): 57; no. 18 (Apr. 1892): 113–14; [NYAWGS], *Fourth Annual Report* [for the year ending April 1888], pp. 20–23; *Club Worker* 4, no. 7 (May 1903): 145. Quotation is from Betts, *Leaven in a Great City*, p. 237.

5. Rhine, "Work of Women's Clubs," p. 527; Betts, *Leaven in a Great City*, pp. 237–38. Quotation is from Betts, p. 238.

6. Bailey, "'Will the Real Bill Banks,'" quotation is from p. 338.

7. AWGS Convention 1894, pp. 9–10, quotations are from p. 10.

8. Ibid., p. 157; Gompers, *Seventy Years*, vol. 1, p. 434; *Far and Near*, no. 12 (Oct. 1891): 222; no. 30 (Apr. 1893): 113; no. 32 (June 1893): 157; no. 37 (Nov. 1893): 7; no. 39 (Jan. 1894): 44; no. 42 (Apr. 1894): 83–84. Quotation is from *Far and Near*, no. 39.

9. *Far and Near*, no. 1 (Nov. 1890): 2; no. 7 (May 1891): 127; no. 12 (Oct. 1891): 225; no. 42 (Apr. 1894): 83; G. Dodge, *Thoughts of Busy Girls*, pp. 12–14, and "Outline of Address to Mothers, at Sunny Side Day Nursery, February 21, 1890," bound in "Personal Work, Papers and Addresses," p. 47, Dodge Papers. Quotations are from Dodge, *Thoughts*, p. 13; *Far and Near*, no. 1; no. 12.

10. *Far and Near*, no. 21 (July 1892): 180; no. 23 (Sept. 1892): 223–24; no. 46 (Aug. 1894): 138–39; Peiss, *Cheap Amusements*, pp. 45–51. Quotations are from *Far and Near*, no. 46, p. 138; no. 23, p. 223.

11. *Far and Near*, no. 9 (July 1891): 166; no. 13 (Nov. 1891): 2; no. 42 (Apr. 1894): 85; quotations are from no. 9; no. 13. For general discussions of working wom-

en's attitudes regarding their dress, see Van Vorst, *Woman Who Toils;* Addams, *Democracy and Social Ethics,* pp. 34–36; McDowell, "Our Proxies in Industry," (typescript, n.d.), folder 15, p. 1, Mary McDowell Papers, Chicago Historical Society; Peiss, *Cheap Amusements,* pp. 62–67.

12. *Far and Near,* no. 23 (Sept. 1892): 229; Betts, *Leaven in a Great City,* pp. 154–55, 245–47; G. Dodge, *Thoughts of Busy Girls,* pp. 74–76.

13. Bailey, "'Will the Real Bill Banks,'" p. 343.

14. NYBSL, *[Third] Annual Report for the Year 1885,* pp. 291–94; "The Factory Girl," *New York Times,* Mar. 9, 1892, p. 8; G. Dodge, "Notes for Two Addresses, Hartford, Conn., December 12, 1889," bound in "Personal Work, Papers and Addresses," p. 24, Dodge Papers; S. White, *Business Openings for Girls,* pp. 75–77; Lanza, "Women Clerks in New York," pp. 445–47, 450–51; *Far and Near,* no. 17 (Mar. 1892): 95. Quotation is from "Labor's Demonstration," *New York Times,* Sept. 8, 1885, p. 8.

15. Quotation is from *Far and Near,* no. 10 (Aug. 1891): 178; see also no. 11 (Sept. 1891): 208.

16. Betts, *Leaven in a Great City,* pp. 205–21, esp. 219–20; *Far and Near,* no. 15 (Jan. 1892): 55–56. For an instructive discussion of female purity's importance in working-class London at the turn of the century, see Ellen Ross, "'Not the Sort that Would Sit on the Doorstep,'" pp. 49–51.

17. William T. Elsing, "Life in New York Tenement-Houses as Seen by a City Missionary," in Woods, Elsing, Riis, Parsons, Wendell, Flagg, Tucker, Kirkland, Besant, Spearman, Mario, and Craig, *Poor in Great Cities,* p. 72. See also G. Dodge, *Bundle of Letters,* pp. 32–42, 103–4.

18. Lockwood, "Women Who Do the Work," p. 794; Betts, *Leaven in a Great City,* p. 237.

19. An illuminating discussion of the class origins of "good etiquette" appears in Veblen, *Theory of the Leisure Class,* pp. 48–52.

20. AWGS Convention 1894, p. 22.

21. For evidence of widespread democratization, see the "Club Notes" section of *Far and Near,* Dec. 1890 onward; [AWGS], *Report on the Proceedings of the Third National Convention . . . 1897,* pp. 111–14 (hereafter cited as AWGS Convention 1897). Regarding professional women's role in the clubs, see *Far and Near,* no. 5 (Mar. 1891): 88; no. 8 (July 1891): 146; no. 13 (Nov. 1891): 20; no. 16 (Feb. 1892): 79–80; Rose Pastor Stokes, "Ms. autobiography—incomplete; second draft," series 2, box 6, folder 6C, p. 83, Rose Pastor Stokes Papers, Mss. Group no. 573, Sterling Library, Yale University. Workers' suggestions and opinions regarding club programs appeared regularly in the *Far and Near* column "Thoughts from Club Members," which ran from January through September 1891, and in the "Correspondence Column" featured in subsequent issues.

22. AWGS Convention 1894, pp. 24, 11.

23. AWGS Convention 1890, pp. 29–40, quotations are from pp. 30, 31, 37, 38.

24. Ibid., pp. 33–36, quotations are from p. 35.

25. AWGS Convention 1894, pp. 71–79; *Far and Near,* no. 4 (Feb. 1891): 66; no. 20 (June 1892): 168; no. 22 (Aug. 1892): 211; G. Dodge, "[Paper] Presented at the Labor Congress, Chicago, Aug. 6, 1893," bound in "Personal Work, Papers and Address," pp. 191–92, Dodge Papers. Quotation is from AWGS Convention, p. 72.

26. AWGS Convention 1894, pp. 71–79; New Century Guild, *100th Anniversary*, p. 38. Quotation is from AWGS Convention, p. 71. Reports on club classes in vocational skills appear in the "Club Notes" section of *Far and Near* from March 1891 onward.

27. AWGS Convention 1894, pp. 71–79; AWGS Convention 1890, pp. 29–31. Quotations are from AWGS Convention 1894, pp. 75, 77.

28. AWGS Convention 1890, pp. 41–43. Quotations are from AWGS Convention, p. 42; G. Dodge, "[Notes for a Talk at] Plymouth, Conn., February 14[, 1890,] Evening," bound in "Personal Work, Papers and Addresses," p. 45, Dodge Papers.

29. *Far and Near*, no. 21 (July 1892): 187; no. 29 (Mar. 1893): 105; no. 31 (May 1893): 149; AWGS Convention 1894, pp. 98–121.

30. AWGS Convention 1894, pp. 98–121, quotations are from pp. 103, 105, 109, 101.

31. Wharton, *House of Mirth*, pp. 158–60; Hapke, *Tales of the Working Girl*, p. 50; M. Jones, "Women's Opportunities in Town and Country." Quotations are from Wharton, p. 159; AWGS Convention 1894, p. 103. Some of club sponsors' peers thought them wrong to form emotional attachments to individual working women; for a fictional argument to that effect, see M. Deland, "Law, or the Gospel," in Deland, *Wisdom of Fools*, pp. 191–248.

32. AWGS Convention 1894, pp. 10–25, quotations are from pp. 16, 19, 11, 25. On women's friendships, see Smith-Rosenberg, "Female World of Love and Ritual."

Chapter 4: The Woman Question

1. G. Dodge, "Working Girls' Societies," p. 223, and "[Notes for a Talk] at the Elizabeth Home, Dec. 13, 1892," bound in "Personal Work, Papers and Addresses," p. 163, Dodge Papers; *Working Woman's Journal* 2, no. 6 (May 1889): 2; AWGS Convention 1890, pp. 42, 69; *Far and Near*, no. 10 (Aug. 1891): 178; no. 18 (Apr. 1892): 115; no. 23 (Sept. 1892): 228–29. Quotations are from *Far and Near*, no. 23, pp. 228–29; no. 10.

2. U.S. Congress, *Report of the Secretary of the Interior*, p. 36; *Far and Near*, no. 12 (Oct. 1891): 226; no. 16 (Feb. 1892): 72–73.

3. *Far and Near*, no. 2 (Dec. 1890): 29–30; no. 3 (Jan. 1891): 42–43; no. 4 (Feb. 1891): 62–63; no. 37 (Nov. 1893): 15; Graham, *Grace H. Dodge*, pp. 55–61, 72–77; Boyer, *Urban Masses and Moral Order*, pp. 150–53; Ehrenreich and English, *For Her Own Good*, pp. 170–78. Quotation is from Graham, p. 175.

4. F. Kelley, *Notes of Sixty Years*, pp. 45–68; *Far and Near*, no. 8 (June 1891): 146; McHenry, *Famous American Women*, pp. 294–95. Quotation is from Kelley, p. 45.

5. Graham, *Grace H. Dodge*, pp. 31–42; P. Dodge, *Tales of the Phelps-Dodge Family*, pp. 245, 248. Quotation is from Hamilton, *Exploring the Dangerous Trades*, p. 35. For a contemporary critique of the education of upper-class women in the late nineteenth century, see Porter, "Physical Hindrances to Teaching Girls."

6. AWGS Convention 1890, pp. 89–92, quotation is from p. 91.

7. AWGS Convention 1894, pp. 55–71, quotations are from p. 56.

8. Ibid., pp. 62–65; *Far and Near*, no. 16 (Feb. 1892): 72–73; *Working Woman's*

Journal 5, no. 3 (Mar. 1892): 23–24. Quotations are from AWGS Convention 1894, pp. 62, 63, 64.

9. *Far and Near*, no. 24 (Oct. 1892): 245–46; no. 38 (Dec. 1893): 23–24; no. 39 (Jan. 1894): 39–40.

10. *Far and Near*, no. 32 (June 1893): 162; AWGS Convention 1894, pp. 157–61; *Working Woman's Journal* 7, no. 9 (Nov. 1894): 68–70; 8, no. 10 (Dec. 1895): 75–77. Quotation is from AWGS Convention 1894, p. 159.

11. Betts, *Leaven in a Great City*, pp. 251–53; Wright, "Why Women Are Paid Less than Men"; Peiss, *Cheap Amusements*, pp. 51–58, 108–14.

12. G. Dodge, *Bundle of Letters*, pp. 100–107, and "Practical Suggestions Relating to Moral Elevation," p. 88; E. Turner, *Confidential*; Betts, *Leaven in a Great City*, pp. 251–53. Quotations are from Dodge, *Bundle of Letters*, pp. 103–4; Betts, p. 253. In the late 1880s and early nineties, many club sponsors were devotees of the White Cross Society, a sexual purity movement spearheaded by the Episcopal Church, which imported it from England in 1886. See Campbell, "Association in Clubs," p. 65; Pivar, *Purity Crusade*, pp. 110–15.

13. *Working Woman's Journal* 3, no. 5 (May 1890): 2.

14. *Far and Near*, no. 16 (Feb. 1892): 65; no. 18 (Apr. 1892): 124; no. 34 (Aug. 1893): 211–12; AWGS Convention 1894, pp. 106–7, 110–14, 119–21; Humphreys, "New York Working Girl," p. 513. Quotations are from AWGS Convention, pp. 113, 107.

15. *Far and Near*, no. 17 (Mar. 1892): 101; AWGS Convention 1894, p. 108.

16. AWGS Convention 1894, pp. 110–14; Graham, *Grace H. Dodge*, pp. 47–57; Emily Sophie Brown, "Biographical Sketch of Emily Malbone Morgan," in Scudder, *Letters to Her Companions*, pp. 6–7; *Far and Near*, no. 9 (July 1891): 160–62; Sinclair, *Emancipation of the American Woman*, pp. 118–23. Quotations are from AWGS Convention, p. 112; *Far and Near*, p. 161. For a sketch of late nineteenth-century debutantes' social life, see Lewis, *Edith Wharton*, pp. 32–37.

17. Quotations are from "Men Are Excluded," *New York Times*, Apr. 19, 1889, p. 2; *Far and Near*, no. 24 (Oct. 1892): 255; *Working Woman's Journal* 8, no. 1 (Jan. 1895): 1.

18. *Club Worker* 2, no. 4 (Apr. 1900): 4; NYBSL, *Eighteenth Annual Report for the Year 1900*, pp. 341–43; O'Reilly, "Diaries and Notebooks," vol. 7, entries for June 1 and 2, 1899, Leonora O'Reilly Papers, Schlesinger Library, Radcliffe College. Quotations are from *Club Worker*; O'Reilly, June 2.

19. G. Dodge, *Bundle of Letters*, pp. 40–42, 53–62; [NYAWGS], *Fourth Annual Report* [for the year ending Apr. 1888], pp. 20–23. Quotation is from *Annual Report*, p. 20. For a general discussion of working women's vision of marriage as an escape from overwork and the genteel efforts to whet their interest in domestic training by romanticizing housework, see Eisenstein, *Give Us Bread*, pp. 129, 139–42.

20. G. Dodge, *Thoughts of Busy Girls*, pp. 18–20; *Working Woman's Journal* 7, no. 4 (Apr. 1894): 27; *New Century Journal of Women's Interests* 9, no. 4 (Apr. 1896): 30. Quotation is from Dodge, p. 18.

21. *Far and Near*, no. 22 (Aug. 1892): 209–10; *Working Woman's Journal* 3, no. 3 (Mar. 1889): 2–3; Matthaei, *Economic History of Women*, pp. 124–33; Jensen, "Cloth, Butter and Boarders," pp. 18–21; Kleinberg, "Technology and Women's Work";

Strasser, *Never Done*, pp. 11–161. Quotations are from *Far and Near*, p. 210; *Working Woman's Journal*, p. 2.

22. For a description of the patterns of married life that club members aimed to avoid, see Peiss, *Cheap Amusements*, pp. 16–26.

23. G. Dodge, *Thoughts of Busy Girls*, pp. 27–29; *Working Woman's Journal* 3, no. 4 (Apr. 1890): 4; *New Century Journal of Women's Interests* 9, no. 6 (June 1896): 46. Quotations are from Dodge, pp. 28, 29; *New Century Journal*.

24. NYBSL, *Tenth Annual Report for the Year 1892*, pp. 170–89; *Far and Near*, no. 24 (Oct. 1842): 248.

25. "Women Who Work," *Chicago Tribune*; AWGS Convention 1897, pp. 8–10; Beadle and the Centennial History Committee, *Fortnightly of Chicago*, pp. 81–82.

26. AWGS Convention 1890, pp. 89–92; [NYAWGS], *Association of Working Girls' Societies* [annual report for the year ending Mar. 1886], pp. 1–3; AWGS Convention 1894, pp. 169–70; "Sarah Ollesheimer" [obituary], *New York Times*, Dec. 1, 1923, p. 13; *Club Worker* 17, no. 8 (May 1918): 12; 17, no. 12 (Sept. 1918): 6–7; "Mrs. Richard Irvin" [obituary], *New York Times*, June 7, 1918, p. 13; *Far and Near*, no. 6 (Apr. 1891): 109; *National Civic Federation Review* 3, no. 4 (May 1908): 14; Stein, *Edie*, pp. 12, 28, 430–31, quotation is from p. 28.

27. New Century Guild, *100th Anniversary*, pp. 11–21; *Working Woman's Journal* 5, no. 1 (Jan. 1892): 2–4, quotation is from p. 4.

28. Betts, *Leaven in a Great City*, p. 166; AWGS Convention 1894, pp. 167–69; *Far and Near*, no. 38 (Dec. 1893): 38; *Club Worker* 2, no. 3 (Mar. 1900): 3; 2, no. 7 (Oct. 1900): 1–3; 3, no. 9 (Dec. 1901): 7; "List of Topics for Domestic Circle—1898," bound in "Personal Work, Papers and Addresses," p. 246, Dodge Papers. Quotations are from "List of Topics"; *Club Worker* 2, no. 3.

29. *Working Woman's Journal* 7, no. 4 (Apr. 1894): 27.

30. G. Dodge, *Thoughts of Busy Girls*, pp. 19–22, quotation is from pp. 20–21.

31. *Working Woman's Journal* 6, no. 8 (Oct. 1893): 62–64; 6, no. 10 (Dec. 1893): 80–81; *Club Worker* 3, no. 1 (Jan. 1901): 7; 18, no. 3 (Dec. 1918): 8; "Maria Chapin" [obituary], *New York Times*, Mar. 9, 1934, p. 19; Betts, *Leaven in a Great City*, p. 254; *Lend a Hand* 5, no. 12 (Dec. 1890): 877–78; AWGS Convention 1894, p. 167; *Far and Near*, no. 4 (Feb. 1891): 61–62; no. 12 (Oct. 1891): 214–15; no. 21 (July 1892): 187; G. Dodge, "[Notes for a Talk at] New Haven, Conn., Dec. 7, 1892," bound in "Personal Work, Papers and Addresses," p. 159, Dodge Papers; P. Dodge, *Tales of the Phelps-Dodge Family*, p. 247. Quotation is from *Far and Near*, no. 12, pp. 214–15.

32. G. Dodge, *Thoughts of Busy Girls*, pp. 22–26. Quotations are from Dodge, pp. 23–24, 25–26; Betts, *Leaven in a Great City*, p. 254.

33. Wright, "Why Women Are Paid Less than Men," pp. 236–38; Smith, "Family Limitation," pp. 223–24; Degler, *At Odds*, pp. 165–75. Quotation is from Wright, p. 237.

34. "New Woman," *Review of Reviews*; "New Woman under Fire," *Review of Reviews*; AWGS Convention 1897, p. 168; Graham, *Grace H. Dodge*, pp. 92–93, quotation is from p. 92.

35. For a discussion of the "true woman" ideal, see Welter, "Cult of True Womanhood." As suggested by club sponsors' and members' many references to "true womanhood," this ideal remained influential in the late nineteenth century, al-

beit in a tattered form. For a sterling example of sponsors' self-presentation as altruists, see AWGS Convention 1890, pp. 16–20, esp. 16.

36. AWGS Convention 1894, pp. 16–18; G. Dodge, "Practical Suggestions Relating to Moral Elevation," pp. 82–84; *Far and Near*, no. 16 (Feb. 1892): 65. Quotation is from AWGS Convention, p. 17.

It is instructive that New York City's Endeavor Club, which originated the council form of club government, was also the first to integrate men into club life. Sarah Minturn, the first club sponsor to speak for the record about domesticity's disadvantages, was connected with this club. See *Far and Near*, no. 5 (Mar. 1891): 86; no. 9 (July 1891): 158; AWGS Convention 1890, pp. 91–92.

37. *Far and Near*, no. 9 (July 1891): 157; no. 13 (Nov. 1891): 8–9; AWGS Convention 1894, pp. 10–11, 14, 16–19, 23–25, 35, 197, 199. Quotation is from *Far and Near*, no. 13, p. 8.

Chapter 5: The Labor Question

1. Campbell, "Working Girls' Clubs."

2. Tax, *Rising of the Women*, pp. 39–41; *Far and Near*, no. 33 (July 1893): 180. Quotations are from Lizzie Swank Holmes, "Women Workers of Chicago," *American Federationist* 12, no. 8 (Aug. 1905): 509, cited in Tax, p. 40.

3. Graham, *Grace H. Dodge*, pp. 66–72, quotation is from p. 67.

4. Fawcett, "Woes of the New York Working-Girl"; *Far and Near*, no. 19 (May 1892): 144. Quotations are from Fawcett, p. 30; *Far and Near*.

One notable exception to the silence regarding work life was Philadelphia's New Century Guild; see, for example, *Working Woman's Journal* 2, no. 7 (Sept. 1889): 2–3; 2, no. 9 (Nov. 1889): 5–7; 2, no. 10 (Dec. 1889): 4–5.

5. [NYAWGS], *Seventh Annual Report* [for the year ending Mar. 1891], pp. 5–6; AWGS Convention 1894, pp. 137–39, 169–74; Alliance Employment Bureau, *Annual Report Bureau* [for 1897]; AWGS Convention 1897, pp. 76–77; *Far and Near*, no. 7 (May 1891): 128; no. 9 (July 1891): 170; no. 11 (Sept. 1891): 211; no. 18 (Apr. 1892): 125; no. 23 (Sept. 1892): 234; no. 31 (May 1893): 148.

6. *Working Woman's Journal* 3, no. 3 (Mar. 1890): 5–7; G. Dodge, *Thoughts of Busy Girls*, pp. 102–3, 106; Graham, *Grace H. Dodge*, pp. 96–98; Weimann, *Fair Women*, pp. 511–14. Quotation is from Graham, p. 98.

7. *Far and Near*, no. 4 (Feb. 1891): 67.

8. Ibid., no. 5 (Mar. 1891): 71–72.

9. Ibid., no. 6 (Apr. 1891): 109; no. 7 (May 1891): 125; no. 9 (July 1891): 152–53; no. 10 (Aug. 1891): 171–72; no. 14 (Dec. 1891): 40; G. Dodge, "[Notes for a Talk at] Wilmington, Del., Feb. 11, 1891," bound in "Personal Work, Papers and Addresses," pp. 73–74, Dodge Papers; Wolfe, "Women, Consumerism, and the National Consumers' League," pp. 383–84. Quotations are from *Far and Near*, no. 9, p. 153; no. 10, p. 172.

10. *Far and Near*, no. 12 (Oct. 1891): 222; no. 13 (Nov. 1891): 16. Quotations are from no. 13; no. 12; no. 13. The full text of Burke's letter is reprinted in Appendix 3.

11. Ibid., no. 13 (Nov. 1891): 18; no. 20 (June 1892): 168.

12. Ibid., no. 15 (Jan. 1892): 45–46; no. 17 (Mar. 1892): 85–86; no. 18 (Apr. 1892):

107–8, 115; no. 19 (May 1892): 136–37. Quotations are from no. 19, p. 137; no. 15, p. 46; no. 17, p. 85; no. 18, p. 108.

13. Ibid., no. 18 (Apr. 1892): 115, 121–22; no. 19 (May 1892): 129. Quotations are from no. 18, pp. 121, 115; no. 19.

14. G. Dodge, "Glimpses into Working Girls' Club Life and Principles," p. 68; *Far and Near* no. 45 (July 1894): 131.

15. Wertheimer, *We Were There*, pp. 198–206.

16. Foner, *Women and the American Labor Movement*, pp. 215–18; Kocka, *White Collar Workers*, pp. 55, 67–68; Grob, *Workers and Utopia*, pp. 120–27; Commons et al., *History of Labour*, vol. 2, pp. 486–87: Montgomery, *Fall of the House of Labor*, pp. 164–65.

17. Foner, *Women and the American Labor Movement*, pp. 223–27.

18. O'Sullivan, "Autobiography of Mary Kenney O'Sullivan" [Ms.], pp. 33a, 62, 76, Schlesinger Library, Radcliffe College; *Far and Near*, no. 11 (Sept. 1891): 212; no. 13 (Nov. 1891): 21; AWGS Convention 1894, pp. 50–51; Foner, *Women and the American Labor Movement*, pp. 228–29; Tax, *Rising of the Women*, pp. 59–61. Quotation is from O'Sullivan, p. 62.

19. *Far and Near*, no. 21 (July 1892): 181; Sewall, *World's Congress*, pp. 871–74; Graham, *Grace H. Dodge*, p. 97. Quotations are from *Far and Near*.

20. AWGS Convention, 1890, pp. 79–80, 95–97; Montgomery, *Workers' Control in America*, p. 20. Quotations are from AWGS Convention 1890, pp. 79–80, 95, 97.

21. *New York Times*, Aug. 6, 1889, p. 8; G. Dodge, "Notes for Two Addresses, Hartford, Conn., December 12, 1889," bound in "Personal Work, Papers and Addresses," p. 24, Dodge Papers; NYBSL, *Seventh Annual Report for the Year 1889*, pp. 484, 651–52, 714, and *Eighth Annual Report for the Year 1890*, pp. 790, 1024–26, 1096–97; [NYAWGS], *Seventh Annual Report* [for the year ending Mar. 1891], pp. 32–33. Quotations are from AWGS Convention 1890, pp. 80, 79, 80.

22. *Far and Near*, no. 19 (May 1892): 146; Board of Lady Managers, Reports on American and Foreign Exhibitors, World's Columbian Exposition Papers, vol. 41, entries for New York State and Rhode Island, unnumbered pages; Foner, *Women and the American Labor Movement*, pp. 185–212; Blewett, *Men, Women, and Work*, pp. 225–66.

23. Jelley, *Voice of Labor*, pp. 197–201; *Far and Near*, no. 3 (Jan. 1891): 37–38; no. 4 (Feb. 1891): 57; no. 9 (July 1891): 157; no. 16 (Feb. 1892): 81; no. 19 (May 1892): 147; no. 26 (Dec. 1892): 29; Foner, *History of the Labor Movement*, vol. 2, pp. 47–55, 157–67, 300–310; Fink, *Workingmen's Democracy*, pp. 3–37. Quotations are from *Far and Near*, no. 3, p. 37; no. 16.

24. AWGS Convention 1894, p. 155.

25. *Far and Near*, no. 10 (Aug. 1891): 191; *Journal of the Knights of Labor*, May 17, 1894, p. 3; *Club Worker* 7, no. 2 (Dec. 1905): 395–97; 17, no. 5 (Feb. 1918): 3–4.

26. Tax, *Rising of the Women*, pp. 60–63, 66–89; Peiss, *Cheap Amusements*, p. 172.

27. "A Work Full of Promise," *New York Times*, Apr. 18, 1890, p. 8; "Living Questions for Working Girls," *New York Herald*, Apr. 18, 1890, p. 3; AWGS Convention 1890, p. 99; Foner, *History of the Labor Movement*, vol. 2, pp. 54, 166; Wertheimer, *We Were There*, pp. 186–89. Quotations are from "Work Full"; Orth, *Armies of Labor*, p. 78.

28. AWGS Convention 1890, pp. 99–100; *Far and Near,* no. 20 (June 1892): 157; no. 22 (Aug. 1892): 206; no. 23 (Sept. 1892): 222–23; no. 28 (Feb. 1893): 65–67; Montgomery, *Fall of the House of Labor,* pp. 165–68; Foner, *History of the Labor Movement,* vol. 2, pp. 206–18.

29. *Far and Near,* no. 17 (Mar. 1892): 95.

30. Foner, *Women and the American Labor Movement,* pp. 228–30, and *History of the Labor Movement,* vol. 2, pp. 206–34, 253–54.

31. *Far and Near,* no. 26 (Dec. 1892): 41; no. 27 (Jan. 1893): 48–49, 53; no. 29 (Mar. 1893): 87–88, 92–93; Commons et al., *History of Labour,* vol. 2, pp. 499–500, 509. Quotations are from *Far and Near,* no. 27, p. 53; no. 29, p. 92.

32. Board of Lady Managers, Reports on American and Foreign Exhibitors, World's Columbian Exposition Papers, vol. 41, entry for the Far and Near Club, New York State, unnumbered page; G. Dodge, "[Paper] Presented at the Labor Congress, Chicago, Aug. 6, 1893. Read by Miss De Graffenried," bound in "Personal Work, Papers and Addresses," p. 193, Dodge Papers; *Far and Near,* no. 27 (Jan. 1893): 60; no. 32 (June 1893): 170. Quotations are from *Far and Near,* no. 29 (Mar. 1893): 92; Dodge, "Glimpses into Working Girls' Club Life and Principles," p. 68.

33. *Far and Near,* no. 13 (Nov. 1891): 16.

34. NYBSL, *Eleventh Annual Report for the Year 1893,* pt. 2, pp. 3212, 3318, 3241, 3273; Foner, *History of the Labor Movement,* vol. 2, pp. 235–36; Lebergott, *Manpower in Economic Growth,* pp. 522, 528.

35. *Far and Near,* no. 38 (Dec. 1893): 28–29, 37–38; no. 39 (Jan. 1894): 50; no. 41 (Mar. 1894): 74. Quotation is from *Far and Near,* no. 38, p. 28.

36. G. Dodge, "Statement Presented to Committee on Holiday Houses," bound in "Personal Work, Papers and Addresses," p. 208, Dodge Papers; *Working Woman's Journal* 7, no. 3 (Mar. 1894): 20; *Far and Near,* no. 31 (May 1893): 149; no. 42 (Apr. 1894): 89.

37. *Far and Near,* no. 5 (Mar. 1891): 72.

38. Ibid., no. 35 (Sept. 1893): 226; no. 36 (Oct. 1893): 242; no. 37 (Nov. 1893): 15; no. 38 (Dec. 1893): 24, 28–29, 37; no. 39 (Jan. 1894): 40–43, 50; no. 40 (Feb. 1894): 53; no. 41 (Mar. 1894): 73–75, 78; no. 45 (July 1894): 122–23. Quotation is from no. 35.

39. Ibid., no. 39 (Jan. 1894): 42–43, 48–50; Richmond, *Long View,* p. 35. Quotations are from *Far and Near,* pp. 48, 50.

40. *Far and Near,* no. 38 (Dec. 1893): 28–29; no. 39 (Jan. 1894): 41; no. 40 (Feb. 1894): 63; AWGS Convention 1894, p. v; Foner, *Women and the American Labor Movement,* pp. 236–37; Blair, *Clubwoman as Feminist,* pp. 82–83.

41. *Far and Near,* no. 35 (Sept. 1893): 234; no. 37 (Nov. 1893): 20–21; no. 38 (Dec. 1893): 37–38; no. 39 (Jan. 1894): 49–50; no. 42 (Apr. 1894): 82, 89, 91; no. 43 (May 1894): 106.

42. Ibid., no. 43 (May 1894): 99, 105; AWGS Convention 1894, pp. 127–37, 139–42, 157–61.

Chapter 6: Labor Reform

1. *Far and Near,* no. 42 (Apr. 1894): 82; Graham, *Grace H. Dodge,* pp. 108–10. Quotation is from *Far and Near.*

2. Pelzer, "Social Problem," *Rights of Labor,* Apr. 5, 1890, p. 4; Nov. 29, 1890, p. 4; Riis, *How the Other Half Lives,* pp. 183–89; AWGS Convention 1894, pp. 127–33; MBSL, *Twenty-Fifth Annual Report* [Mar. 1895] (Boston: Wright and Potter, 1895), p. 40, cited in Kessler-Harris, *Out to Work,* p. 100; M. Jones, "Women's Opportunities in Town and Country," pp. 200–201. Quotations are from Pelzer, Apr. 5, 1890; Riis, p. 183; MBSL.

3. AWGS Convention 1894, pp. 127–29, quotations are from pp. 128, 129, 128. Wage-earning wives also drew fire when Boston's Shawmut Avenue Club debated the pin money question in 1892; see *Far and Near,* no. 17 (Mar. 1892): 99. This was apparently an especially hot issue in Boston, where in 1899 unmarried working women formed an organization that petitioned employers not to hire married women; see MBSL, *Thirtieth Annual Report, March 1900,* p. 222.

4. AWGS Convention 1894, pp. 129–33, quotation is from p. 131.

5. Ibid., pp. 131–33.

6. Ibid., pp. 139–42, quotation is from p. 139.

7. Ibid., p. 141.

8. Ibid., p. 142.

9. Ibid., pp. 142–47, 153–61, quotations are from pp. 159, 158, 146, 144, 156.

10. Ibid., pp. 147–53, quotation is from p. 151.

11. Ibid., p. 151. Regarding women's exclusion from union shops, see [WTULM], *History of Trade Unionism,* pp. 10–13; DuBois, *Feminism and Suffrage,* pp. 126–61.

12. AWGS Convention 1894, pp. 147–48.

13. *Far and Near,* no. 46 (Aug. 1894): 139–40; no. 48 (Oct. 1894): 164; G. Dodge, "[Letter] to the Several Committees on 'Far and Near' and Others Interested in the Paper, Nov. 10, 1893," in "Personal Work, Papers and Addresses," pp. 208–10, Dodge Papers; Graham, *Grace H. Dodge,* pp. 115–16; Gompers, *Seventy Years,* vol. 1, p. 434; M. Kelley, "Women and the Labor Movement." On working women's labor conditions during the latter half of the depression, see NYBSL, *Fourteenth Annual Report for the Year 1896,* pp. 913–45; New York [State] Legislative Assembly, *Report and Testimony.*

14. AWGS Convention 1897, pp. 7–9, 118; Henrotin, *Attitude of Women's Clubs,* pp. 515; National Council of Women, *Report,* p. 185.

15. *Far and Near,* no. 47 (Sept. 1894): 149–51; AWGS Convention 1897, pp. 6–7, 69–70; Wilkinson, "Women and Their Work."

16. AWGS Convention 1897, pp. 102–3.

17. "Women's Clubs: Trade Unionism and Working Hours Discussed," clipping from the *Public Ledger* (Philadelphia), probably April 30, 1897, in Maud Nathan Papers, Scrapbooks, vol. 2, unnumbered page, Schlesinger Library, Radcliffe College; AWGS Convention 1897, pp. vii, 70–73, 80–83, 91, 102–3. Quotation is from [NYAWGS], *Report* [fourteenth annual report, for the year ending Apr. 1898], p. 13.

18. AWGS Convention 1894, p. 199; AWGS Convention 1897, pp. 3–4, 7; Board of Lady Managers, Reports on American and Foreign Exhibitors, World's Columbian Exposition Papers, vol. 41, entries for Connecticut and Pennsylvania, unnumbered pages; New Century Guild, *100th Anniversary,* p. 41; NLWW, *History,* p. 26.

19. AWGS Convention 1897, pp. 62–70, quotations are from p. 68.

20. Ibid., pp. vii-viii; *Club Worker* 2, no. 1, suppl. (Jan. 1900).

21. AWGS Convention 1897, pp. 188–92, 207–11, quotations are from pp. 191–92, 209.

22. [NYAWGS], *Report* [fourteenth annual report, for the year ending Apr. 1898], pp. 13–14; *Club Worker* 2, no. 1, suppl. (Jan. 1900): 1–5; 4, no. 3 (Jan. 1903): 67–68. Industrial training and vocational opportunities for women were the only social issues discussed at the club movement's first convention under the NLWW's auspices; see [NLWW], *Report of the Proceedings of the Fourth National Convention . . . 1901* (hereafter cited as NLWW Convention 1901).

23. [MAWW], *MAWW: The Work, the Method, the Result,* p. 69; *Club Woman* 1, no. 2 (Nov. 1897): 56; 2, no. 2 (May 1898): 58; Consumers' League of the City of New York, *Report,* pp. 2–3; *Club Worker* 3, no. 2 (Feb. 1901): 4–5; 4, no. 1 (Nov. 1902): 21; 4, no. 2 (Dec. 1902): 41; 4, no. 3 (Jan. 1903): 67–68, 72; 4, no. 4 (Feb. 1903): 91; 5, no. 6 (Apr. 1904): 138; Wolfe, "Women, Consumerism, and the National Consumers' League," pp. 384, 386.

24. Woolman, *Making of a Trade School,* pp. 1–14; New York [State] Department of Labor, Bureau of Labor Statistics, *Twenty-Sixth Annual Report for the Year Ended September 30, 1908,* pt. 1, pp. 332–33; "Meeting of the Board of Administrators of the Manhattan Trade School of Girls Held at the School Building, October 26th, 1910," series 7, folder 674, James Earl Russell Papers, Milbank Memorial Library, Teachers College, Columbia University; MBSL, *Thirty-Sixth Annual Report, March 1906,* pp. 35–37; *Club Worker* 9, no. 3 (Dec. 1907): 690–91; 10, no. 5 (Feb. 1909): 876; 18, no. 3 (Dec. 1918): 8; WEIUB, *Industrial Experience of Trade-School Girls,* pp. 257–58. Publications of the Girls' Trade Education League include H. Dodge, *Survey of Occupations;* Vocation Office for Girls, *Bookbinding, Dressmaking, Millinery, Paper Box Making, Salesmanship, Stenography and Typewriting,* and *Telephone Operating.* For descriptions of the Manhattan Trade School and Boston Trade School for Girls in the mid-1910s, see New York [State], *Fourth Report of the Factory Investigating Commission, 1915,* pp. 1432–36.

25. Cremin, *Transformation of the School,* pp. 24–38; Bowles and Gintis, *Schooling in Capitalist America,* pp. 192–93; Spring, *Education and the Rise of the Corporate State,* pp. 41–43.

26. AWGS Convention 1894, pp. 152–53; *Club Worker* 4, no. 3 (Jan. 1903): 63–66, 68; Lagemann, *Generation of Women,* pp. 101–6. Quotations are from *Club Worker,* pp. 66, 65; Leonora O'Reilly to Virginia Potter, n.d. [c. 1902], cited in Lagemann, p. 102. For a testament to O'Reilly's initial enthusiasm for the NLWW's vocational education campaign, see NLWW Convention 1901, pp. 25–29.

27. *Club Worker* 18, no. 7 (Apr. 1919): 8; Alliance Employment Bureau, *Annual Report* [for 1900], and *Annual Report, 1910.*

28. MBSL, *Thirty-Sixth Annual Report, March 1906,* pp. 3–4, 29–30; Woolman, *Making of a Trade School,* pp. 14–16; National Council of Women, *Report,* p. 188; Alliance Employment Bureau, *Annual Report, 1905,* p. 5; Vocation Office for Girls, *Stenography and Typewriting,* pp. 7–8; New York [State] Department of Labor, *Annual Report of the Industrial Commission,* pp. 233–36. Regarding the availability of commercial education in public schools and nonprofit trade schools, see MBSL, "Occupations of Girl Graduates," and "Trade and Technical Education."

29. Mary O'Hagan, "The Manhattan Trade School for Girls," *New York Herald*, reprinted in *Club Worker* 4, no. 4 (Feb. 1903): 83–85; Mary S. Woolman, [untitled report on the work of the Manhattan Trade School, dated Nov. 13, 1905], series 7, folder 674, Russell Papers; "Manhattan Trade School for Girls" [prospectus, 1903], in "Speeches and Writings," O'Reilly Papers. Quotations are from *Club Worker*, p. 83; Woolman. Regarding general trends in women's trade education in the Progressive Era, see Finlayson, "Vocational Schools for Girls."

30. See, for example, *Club Worker* 4, no. 3 (Jan. 1903): 66, 68; 4, no. 5 (Mar. 1903); 101–2; 7, no. 1 (Nov. 1905): 380; MBSL, *Thirty-Sixth Annual Report, March 1906*, p. 37. Quotations are from *Club Worker* 7, no. 1; *Far and Near*, no. 42 (Apr. 1894): 82.

31. Quotations are from NLWW, *History*, pp. 14, 15.

32. Bremner, *From the Depths*, pp. 138–63; Lubove, *Professional Altruist*, pp. 140–56; Slaughter and Silva, "Looking Backwards," pp. 57–62.

33. *Club Worker* 3, no. 7 (Oct. 1901): 4–5; 7, no. 6 (Apr. 1906): 451–52; 9, no. 4 (Jan. 1908): 699; NLWW, *History*, pp. 17–21, 26–34, and *Suggested Bibliography for Club Workers*.

34. "University Settlement Society," *Critic*; Lubove, *Professional Altruist*, pp. 12–18, esp. 17; Davis, *Spearheads for Reform*, pp. 18–21; Boyer, *Urban Masses and Moral Order*, pp. 150–61. Quotation is from G. Dodge, "Notes for Two Addresses, Hartford, Conn., December 1889," in "Personal Work, Papers and Addresses," p. 23, Dodge Papers. For a useful analysis of Progressive reformers' faith in "scientific methods," see Haber, *Efficiency and Uplift*, pp. 75–116.

35. AWGS Convention 1897, pp. 77–80, 195–201; *Century Club Advance* [after Mar. 1903, *Woman's Welfare*] 1, no. 2 (Jan.-Mar. 1903): 65–67, 81–84, 103–7, 125–26; *Woman's Welfare* 1, no. 4 (Oct. 1903): 195–204; 2, no. 1 (Mar. 1904): 1, 4; 2, no. 2 (June 1904): 77–80. Quotation is from *Century Club Advance*, p. 67. For data on corporate welfare programs for women workers, see New York [State] Department of Labor, *Third Annual Report of the Commissioner*, pp. 227–329; Otey, *Employers' Welfare Work*; Brandes, *American Welfare Capitalism*, pp. 10–29, 111–18; Nelson, *Managers and Workers*, pp. 101–21. Regarding genteel women's activities as welfare secretaries, see Ferris, "College Graduate in Welfare Work"; Gilson, *What's Past Is Prologue*; Tracy, *How My Heart Sang*; "Work of Welfare Secretary," *Bulletin*.

36. NLWW, *NLWW: Brief History*, pp. 20–23; *Club Worker* 13, no. 5 (Feb. 1912): 319–20; *National Civic Federation Review* 3, no. 4 (May 1908): 14; 3, no. 5 (Sept. 1908): 8; Morgan, *American Girl*, pp. 38–41; Green, *National Civic Federation*, pp. 267–84; Foner, *Women and the American Labor Movement*, pp. 290–323.

37. Foner, *Women and the American Labor Movement*, pp. 303–91; Dye, *As Equals and As Sisters*, pp. 61–109; Glenn, "Partners in the Struggle"; Feldberg, "'Union Fever,'" pp. 60–61. For useful summaries of genteel women's labor reform activity, see Wood, *History of the General Federation of Women's Clubs*, pp. 211–12; Lieberman, "Their Sisters' Keepers"; Blair, *Clubwoman as Feminist*, pp. 73–91; Wolfe, "Women, Consumerism, and the National Consumers' League," pp. 384–88; Kessler-Harris, *Out to Work*, pp. 171–79.

38. For a sterling example of employers' overtures to women labor reformers, see Filene, "Betterment of the Conditions of Working Women," written by the proprietor of the William Filene's Sons department store in Boston. Genteel

women's commitments to ethical shopping encouraged especially elaborate welfare programs in department stores, which emphasized programs for women workers in particular. See, for example, MBSL, *Thirty-Second Annual Report, March 1902*, pp. 223–24, and *Thirty-Third Annual Report, March 1903*, p. 69; Otey, *Employers' Welfare Work*, pp. 48–60; Hemenway, "Training of Department Store Employees"; Benson, *Counter Cultures*, pp. 124–67. On employers' antiunion propaganda, see Foner, *History of the Labor Movement*, vol. 3, pp. 49–55. Regarding labor reformers' orientation toward alternatives to unionism, see MacLean, "Trade Unionism versus Welfare Work"; Kessler-Harris, *Out to Work*, pp. 164–79, 187–88, 198–201; Wolfe, "Women, Consumerism and the National Consumers' League," pp. 388–89; Dye, *As Equals and As Sisters*, pp. 140–61.

39. [WTUL], *History of Trade Unionism;* National Women's Trade Union League, *How to Organize;* Kessler-Harris, "'Where Are the Organized Women Workers?'" Quotation is from National Women's Trade Union League, p. 16.

40. *Club Worker* 5, no. 5 (Mar. 1904): 98–99; 8, no. 7 (Apr. 1907): 608; 12, no. 2 (Nov. 1910): 162; 14, no. 9 (Jan. 1915): 11–12; 15, no. 1 (Oct. 1915): 3.

41. Ibid., 4, no. 7 (May 1903): 144; 7, no. 1 (Nov. 1905): 370–72; 10, no. 8 (May 1909): 912–13; 10, no. 9 (June 1909): 940; unnumbered issue (Jan. 1913): 399; 14, no. 11 (Mar. 1915): 4–6. Quotations are from 4, no. 7; 7, no. 1, p. 371; 14, no. 11, p. 4; 10, no. 9.

42. Ibid., 4, no. 7 (May 1903): 149; 7, no. 2 (Dec. 1905): 387–88; 13, no. 1 (Oct. 1911): 266–67. Quotation is from NLWW, *History*, p. 14.

Chapter 7: Disintegration

1. *Club Worker* 2, no. 1, suppl. (Jan. 1900): 4; 15, no. 8 (May 1916): 2; 21, no. 3 (Nov. 1920): 12. Quotation is from [NLWW], *Convention Proceedings . . . 1916*, p. 18 (hereafter cited as NLWW Convention 1916).

2. NLWW, *History*, pp. 14–16, quotations are from p. 15.

3. *Club Worker* 14, no. 2 (Mar. 1914): 6–8; 14, no. 3 (Apr. 1914): 9–10; 15, no. 1 (Oct. 1915): 2–5; NLWW Convention 1916, p. 5; [NLWW], *Proceedings of the Tenth Biennial . . . 1918*, p. 3 (hereafter cited as NLWW Convention 1918). Quotation is from *Club Worker* 14, no. 3, p. 10.

4. NLWW Convention 1916, pp. 2–4; NLWW Convention 1918, pp. 3–4; *Club Worker* 14, no. 5 (June 1914): 7–9; 14, no. 9 (Jan. 1915): 11–12; 15, no. 4 (Jan. 1916): 2–7; 16, no. 3 (Dec. 1916): 4–7.

5. *Club Worker* 3, no. 9 (Dec. 1901): 4–5; 7, no. 8 (June 1906): 486–88; 8, no. 3 (Dec. 1906): 538; 13, no. 1 (Oct. 1911): 265–69; NLWW, *Junior Clubs*. Quotation is from *Club Worker* 13, no. 1, pp. 268.

6. *Club Worker* 10, no. 7 (Apr. 1909): 893–99; 10, no. 8 (May 1909): 913–21; 10, no. 9 (June 1909): 927–37, quotation is from p. 931.

7. Ibid., 4, no. 2 (Dec. 1902): 54; 5, no. 5 (Mar. 1904): 102; 7, no. 4 (Feb. 1906): 420–21; NLWW Convention 1916, p. 17. Quotation is from *Club Worker* 10, no. 7 (Apr. 1909): 893.

8. *Club Worker* 6, no. 9 (June 1905): 332; 8, no. 4 (Jan. 1907): 557; 9, no. 2 (Nov. 1907): 673–75; 11, no. 3 (Dec. 1909): 47. Quotation is from 9, no. 2, p. 674.

9. Kennard, *National League of Women Workers;* [NLWW], *National League of Women Workers; Club Worker* 14, no. 10 (Feb. 1915): 11–12; 14, no. 11 (Mar. 1915):

4–6; 17, no. 8 (May 1918): 3; NLWW Convention 1916, pp. 17–18, 23–25; NLWW Convention 1918, pp. 19–21, 34. Quotations are from Kennard, p. 7; [NLWW], unnumbered page; *Club Worker* 17, no. 8.

10. NLWW Convention 1916, pp. 12, 15, 20–24; NLWW Convention 1918, pp. 24–26, 41, 44–52; *Club Worker* 19, no. 2 (Oct. 1919): 3. Quotation is from NLWW Convention 1918, p. 25.

11. *Club Worker* 14, no. 14 (June 1915): 16–18; [NLWW], *National League of Women Workers;* Massachusetts League of Women Workers, *Life and the Woman Worker.* Quotation is from *Club Worker,* p. 16.

12. *Club Worker* 14, no. 2 (Mar. 1914): 6–11, quotation is from p. 8.

13. Ibid., 16, no. 1 (Oct. 1916): 4–6, quotation is from p. 4.

14. Quotations are from Graham, *Grace H. Dodge,* p. 85; AWGS Convention 1890, p. 84.

15. Edwards, *Comparative Occupation Statistics,* pp. 110–12, 127–29; M. Deland, "Change in the Feminine Ideal"; "The Point of View," *Scribner's Magazine,* pp. 121–23; Bachelor Maid, "Work for Women"; Laut, "New Spirit"; "After Vassar, What?" *Outlook.* Quotations are from "Point of View," p. 122; Laut, p. 930; "Work for Women," p. 182. See also Cott, *Grounding of Modern Feminism,* pp. 217–39; Matthaei, *Economic History of Women,* pp. 256–63. A broad comparison of genteel attitudes toward working women in the late nineteenth and early twentieth centuries appears in Eisenstein, *Give Us Bread,* pp. 55–112.

16. Thomas, "Secretarial Work and the College Woman"; Shuler, "Organization of Business Women"; MBSL, *Thirty-Sixth Annual Report, March 1906,* pp. 3–4, 29–30; Edwards, *Comparative Occupation Statistics,* pp. 122, 129; Cott, *Grounding of Modern Feminism,* pp. 132–34, 328n.26. Quotation is from Shuler, p. 309. For an illuminating study of the class origins and ambiguous class status of clerical workers of both sexes, see DeVault, *Sons and Daughters of Labor.* A rich analysis of clerical women's aspirations and disappointments in the 1910s and 1920s appears in Fine, *Souls of the Skyscraper,* pp. 139–89.

17. Graham, *Grace H. Dodge,* p. 85. For useful surveys of racialist thinking in the Progressive Era, see Higham, *Strangers in the Land,* pp. 131–263; Gossett, *Race,* pp. 253–369; Hofstadter, *Social Darwinism,* pp. 143–200.

18. Ripley, "Races in the United States"; L. Deland, "Lawrence Strike"; Lauck, "Cotton-Mill Operatives of New England"; Grant, *Passing of the Great Race.* See also Kraut, *Huddled Masses,* pp. 12–27; J. Jones, *Labor of Love, Labor of Sorrow,* pp. 152–60; Wiebe, *Businessmen and Reform,* pp. 180–93; Gossett, *Race,* pp. 353–63.

19. G. Turner, "Daughters of the Poor"; Kellor, "Protection of Immigrant Women"; Ovington, *Half a Man,* pp. 153–55; Kneeland, *Commercialized Prostitution.* Quotations are from Turner, pp. 58, 54, 54; Kneeland, p. 21. See also *Prostitution in America;* Pivar, *Purity Crusade,* pp. 78–203; Feldman, "Prostitution, the Alien Woman, and the Progressive Imagination"; Katzman, *Seven Days a Week,* pp. 213–14, 331n44.

20. MacLean, *Wage-Earning Women;* Davenport, *Heredity,* pp. 212–19; Edward Ross, "Lesser Immigrant Groups"; Popenoe and Johnson, *Applied Eugenics,* pp. 280–317; Eisenstein, *Give Us Bread,* pp. 108–9. Quotations are from MacLean, p. 41; Popenoe and Johnson, pp. 283, 302; Mary A. Laselle and Katherine E. Wiley, *Vocations for Girls* (Boston: Houghton Mifflin, 1913), p. 31, cited in Eisenstein, p.

108. On *The Clansman* and similar works, see Williamson, *Rage for Order,* pp. 98–115. On African American women's portrayal in the popular press, see Guy-Sheftall, *Daughters of Sorrow,* pp. 37–90.

21. *Club Worker* 14, no. 1 (Feb. 1914): 18–20, quotations are from p. 20. For a discussion of the "rough" dance styles popular among working-class youth, see Peiss, *Cheap Amusements,* pp. 100–104.

22. *Club Worker* 15, no. 3 (Dec. 1915): 11–12; 16, no. 3 (Dec. 1916): 7; 16, no. 9 (June 1917): 1–2; 17, no. 2 (Nov. 1917): 11–13; 17, no. 5 (Feb. 1918): 9–11; 17, no. 12 (Sept. 1918): 1–3; 18, no. 9 (June 1919): 6–7; Lighthouse Girls' Club Scrapbook, 1914–17, Lighthouse Papers, Historical Society of Pennsylvania; NLWW Convention 1916, pp. 10–13; NLWW Convention 1918, pp. 5–13, 15–18; [NLWW], *National League of Women Workers.*

23. *Club Worker* 16, no. 8 (May 1917): 2–6; 16, no. 9 (June 1917): 1–2; 17, no. 6 (Mar. 1918): 3–4. Quotations are from 17, no. 6, p. 3.

24. NLWW Convention 1918, pp. 5–7, 25, 28–29, 37–38; *Club Worker* 17, no. 4 (Jan. 1918): 6–8, 11, 13; 18, no. 4 (Jan. 1919): 1–2; 18, no. 7 (Apr. 1919): 6–7; 18, no. 8 (May 1919): 7; Lighthouse Girls' Club Scrapbook, 1917–26, Lighthouse Papers. Quotations are from NLWW Convention 1918, p. 38; *Club Worker* 18, no. 7, p. 6.

25. [NLWW], *National League of Women Workers;* Trachtenberg, *American Labor Year Book,* pp. 185–89; *Club Worker* 18, no. 7 (Apr. 1919): 1; 18, no. 8 (May 1919): 1–2, 7; 19, no. 2 (Oct. 1919): 1; 19, no. 3 (Nov. 1919): 1, 3; 19, no. 5 [misnumbered] (Feb. 1920): 1–2, 12; 19, no. 7 (Mar. 1920): 1–2, 6–7; 19, no. 8 (Apr. 1920): 12; 19, no. 9 (May 1920): 9–12; 19, no. 10 (June 1920): 9. See also "News of the Leagues" and "From Near and Far" columns in monthly issues of the National Women's Trade Union League journal, *Life and Labor,* for 1919. Quotation is from [NLWW], unnumbered page.

For useful studies of female labor militancy during World War I and the postwar era, see Greenwald, *Women, War, and Work,* pp. 87–232; Norwood, *Labor's Flaming Youth,* pp. 156–215. In counterpoint to rising militancy among workers of both sexes, employers expanded corporate welfare programs, which often included company-sponsored clubs. Regarding this trend, see Norton, "Welfare Work for Civilian Employees"; U.S. Department of Labor, Bureau of Labor Statistics, *Welfare Work.*

26. NLWW Convention 1918, pp. 52, 55; Trachtenberg, *American Labor Year Book,* pp. 292–93; *Club Worker* 19, no. 1 (Sept. 1919): 7–8; 19, no. 2 (Oct. 1919): 8; 19, no. 9 (May 1920): 6.

27. *Far and Near,* no. 8 (June 1891): 148; no. 12 (Oct. 1891): 230; *Club Worker* 3, no. 8 (Nov. 1901): 6–7; 9, no. 3 (Dec. 1907): 687; 14, no. 3 (Apr. 1914): 12–13; 18, no. 1 (Oct. 1918): 1–2; 19, no. 7 (Mar. 1920): 3; 19, no. 8 (Apr. 1920): 10; 19, no. 9 (May 1920): 4. Quotations are from *Club Worker* 9, no. 3; 14, no. 3, p. 13; 19, no. 9.

28. *Working Woman's Journal* 5, no. 5 (May 1892): 40; [MAWW], *MAWW: The Work, the Method, the Result,* p. 39; Ovington, *Half a Man,* pp. 161–63; WEIUB, *Industrial Experience of Trade-School Girls,* pp. 176–78; *Club Worker* 19, no. 2 (Oct. 1919): 4, 6–7. Quotations are from *Club Worker* 20, no. 1 [misnumbered] (Jan. 1920): 2; 19, no. 2, pp. 4, 6.

29. *Club Worker* 20, no. 1 [misnumbered] (Jan. 1920): 2, 12; 19, no. 9 (May 1920): 10; Neverdon-Morton, *Afro-American Women,* pp. 183–87. Quotation is from *Club*

Worker 19, no. 9. Regarding cross-class organizing among African American women, see McDougald, "Task of Negro Womanhood"; Brown, "Womanist Consciousness"; Giddings, *When and Where I Enter*, pp. 136–97; D. White, "Cost of Club Work."

30. *Far and Near*, no. 6 (Apr. 1891): 96–97; *Club Worker* 1, no. 6 (Dec. 1899): 4; 6, no. 1 (Oct. 1904): 215; 8, no. 6 (Mar. 1907): 595; 19, no. 10 (June 1920): 9, 12; NLWW, *NLWW: Brief History*, pp. 21–22. Quotation is from *Club Worker* 19, no. 10, p. 12.

31. Quotations are from *Club Worker* 18, no. 6 (Mar. 1919): 2; 19, no. 10 (June 1920): 12.

32. Azadian, "Education of the Working Girl," quotation is from p. 3.

33. Ibid.; *Club Worker* 21, no. 8 (Apr. 1921): 12. Quotations are from Azadian, pp. 41, 29.

34. Quotation is from Barbour, "Girls' Clubs." Regarding racial-ethnic exclusivity at Bryn Mawr and similar institutions, see Solomon, *In the Company of Educated Women*, pp. 143–44.

35. Hackett, "Girls' Club Worker"; *Club Worker* 19, no. 7 (Mar. 1920): 5; 19, no. 10 (June 1920): 12; 21, no. 3 (Nov. 1920): 12.

36. Barbour, "Girls' Clubs"; *Club Worker* 21, no. 5 (Jan. 1921): 5; 21, no. 6 (Feb. 1921): 2–3; 21, no. 7 (Mar. 1921): 6–8, 10; 21, no. 8 (Apr. 1921): 2–3; 21, no. 9 (May-June 1921): 10–11. Quotation is from Barbour.

37. *Club Worker* 21, no. 5 (Jan. 1921): 12; 21, no. 9 (May-June 1921): 2; "NLGC, Meeting of the National Board of Directors, June 18th and 22nd, 1924," folder 6, pp. 7–8, Marion Niles Papers, Schlesinger Library, Radcliffe College; "The National League of Girls' Clubs: Minutes of the Business Meetings, Thirteenth National Biennial Convention, Smith College, June 20–21, 1924," folder 6, p. 7, Niles Papers; "National League of Girls' Clubs, Meeting of the Board of Directors, June 21, 1928," folder 6, Niles Papers; "National League of Girls' Clubs, Convention Business Meeting, June 23, 1928," folder 6, Niles Papers; Johnson and Dodge, *Thirty Years*, p. 10.

On the NLGC's education campaign, see [Marion Niles], "National League of Girls' Clubs: Report of the Secretary of the Education Department to the Thirteenth Biennial Convention, Smith College, June 1924," folder 6, Niles Papers; "Adventures in Education," *Survey*; Foster, "Workers Who Like to Use Their Minds"; NLGC, *Evolution of a Summer School*.

38. Johnson and Dodge, *Thirty Years*, p. 10.

Conclusion

1. Ginzberg, *Women and the Work of Benevolence*, pp. 195–202; Boyer, *Urban Masses and Moral Order*, pp. 142–61; A. Scott, *Natural Allies*, pp. 104–8; Blair, *Clubwoman as Feminist*, pp. 73–91. See also Pascoe, *Relations of Rescue*.

2. NYBSL, *Eighteenth Annual Report for the Year 1900*, "Part II: Social Settlements," pp. 247–431; Carson, *Settlement Folk*, pp. 65–84; Davis, *Spearheads for Reform*, pp. 3–29; Wood, *History of the General Federation of Women's Clubs*, pp. 103–5; Lieberman, "Their Sisters' Keepers," pp. 47–94; Blewett, *Men, Women, and Work*, pp. 274–80; Bordin, *Woman and Temperance*, pp. 140–55.

3. *Club Worker* 2, no. 9 (Dec. 1900): 3–4; A. Scott, *Natural Allies*, pp. 141–74; Deutsch, "Learning to Talk More Like a Man"; Sklar, "Historical Foundations of

Women's Power"; Skocpol, *Protecting Soldiers and Mothers,* pp. 310–539. On the WTUL, see Dye, *As Equals and As Sisters;* Jacoby, "Women's Trade Union League." For instructive studies of two Progressive Era women reformers, see Payne, *Reform, Labor, and Feminism;* Perry, *Belle Moskowitz,* pp. 23–114.

4. *Club Worker* 4, no. 5 (Mar. 1903): 98–100; 7, no. 3 (Jan. 1906): 406; 7, no. 4 (Feb. 1906): 430; 7, no. 6 (Apr. 1906): 451–52; 8, no. 4 (Jan. 1907): 552; NLWW, *History,* p. 14.

5. On genteel women reformers' reach for professionalism, see Muncy, *Creating a Female Dominion.* Pascoe links new reform trends to the erosion of the Victorian gender system; see her *Relations of Rescue,* pp. 177–207.

6. Quotation is from *Far and Near,* no. 13 (Nov. 1891): 8.

Bibliography

Primary Sources

Archival and Manuscript Material

Schlesinger Library, Radcliffe College, Cambridge, Mass.
    Maud Nathan Papers
    Marion H. Niles Papers
    Leonora O'Reilly Papers
    Mary Kenney O'Sullivan Manuscript Autobiography
Chicago Historical Society, Chicago, Ill.
    Mary McDowell Papers
    World's Columbian Exposition, Chicago, 1893, Collected Papers
Sterling Library, Yale University, New Haven, Conn.
    Rose Pastor Stokes Papers
Milbank Memorial Library, Teachers College, Columbia University, New York, N.Y.
    Anna Cooley Papers
    Grace Hoadley Dodge Papers
    James Earl Russell Papers
Historical Society of Pennsylvania, Philadelphia, Pa.
    Lighthouse Papers

Club Movement Publications, Documents, Accounts, and Commentaries

"Adventures in Education." *Survey* 54, no. 4 (May 15, 1925): 237–38.
Allen, Frederick B. "Must Working Girls Clubs Be Self Sustaining?" *Christian Union* 43, no. 9 (Feb. 26, 1891): 278–79.
Alliance Employment Bureau (New York, N.Y.). *Annual Report.* Title varies. New York: [Alliance Employment Bureau], 1897–1915.

Associations of Working Girls' Societies (AWGS). *The Discussions of the Convention Held in New York City, April 15th, 16th, and 17th, 1890.* New York: Trow's
Printing and Bookbinding, 1890.

[―――]. *Report of Proceedings of the Second National Convention of Working Girls'
Clubs, Boston, May 9–11, 1894.* Boston: Everett Press, 1894.

[―――]. *Report of the Proceedings of the Third National Convention of Working Wom-
en's Clubs of New York, Brooklyn, Massachusetts, Connecticut, Illinois and Pennsylvania Associations. Philadelphia, April 28, 29, 30, 1897.* N.p., n.d.

Azadian, Arous Hovanes. "The Education of the Working Girl." Master's thesis, Teachers College, Columbia University, 1921.

Barbour, Violet. "Girls' Clubs." *Survey* 48, no. 12 (June 15, 1922): 532.

Betts, Lillian W. *The Leaven in a Great City.* New York: Dodd, Mead, 1902.

Campbell, Helen. "Association in Clubs with Its Bearing on Working-Women."
Arena 5, no. 25 (Dec. 1891): 61–67.

―――. "Working Girls' Clubs." *Public Opinion* 18, no. 22 (May 30, 1895): 600.

[Civic Club, Philadelphia]. *A Directory of the Charitable, Social Improvement, Educational and Religious Associations and Churches of Philadelphia.* Philadelphia: n.p.,
1903.

Coleman, Mary Winiett. "Model Working Girls' Clubs—An American Point of
View." *Charities Review* 4, no. 6 (Apr. 1895): 307–14.

Davidge, Clara Sidney. "Working-Girls' Clubs." *Scribner's Magazine* 15, no. 5 (May
1894): 619–28.

Dodge, Grace H. "Association of Working Girls' Societies." *Woman's Cycle* 1, no.
18 (May 15, 1890): 18–19.

―――. *A Bundle of Letters to Busy Girls on Practical Matters.* New York: Funk and
Wagnalls, 1887.

―――. "Glimpses into the Lives of Working-Women." 2 pts. *Harper's Bazar* 23,
no. 2 (Jan. 11, 1890): 23; 23, no. 4 (Jan. 25, 1890): 67.

―――. "Glimpses into Working Girls' Club Life and Principles." *American Federationist* 1, no. 4 (June 1894): 68–69.

―――. *Moral Elevation of Girls: Suggestions Relating to Preventive Work.* New York:
Committee on the Elevation of the Poor in Their Homes, 1885.

―――. *Paper on the Association of Working Girls' Societies.* Offprint from Proceedings of the Convention of Christian Workers in the United States and Canada,
Broadway Tabernacle, New York City, September 21–28, 1887. N.p., n.d.

―――. "Practical Suggestions Relating to Moral Elevation and Preventive Work
among Girls." Paper delivered at the Eighth International Conference of Wom-
en's Christian Associations, Cincinnati, 1885, reprinted in "In Memory of Grace
H. Dodge," *Association Monthly* 9, no. 2 (Mar. 1915), sec. 2, pp. 82–90.

―――. *A Private Letter to Girls.* New York: Philanthropist, 1889.

―――, ed. *Thoughts of Busy Girls.* New York: Cassell, 1892.

―――. "Working Girls' Societies." *Chautauquan* 9, no. 4 (Jan. 1889): 223–25.

Dodge, Harriet. *Survey of Occupations Open to the Girl of Fourteen to Sixteen Years.*
Boston: Girls' Trade Education League, 1912.

Foster, Hazel E. "Workers Who Like to Use Their Minds." *Survey* 55, no. 4 (Nov.
15, 1925): 219, 223.

Hackett, Sarah B. "The Girls' Club Worker." In *Careers for Women*, ed. Catherine Filene, pp. 484–86. Boston: Houghton Mifflin, 1920.

Hamilton, Agnes. *Club Democracy: Is a Division into Club Leaders and Club Members Inevitable?* New York: National League of Women Workers, n.d. [probably 1914 or 1915].

Hamilton, Jean. "Recreation for Girls." *Survey* 37, no. 13 (Dec. 30, 1916): 371.

Humphreys, Mary Gay. "The New York Working Girl." *Scribner's Magazine* 20, no. 4 (Oct. 1896): 502–13.

Jones, Mary Cadwalader. "Women's Opportunities in Town and Country." In *The Women's Book*, vol. 2, pp. 181–214. New York: Charles Scribner's Sons, 1894.

Kennard, Beulah E. "The National League of Women Workers." *Survey* 32, no. 16 (July 18, 1914): 410.

———. *National League of Women Workers: Distinctive Characteristics*. [New York]: NLWW, n.d. [probably 1914 or 1915].

Lockwood, Florence. "The Women Who Do the Work." *Century* 41, no. 5 (Mar. 1891): 793–94.

[Massachusetts Association of Women Workers (MAWW)]. *Massachusetts Association of Women Workers: The Work, the Method, the Result*. N.p.: n.p., 1902.

Massachusetts League of Women Workers. *Life and the Woman Worker*. N.p., n.d. [probably 1919].

Morse, Ruth. "'Thoughts of Busy Girls.'" *Chautauquan* 17, no. 4 (July 1893): 458–59.

National Council of Women of the United States. *Report of Its Tenth Annual Executive and Its Third Triennial Sessions*, ed. May Wright Sewall. Indianapolis, Ind.: Hollenbeck Press, [1899].

National League of Girls' Clubs (NLGC). *The Evolution of a Summer School*. N.p., n.d.

[National League of Women Workers (NLWW) (from September 1920, National League of Girls' Clubs)]. *Convention Proceedings, Ninth Biennial Convention of the National League of Women Workers, Pittsfield, Massachusetts, May 31–June 4, 1916*. N.p., n.d.

———. *"Getting Together": A Plea for Coordination in Recreation Work*. New York: NLWW, 1917.

———. *History of the National League of Women Workers, 1914*. N.p., n.d.

———. *Junior Clubs*. N.p., n.d. [probably 1914].

[———]. *The National League of Women Workers*. [New York]: NLWW, 1918.

———. *The National League of Women Workers: Brief History of Its First Decade, from 1898–1908*. Philadelphia: Devine Printing, 1908.

[———]. *Proceedings of the Tenth Biennial of the National League of Women Workers, Held at Wellesley College, June 20–24, 1918*. New York: NLWW, n.d.

[———]. *Report of the Proceedings of the Fourth National Convention of Clubs Belonging to the National League of Women Workers of the New York, Long Island, Massachusetts, Connecticut and Pennsylvania Associations, Buffalo, August 27, 28, 29, 30, 1901*. Syracuse, N.Y.: Mason Press, n.d.

———. *A Suggested Bibliography for Club Workers*. N.p., n.d.

New Century Guild. *100th Anniversary: 1882–1982*. N.p., n.d.

[New York] Association of Working Girls' Societies (NYAWGS). *Annual Report.* New York: 1886–1903. Title varies.

———. *How to Start a Working Girls' Society or Club.* W.G.S. Series, no. 1. N.p.: n.p., 1891.

———. *Reasons for Advancing the Principle of Self-Support.* W.G.S. Series, no. 6. New York: NYAWGS, n.d.

———. *Suggestions for Club Work.* W.G.S. Series, no. 3. New York: AWGS, n.d.

Rhine, Alice Hyneman. "The Work of Women's Clubs." *Forum* 12, no. 4 (Dec. 1891): 519–28.

Turner, E. S. [Eliza Sproat]. "Report of the New Century Guild." *Woman's Cycle* 1, no. 18 (May 15, 1890): 9–10.

Vocation Office for Girls. *Bookbinding.* Vocations for Boston Girls, Bulletin no. 2. Boston: Girls' Trade Education League, 1911.

———. *Dressmaking.* Vocations for Boston Girls, Bulletin no. 5. Boston: Girls' Trade Education League, 1911.

———. *Millinery.* Vocations for Boston Girls, Bulletin no. 6. Boston: Girls' Trade Education League, 1911.

———. *Paper Box Making.* Vocations for Boston Girls, Bulletin no. 12. Boston: Girls' Trade Education League, 1912.

———. *Salesmanship.* Vocations for Boston Girls, Bulletin no. 10. Boston: Girls' Trade Education League, 1912.

———. *Stenography and Typewriting.* Vocations for Boston Girls, Bulletin no. 3. Boston: Girls' Trade Education League, 1911.

———. *Telephone Operating.* Vocations for Boston Girls, Bulletin no. 1. Boston: Girls' Trade Education League, 1911.

"Wendell Phillips." *Woman's Journal* 15, no. 10 (Mar. 8, 1884): 77–79, 81, 84.

"Which Is the More Important?" *Outlook* 49, no. 4 (Jan. 27, 1894): 177.

Wilkinson, Charlotte Coffyn. "Women and Their Work." New York *Evening Post,* Mar. 22, 1899, p. 7.

Wooding, Marie Isabel. "A Plea for the Working Girl." *Chautauquan* 21, no. 5 (Aug. 1895): 625–28.

Woolman, Mary Schenk. *The Making of a Trade School.* Boston: Whitcomb and Barrows, 1910.

Government Documents

Ferguson, Mary S. *Boarding Homes and Clubs for Working Women.* Bulletin of the Bureau of Labor, no. 15. Washington, D.C.: Government Printing Office, 1898.

Henrotin, Ellen. *The Attitude of Women's Clubs and Associations toward Social Economics.* Bulletin of the Bureau of Labor, no. 23. Washington, D.C.: Government Printing Office, 1899.

Kansas. *Annual Report of the Bureau of Labor and Industrial Statistics.* Fifth Annual Report [for 1889]. Topeka: Kansas Publishing House, 1890.

Maine. *Annual Report of the Bureau of Industrial and Labor Statistics.* Second Annual Report, 1888. Augusta: Burleigh and Flynt, 1889.

Massachusetts Bureau of Statistics of Labor (MBSL). *Annual Report.* Boston: Wright and Potter Printing, 1889–1906. Title varies.

———. "Occupations of Girl Graduates." *Labor Bulletin of the Commonwealth of Massachusetts*, no. 41 (May 1906): 133–42.

———. "Trade and Technical Education in Massachusetts." *Labor Bulletin of the Commonwealth of Massachusetts*, no. 26 (May 1903): 57–88.

New York [State]. *Fourth Report of the Factory Investigating Commission, 1915*. Albany: James B. Lyon, 1915.

New York [State] Bureau of Statistics of Labor (NYBSL). *Annual Report*. New York: 1885–1901. Title and publisher vary.

New York [State] Department of Labor. *Annual Report of the Industrial Commission for the Twelve Months Ended June 30, 1917*. Albany: State Department of Labor, 1918.

———. *Third Annual Report of the Commissioner of Labor. For the 12 Months Ended September 30, 1903*. Albany: Oliver A. Quayle, 1904.

New York [State] Department of Labor. Bureau of Labor Statistics. *Twenty-Sixth Annual Report for the Year Ended September 30, 1908*. Albany: State Department of Labor, 1909.

New York [State] Legislative Assembly. *Report and Testimony taken before the Special Committee of the Assembly Appointed to Investigate the Condition of Female Labor in the City of New York*. 2 vols. Albany: Wynkoop Hallenbeck Crawford, 1896.

Norton, Augustus P. "Welfare Work for Civilian Employees of the United States." *Monthly Labor Review* 7, no. 2 (Aug. 1918): 218–31.

Otey, Elizabeth L. *Employers' Welfare Work*. Bulletin of the U.S. Bureau of Labor Statistics, no. 123. Washington, D.C.: Government Printing Office, 1913.

Pennsylvania. *Annual Report of the Secretary of Internal Affairs of the Commonwealth of Pennsylvania* [for 1894]. Vol. 22, pt. 3, Industrial Statistics. [Harrisburg]: Clarence M. Busch, 1895.

Rhode Island. *Annual Report of the Commissioner of Industrial Statistics, Made to the General Assembly*. Third Annual Report [for 1889]. Providence: E. L. Freeman and Son, 1890.

U.S. Bureau of Labor. *Work and Wages of Men, Women and Children*. Eleventh Annual Report of the Commissioner of Labor, 1895–96. Washington, D.C.: Government Printing Office, 1897.

U.S. Congress. House. *Report of the Secretary of the Interior*. 50th Cong., 2d sess., E. Doc. 1, Pt. 5, Vol. 6.

U.S. Department of Labor. Bureau of Labor Statistics. *Welfare Work for Employees in Industrial Establishments in the United States*. Bulletin of the U.S. Bureau of Labor Statistics, no. 250. Washington, D.C.: Government Printing Office, 1919.

Women's Educational and Industrial Union, Boston (WEIUB). *Industrial Experience of Trade-School Girls in Massachusetts*. Bulletin of the U.S. Bureau of Labor Statistics, no. 215. Washington, D.C.: Government Printing Office, 1917.

Wright, Carroll D. *The Working Girls of Boston* [from the *Fifteenth Annual Report of the Massachusetts Bureau of Statistics of Labor, 1884*]. Boston: Wright and Potter Printing, 1889; New York: Arno Press, 1969.

Contemporary Material

Abbott, Edith. *Women in Industry: A Study in American Economic History*. New York: D. Appleton, 1910.

Addams, Jane. *Democracy and Social Ethics.* 1902; Cambridge, Mass.: Harvard University Press, Belknap Press, 1964.

———. *Twenty Years at Hull-House.* 1910; New York: New American Library, 1981.

"After Vassar, What?" *Outlook* 110 (June 30, 1915): 518–23.

Ames, Azel, Jr. *Sex in Industry: A Plea for the Working-Girl.* Boston: James R. Osgood, 1875.

Bachelor Maid (pseud.). "Work for Women." *Independent* 73, no. 3321 (July 25, 1912): 182–86.

Campbell, Helen. *Prisoners of Poverty: Women Wage-Workers, Their Trades and Their Lives.* 1887; Westport, Conn.: Greenwood Press, 1970.

Consumers' League of the City of New York. *Report for the Year Ending December 1900.* [New York]: n.p., n.d.

Croly, Mrs. J. C. [Jane Cunningham]. *The History of the Woman's Club Movement in America.* New York: Henry G. Allen, 1898.

Davenport, Charles Benedict. *Heredity in Relation to Eugenics.* New York: Henry Holt, 1911.

de Graffenried, Clare. "The Condition of Wage-Earning Women." *Forum* 15, no. 1 (Mar. 1893): 68–82.

Deland, Lorin F. "The Lawrence Strike: A Study." *Atlantic Monthly* 109, no. 5 (May 1912): 694–705.

Deland, Margaret. "The Change in the Feminine Ideal." *Atlantic Monthly* 105, no. 3 (Mar. 1910): 289–302.

———. *The Wisdom of Fools.* Boston: Houghton Mifflin, 1897.

Fawcett, Edgar. "The Woes of the New York Working-Girl." *Arena* 5, no. 25 (Dec. 1891): 26–35.

Ferris, Helen J. "The College Graduate in Welfare Work." *Bookman* 43 (May 1916): 289–91.

Filene, Edward A. "The Betterment of the Conditions of Working Women." *Annals of the American Academy of Political and Social Science* 27, no. 3 (May 1906): 151–61.

Finlayson, Alma Jessie. "Vocational Schools for Girls." Master's thesis, Teachers College, Columbia University, 1912.

Gilson, Mary Barnett. *What's Past Is Prologue: Reflections on My Industrial Experience.* New York: Harper and Brothers, 1940.

Girod, Louise. "The Catholic Women's Association." *Catholic World* 72, no. 430 (Jan. 1901): 497–510.

Gompers, Samuel. *Seventy Years of Life and Labor: An Autobiography.* 2 vols. 1925; New York: E. P. Dutton, 1943.

Grant, Madison. *The Passing of the Great Race.* New York: Charles Scribner's Sons, 1916.

Hamilton, Alice. *Exploring the Dangerous Trades.* 1943; Boston: Northeastern University Press, 1985.

Hemenway, Thomas. "Training of Department Store Employees." Master's thesis, Teachers College, Columbia University, 1921.

Hillel, Felicia. "Working-Girls." *Chautauquan* 10, no. 3 (Dec. 1889): 328–32.

Howells, William Dean. *A Hazard of New Fortunes.* 1889; Bloomington: Indiana University Press, 1976.

Jelley, S. M. *The Voice of Labor*. Philadelphia: H. J. Smith, 1888.

Kelley, Florence. *Notes of Sixty Years: The Autobiography of Florence Kelley*, ed. Kathryn Kish Sklar. Chicago: Charles H. Kerr Publishing, 1986.

Kelley, M. E. J. "Women and the Labor Movement." *North American Review* 166, no. 497 (Apr. 1898): 408–17.

Kellor, Frances A. "The Protection of Immigrant Women." *Atlantic Monthly* 101, no. 2 (Feb. 1908): 246–55.

Kneeland, George. *Commercialized Prostitution in New York City*. New York: Century, 1913.

Lanza, Clara. "Women Clerks in New York." In *The National Exposition Souvenir: What America Owes to Women*, ed. Lydia Hoyt Farmer, pp. 444–51. Buffalo: Charles Wells Moulton, 1893.

Lauck, W. Jett. "The Cotton-Mill Operatives of New England." *Atlantic Monthly* 109, no. 5 (May 1912): 706–13.

Laut, Agnes C. "The New Spirit among Women Who Work." *Century* 89, no. 6 (Apr. 1915): 927–33.

MacLean, Annie Marion. "Trade Unionism versus Welfare Work for Women." *Popular Science Monthly* 87, no. 1 (July 1915): 50–55.

———. *Wage-Earning Women*. New York: Macmillan, 1910.

McDougald, Elise Johnson. "The Task of Negro Womanhood." In *The New Negro*, ed. Alain Locke, pp. 369–82. 1925; New York: Atheneum, 1968.

McEnnis, John J. *The White Slaves of Free America*. Chicago: R. S. Peale, 1888.

McNeill, George E., ed. *The Labor Movement: The Problem of Today*. Boston: A. M. Bridgeman, 1887.

Mission of Our Lady of the Rosary for the Protection of Irish Immigrant Girls. New York: Press of Lauter and Lauterjung, 1900.

Morgan, Anne. *The American Girl: Her Education, Her Responsibility, Her Recreation, Her Future*. New York: Harper and Brothers, 1915.

National Women's Trade Union League of America. *How to Organize: A Problem*. Chicago: NWTULA, 1929.

"A New Field for Catholic Women." *Pilot* 57, no. 20 (May 19, 1894): 4.

"The New Woman." *Review of Reviews: An International Magazine* [U.S. ed.] 9, no. 6 (June 1894): 708–9.

"The New Woman under Fire." *Review of Reviews: An International Magazine* [U.S. ed.] 10, no. 6 (Dec. 1894): 656–57.

Orth, Samuel P. *The Armies of Labor: A Chronicle of Organized Wage-Earners*. New Haven, Conn.: Yale University Press, 1920.

Ovington, Mary White. *Half a Man: The Status of the Negro in New York*. New York: Longmans, Green, 1911.

Pelzer, Otto. "The Social Problem" [series]. *Rights of Labor* [Chicago] 6, nos. 212–59 (Jan. 25, 1890–Jan. 3, 1891).

"The Point of View." *Scribner's Magazine* 48, no. 1 (July 1910): 121–24.

Popenoe, Paul, and Roswell Hill Johnson. *Applied Eugenics*. 1918; New York: Macmillan, 1926.

Porter, Charlotte W. "Physical Hindrances to Teaching Girls." *Forum* 12, no. 1 (Sept. 1891): 41–49.

Powell, Aaron Macy, ed. *The National Purity Congress: Its Papers, Addresses, Portraits*. New York: American Purity Alliance, 1896.

Prostitution in America: Three Investigations, 1902–1914. New York: Arno Press, 1976.

Richardson, Dorothy. *The Long Day: The Story of a New York Working Girl.* 1905. In *Women at Work,* ed. William L. O'Neill. Chicago: Quadrangle Books, 1972.

Richmond, Mary E. *The Long View: Papers and Addresses,* ed. Joanna C. Colcord and Ruth Z. S. Mann. New York: Russell Sage Foundation, 1930.

Rideing, William. "Working Women in New York." *Harper's New Monthly Magazine* 61, no. 361 (June 1880): 25–37.

Riis, Jacob. *How the Other Half Lives.* 1890; New York: Dover Publications, 1971.

Ripley, William Z. "Races in the United States." *Atlantic Monthly* 102, no. 6 (Dec. 1908): 745–59.

Ross, Edward Alsworth. "The Lesser Immigrant Groups in America." *Century Magazine* 88, no. 6 (Oct. 1914): 934–40.

Salmon, Lucy Maynard. *Domestic Service.* New York: Macmillan, 1897.

Scudder, Vida, ed. *Letters to Her Companions by Emily Malbone Morgan.* Privately printed at Adelynrood, South Byfield, Mass.: Society of the Companions of the Holy Cross, 1944.

Sewall, May Wright, ed. *The World's Congress of Representative Women.* Chicago: Rand, McNally, 1894.

Shuler, Marjorie. "An Organization of Business Women." *Review of Reviews: An International Magazine* [U.S. ed.] 66, no. 3 (Sept. 1922): 309–10.

Thomas, Ann E. "Secretarial Work and the College Woman." *Bookman* 43 (May 1916): 291–93.

Toomy, L. A. "Some Noble Work of Catholic Women." *Catholic World* 57, no. 338 (May 1893): 234–43.

Trachtenberg, Alexander, ed. *The American Labor Year Book, 1919–1920.* New York: Rand School of Social Science, 1920.

Tracy, Lena Harvey. *How My Heart Sang: The Story of Pioneer Industrial Welfare Work.* New York: Richard R. Smith, 1950.

Turner, E. S. [Eliza Sproat]. *Confidential.* Philadelphia: n.p., n.d.

Turner, George Kibbe. "The Daughters of the Poor." *McClure's Magazine* 34 (Nov. 1909): 45–61.

"The University Settlement Society." *Critic* 16, no. 416 (Dec. 19, 1891): 352.

Van Vorst, Mrs. John, and Marie Van Vorst. *The Woman Who Toils: Being the Experiences of Two Gentlewomen as Factory Girls.* New York: Doubleday, Page, 1903.

Veblen, Thorstein. *The Theory of the Leisure Class.* 1899; New York: New American Library, 1953.

Wharton, Edith. *The House of Mirth.* 1905; New York: New American Library, 1964.

White, Sallie Joy. *Business Openings for Girls.* Boston: D. Lothrop, 1891.

Willard, Frances E. *Occupations for Women: A Book of Practical Suggestions for the Material Advancement, the Mental and Physical Development, and the Moral and Spiritual Uplift of Women.* New York: Success, 1897.

[Women's Trade Union League of Massachusetts (WTULM)]. *The History of Trade Unionism among Women in Boston.* Boston: WTULM, 1915.

Wood, Mary I. *The History of the General Federation of Women's Clubs.* Norwood, Mass.: Norwood Press, 1912.

Woods, Robert A., W. T. Elsing, Jacob A. Riis, Willard Parsons, Evert J. Wendell,

Ernest Flagg, William Jewett Tucker, Joseph Kirkland, Sir Walter Besant, Edmund R. Spearman, Jessie White Mario, and Oscar Craig. *The Poor in Great Cities: Their Problems and What Is Doing to Solve Them.* New York: Charles Scribner's Sons, 1895.

"Work of Welfare Secretary in a Great Office Building." *Bulletin* [of the League for Business Opportunities for Women] 1, no. 5 (Apr. 1917): 6.

Wright, Carroll D. "Why Women Are Paid Less than Men." *Forum* 13, no. 5 (July 1892): 629–39.

Secondary Sources

Abell, Aaron I. *American Catholicism and Social Action: A Search for Social Justice, 1865–1950.* Westport, Conn.: Greenwood Press, 1960.

"Agency History." Introduction to the Records of the Girls' Friendly Society of the United States of America. Austin, Tex.: Archives of the Episcopal Church, n.d. Typescript.

Bailey, Peter. "'Will the Real Bill Banks Please Stand Up?' Towards a Role Analysis of Mid-Victorian Working Class Respectability." *Journal of Social History* 12, no. 3 (Spring 1979): 336–53.

Baltzell, E. Digby. *The Protestant Establishment: Aristocracy and Caste in America.* 1964; New York: Vintage Books, 1966.

Baron, Ava. "Gender and Labor History: Learning from the Past, Looking to the Future." In *Work Engendered,* ed. Baron, pp. 2–16.

———, ed. *Work Engendered: Toward a New History of American Labor.* Ithaca, N.Y.: Cornell University Press, 1991.

Beadle, Muriel, and Centennial History Committee. *The Fortnightly of Chicago: The City and Its Women: 1873–1973.* Chicago: Henry Regnery, 1973.

Benson, Susan Porter. *Counter Cultures: Saleswomen, Managers, and Customers in American Department Stores, 1890–1940.* Urbana: University of Illinois Press, 1986.

Berlanstein, Lenard R., ed. *Rethinking Labor History: Essays on Discourse and Class Analysis.* Urbana: University of Illinois Press, 1993.

Blair, Karen J. *The Clubwoman as Feminist: True Womanhood Redefined, 1868–1914.* New York: Holmes and Meier, 1980.

Blewett, Mary. *Men, Women, and Work: Class, Gender, and Protest in the New England Shoe Industry, 1780–1910.* Urbana: University of Illinois Press, 1988.

Bordin, Ruth. *Woman and Temperance: The Quest for Power and Liberty, 1873–1900.* Philadelphia: Temple University Press, 1981.

Bowles, Samuel, and Herbert Gintis. *Schooling in Capitalist America: Educational Reform and the Contradictions of Economic Life.* 1976; New York: Basic Books, 1977.

Boyer, Paul. *Urban Masses and Moral Order in America, 1820–1920.* Cambridge, Mass.: Harvard University Press, 1978.

Brandes, Stuart D. *American Welfare Capitalism, 1880–1940.* Chicago: University of Chicago Press, 1976.

Bremner, Robert H. *From the Depths: The Discovery of Poverty in the United States.* New York: New York University Press, 1956.

Broder, Sherri. "Informing the 'Cruelty': The Monitoring of Respectability in

Philadelphia's Working-Class Neighborhoods in the Late Nineteenth Century." *Radical America* 21, no. 4 (July-Aug. 1987): 34–47.

Brown, Elsa Barkley. "Womanist Consciousness: Maggie Lena Walker and the Independent Order of Saint Luke." In *Black Women in America: Social Science Perspectives*, ed. Micheline R. Malson, Elisabeth Mudimbe-Boyi, Jean F. O'Barr, and Mary Wyer, pp. 173–96. Chicago: University of Chicago Press, 1990.

Buhle, Mari Jo. "Gender and Labor History." in *Perspectives on American Labor History*, ed. Moody and Kessler-Harris, pp. 55–79.

Cameron, Ardis. *Radicals of the Worst Sort: Laboring Women in Lawrence, Massachusetts, 1860–1912*. Urbana: University of Illinois Press, 1993.

Carson, Mina. *Settlement Folk: Social Thought and the American Settlement Movement, 1885–1930*. Chicago: University of Chicago Press, 1990.

Chandler, Alfred D., Jr. *The Visible Hand: The Managerial Revolution in American Business*. Cambridge, Mass.: Harvard University Press, Belknap Press, 1977.

Clark, Victor S. *History of Manufactures in the United States*. 3 vols. New York: McGraw-Hill, 1929.

Commons, John R., David J. Saposs, Helen L. Sumner, E. B. Mittelman, H. E. Hoagland, John B. Andrews, Selig Perlman, and Philip Taft. *History of Labour in the United States*. 4 vols. New York: Macmillan, 1926–35.

Conzen, Kathleen Neils. "Ethnicity as Festive Culture: Nineteenth-Century German America on Parade." In *The Invention of Ethnicity*, ed. Werner Sollars, pp. 44–76. New York: Oxford University Press, 1989.

Cott, Nancy F. *The Grounding of Modern Feminism*. New Haven, Conn.: Yale University Press, 1987.

Cremin, Lawrence A. *The Transformation of the School: Progressivism in American Education, 1876–1957*. New York: Alfred A. Knopf, 1961.

Davis, Allen F. *Spearheads for Reform: The Social Settlements and the Progressive Movement, 1890–1914*. New York: Oxford University Press, 1967.

Degler, Carl N. *At Odds: Women and the Family in America from the Revolution to the Present*. New York: Oxford University Press, 1980.

Denning, Michael. *Mechanic Accents: Dime Novels and Working-Class Culture in America*. London: Verso, 1987.

Deutsch, Sarah. "Learning to Talk More Like a Man: Boston Women's Class-Bridging Organizations, 1870–1940." *American Historical Review* 97, no. 2 (Apr. 1992): 379–404.

DeVault, Ileen A. *Sons and Daughters of Labor: Class and Clerical Work in Turn-of-the-Century Pittsburgh*. Ithaca, N.Y.: Cornell University Press, 1990.

———. "Work and Honor: The Daughters of Pittsburgh's Skilled Workers." Paper presented at the annual meeting of the American Historical Association, San Francisco, Dec. 27–30, 1983. Typescript.

Diner, Hasia. *Erin's Daughters in America: Irish Immigrant Women in the Nineteenth Century*. Baltimore: Johns Hopkins University Press, 1983.

Dinnerstein, Leonard, Roger L. Nichols, and David M. Reimers. *Natives and Strangers: Blacks, Indians, and Immigrants in America*. 2d ed. New York: Oxford University Press, 1990.

Dodge, Phyllis B. *Tales of the Phelps-Dodge Family: A Chronicle of Five Generations*. New York: New York Historical Society, 1987.

DuBois, Ellen Carol. *Feminism and Suffrage: The Emergence of the Independent Women's Movement in America, 1848–1869*. Ithaca, N.Y.: Cornell University Press, 1978.

Dye, Nancy Schrom. *As Equals and As Sisters: Feminism, the Labor Movement, and the Women's Trade Union League of New York*. Columbia: University of Missouri Press, 1980.

Edwards, Alba M. *Comparative Occupation Statistics for the United States, 1870–1940*. U.S. Bureau of the Census, Sixteenth Census, 1940. Washington, D.C.: Government Printing Office, 1943.

Ehrenreich, Barbara, and Deirdre English. *For Her Own Good: 150 Years of the Experts' Advice to Women*. Garden City, N.Y.: Doubleday, 1978.

Eisenstein, Sarah. *Give Us Bread But Give Us Roses: Working Women's Consciousness in the United States, 1890 to the First World War*. London: Routledge and Kegan Paul, 1983.

Feldberg, Roslyn L. "'Union Fever': Organizing among Clerical Workers, 1900–1930." *Radical America* 14, no. 3 (May-June 1980): 53–67.

Feldman, Egal. "Prostitution, the Alien Woman, and the Progressive Imagination, 1910–1915." *American Quarterly* 19, no. 2, pt. 1 (Summer 1967): 192–206.

Fine, Lisa M. *The Souls of the Skyscraper: Female Clerical Workers in Chicago, 1870–1930*. Philadelphia: Temple University Press, 1990.

Fink, Leon. *Workingmen's Democracy: The Knights of Labor and American Politics*. Urbana: University of Illinois Press, 1983.

Foner, Philip S. *History of the Labor Movement in the United States*. 6 vols. New York: International Publishers, 1947–82; 2d ed., vol. 2 only, 1975.

———. *Women and the American Labor Movement: From Colonial Times to the Eve of World War I*. New York: Free Press, 1979.

Fones-Wolf, Ken. *Trade Union Gospel: Christianity and Labor in Industrial Philadelphia, 1865–1915*. Philadelphia: Temple University Press, 1989.

Giddings, Paula. *When and Where I Enter: The Impact of Black Women on Race and Sex in America*. 1984; New York: Bantam, 1985.

Ginzberg, Lori D. *Women and the Work of Benevolence: Morality, Politics, and Class in the Nineteenth-Century United States*. New Haven, Conn.: Yale University Press, 1990.

Glenn, Susan A. "Partners in the Struggle: Gender and Class Consciousness among Jewish Women Garment Workers." Paper presented at the annual meeting of the Organization of American Historians, Philadelphia, Apr. 2–5, 1987. Typescript.

Gordon, David M., Richard Edwards, and Michael Reich. *Segmented Work, Divided Workers: The Historical Transformation of Labor in the United States*. New York: Cambridge University Press, 1982.

Gossett, Thomas F. *Race: The History of an Idea in America*. 1963; New York: Schocken Books, 1965.

Graham, Abbie. *Grace H. Dodge: Merchant of Dreams*. New York: Woman's Press, 1926.

Green, Marguerite. *The National Civic Federation and the American Labor Movement, 1900–1925*. Washington, D.C.: Catholic University of America Press, 1956.

Greenwald, Maurine Weiner. *Women, War, and Work: The Impact of World War I on Women Workers in the United States*. Westport, Conn.: Greenwood Press, 1980.

Grob, Gerald N. *Workers and Utopia: A Study of Ideological Conflict in the American Labor Movement, 1865–1900*. Evanston, Ill.: Northwestern University Press, 1961.

Groneman, Carol. "'She Earns as a Child; She Pays as a Man': Women Workers in a Mid-Nineteenth-Century New York City Community." In *Class, Sex and the Woman Worker*, ed. Milton Cantor and Bruce Laurie, pp. 83–100. Westport, Conn.: Greenwood Press, 1977.

Guy-Sheftall, Beverly. *Daughters of Sorrow: Attitudes toward Black Women, 1880–1920*. New York: Carlson Publishing, 1990.

Haber, Samuel. *Efficiency and Uplift: Scientific Management in the Progressive Era, 1890–1920*. Chicago: University of Chicago Press, 1964.

Hapke, Laura. *Tales of the Working Girl: Wage-Earning Women in American Literature, 1890–1925*. New York: Twayne Publishers, 1992.

Higham, John. *Strangers in the Land: Patterns of American Nativism, 1860–1925*. 1955; New York: Atheneum, 1963.

Hofstadter, Richard. *Social Darwinism in American Thought*. Rev. ed. Boston: Beacon Press, 1955.

Hower, Ralph M. *History of Macy's of New York, 1858–1919: Chapters in the Evolution of the Department Store*. Cambridge, Mass.: Harvard University Press, 1943.

Jacoby, Robin Miller. "The Women's Trade Union League and American Feminism." *Feminist Studies* 3, nos. 1–2 (Fall 1975): 126–40.

James, Edward T., ed. *Notable American Women, 1607–1950: A Biographical Dictionary*. 3 vols. Cambridge, Mass.: Harvard University Press, Belknap Press, 1971.

Jensen, Joan M. "Cloth, Butter and Boarders: Women's Household Production for the Market." *Review of Radical Political Economics* 12, no. 2 (Summer 1980): 14–24.

Johnson, Christopher. "Lifeworld, System, and Communicative Action: The Habermasian Alternative in Social History." In *Rethinking Labor History*, ed. Berlanstein, pp. 55–89.

Johnson, Rachel Harris, and Dora Estelle Dodge. *Thirty Years of Girls' Club Experience: Sponsorship, Leadership Training, Program Development*. N.p.: Girls' Clubs of America, n.d. [ca. 1945].

Jones, Jacqueline. *Labor of Love, Labor of Sorrow: Black Women, Work, and the Family from Slavery to the Present*. 1985; New York: Vintage Books, 1986.

Kaplan, Temma. "Female Consciousness and Collective Action: The Case of Barcelona, 1910–1918." *Signs: Journal of Women in Culture and Society* 7, no. 3 (Spring 1982): 545–66.

Katz, Esther, "Grace Hoadley Dodge: Women and the Emerging Metropolis, 1856–1914." Ph.D. dissertation, New York University, 1980.

Katzman, David M. *Seven Days a Week: Women and Domestic Service in Industrializing America*. 1978; Urbana: University of Illinois Press, 1981.

Kessler-Harris, Alice. "A New Agenda for American Labor History: A Gendered Analysis and the Question of Class." In *Perspectives on American Labor History*, ed. Moody and Kessler-Harris, pp. 217–34.

———. *Out to Work: A History of Wage-Earning Women in the United States*. New York: Oxford University Press, 1982.

———. "'Where Are the Organized Women Workers?'" *Feminist Studies* 3, nos. 1–2 (Fall 1975): 92–110.

Kleinberg, Susan. "Technology and Women's Work: The Lives of Working-Class Women in Pittsburgh, 1870–1900." *Labor History* 7, no. 1 (Winter 1976): 58–72.

Kocka, Jurgen. *White Collar Workers in America, 1890–1940: A Social-Political History in International Perspective.* London: Sage, 1980.

Kraut, Alan M. *The Huddled Masses: The Immigrant in American Society, 1880–1921.* Arlington Heights, Ill.: Harlan Davidson, 1982.

Kriegel, Phyllis. "The Daughter of Privilege and the Daughters of Labor: Grace H. Dodge and the Working Girls' Societies, 1884–96." Master's thesis, Sarah Lawrence College, 1977.

Lagemann, Ellen Condliffe. *A Generation of Women: Education in the Lives of Progressive Reformers.* Cambridge, Mass.: Harvard University Press, 1979.

Lebergott, Stanley. *Manpower in Economic Growth: The American Record since 1800.* New York: McGraw-Hill, 1964.

Levine, Susan. *Labor's True Woman: Carpet Weavers, Industrialization, and Labor Reform in the Gilded Age.* Philadelphia: Temple University Press, 1984.

Lewis, R. W. B. *Edith Wharton: A Biography.* New York: Harper and Row, 1975.

Lieberman, Jacob. "Their Sisters' Keepers: The Women's Hours and Wages Movement in the United States, 1890–1925." Ph.D. dissertation, Columbia University, 1971.

Lubove, Roy. *The Professional Altruist: The Emergence of Social Work as a Career, 1880–1930.* 1965; New York: Atheneum, 1977.

Matthaei, Julie. *An Economic History of Women in America: Women's Work, the Sexual Division of Labor, and the Development of Capitalism.* New York: Schocken Books, 1982.

May, Henry F. *Protestant Churches and Industrial America.* New York: Harper and Brothers, 1949.

McHenry, Robert, ed. *Famous American Women: A Biographical Dictionary from Colonial Times to the Present.* 1980; New York: Dover Publications, 1983.

Montgomery, David. *The Fall of the House of Labor: The Workplace, the State, and American Labor Activism, 1865–1925.* New York: Cambridge University Press, 1987.

———. *Workers' Control in America: Studies in the History of Work, Technology and Labor Struggles.* New York: Cambridge University Press, 1979.

Moody, J. Carroll, and Alice Kessler-Harris, eds. *Perspectives on American Labor History: The Problems of Synthesis.* DeKalb: Northern Illinois University Press, 1990.

Muncy, Robyn. *Creating a Female Dominion in American Reform, 1890–1935.* New York: Oxford University Press, 1991.

Nelson, Daniel. *Managers and Workers: Origins of the New Factory System in the United States, 1880–1920.* Madison: University of Wisconsin Press, 1975.

Neverdon-Morton, Cynthia. *Afro-American Women of the South and the Advancement of the Race, 1895–1925.* Knoxville: University of Tennessee Press, 1989.

Norwood, Stephen H. *Labor's Flaming Youth: Telephone Operators and Worker Militancy, 1878–1923.* Urbana: University of Illinois Press, 1990.

Palmer, Bryan. *Descent into Discourse: The Reification of Language and the Writing of Social History.* Philadelphia: Temple University Press, 1990.

Pascoe, Peggy. *Relations of Rescue: The Search for Female Moral Authority in the American West, 1874–1939*. New York: Oxford University Press, 1991.

Payne, Elizabeth Anne. *Reform, Labor, and Feminism: Margaret Dreier Robins and the Women's Trade Union League*. Urbana: University of Illinois Press, 1988.

Peiss, Kathy. *Cheap Amusements: Working Women and Leisure in Turn-of-the-Century New York*. Philadelphia: Temple University Press, 1986.

Perry, Elisabeth Israels. *Belle Moskowitz: Feminine Politics and the Exercise of Power in the Age of Alfred E. Smith*. New York: Routledge, 1992.

Pivar, David J. *Purity Crusade: Sexual Morality and Social Control, 1868–1900*. Westport, Conn.: Greenwood Press, 1973.

Pleck, Elizabeth. "Two Worlds in One: Work and Family." *Journal of Social History* 10, no. 2 (Winter 1976): 178–95.

Reitano, Joanne. "Working Girls Unite." *American Quarterly* 36, no. 1 (Spring 1984): 112–34.

Ross, Ellen. "'Not the Sort that Would Sit on the Doorstep': Respectability in Pre-World War I London Neighborhoods." *International Labor and Working Class History*, no. 27 (Spring 1985): 39–59.

Rothman, Sheila. *Woman's Proper Place: A History of Changing Ideals and Practices, 1870 to the Present*. New York: Basic Books, 1978.

Schofield, Ann. "The Rise of the Pig-Headed Girl: An Analysis of the American Labor Press for Their Attitudes toward Women, 1877–1920." Ph.D. dissertation, State University of New York at Binghamton, 1980.

Scott, Anne Firor. *Natural Allies: Women's Associations in American History*. Urbana: University of Illinois Press, 1992.

Scott, Joan. *Gender and the Politics of History*. New York: Columbia University Press, 1988.

Sinclair, Andrew. *The Emancipation of the American Woman*. New York: Harper and Row, 1965.

Sklar, Kathryn Kish. "The Historical Foundations of Women's Power in the Creation of the American Welfare State, 1830–1930." In *Mothers of a New World: Maternalist Politics and the Origins of Welfare States*, ed. Seth Koven and Sonya Michel, pp. 43–93. New York: Routledge, 1993.

Skocpol, Theda. *Protecting Soldiers and Mothers: The Political Origins of Social Policy in the United States*. Cambridge, Mass.: Harvard University Press, Belknap Press, 1992.

Slaughter, Sheila, and Edward T. Silva. "Looking Backwards: How Foundations Formulated Ideology in the Progressive Period." In *Philanthropy and Cultural Imperialism: The Foundations at Home and Abroad*, ed. Robert F. Arnove, pp. 55–80. 1980; Bloomington: Indiana University Press, 1982.

Smith, Daniel Scott. "Family Limitation, Sexual Control, and Domestic Feminism in Victorian America." In *A Heritage of Her Own: Toward a New Social History of American Women*, ed. Nancy F. Cott and Elizabeth H. Pleck, pp. 222–45. New York: Simon and Schuster, 1979.

Smith-Rosenberg, Carroll. "The Female World of Love and Ritual: Relations between Women in Nineteenth-Century America." *Signs: Journal of Women in Culture and Society* 1, no. 1 (Autumn 1975): 1–29.

Solomon, Barbara Miller. *In the Company of Educated Women: A History of Women in Higher Education in America*. New Haven, Conn.: Yale University Press, 1985.

Spring, Joel H. *Education and the Rise of the Corporate State*. Boston: Beacon Press, 1972.

Stansell, Christine. *City of Women: Sex and Class in New York, 1789–1860*. 1986; Urbana: University of Illinois Press, 1987.

Stein, Jean. *Edie: An American Biography*. New York: Alfred A. Knopf, 1982.

Strasser, Susan. *Never Done: A History of American Housework*. New York: Pantheon Books, 1982.

Tax, Meredith. *The Rising of the Women: Feminist Solidarity and Class Conflict, 1888–1917*. New York: Monthly Review Press, 1980.

Tentler, Leslie. *Wage-Earning Women: Industrial Work and Family Life in the United States, 1900–1930*. New York: Oxford University Press, 1979.

Weimann, Jeanne M. *The Fair Women*. Chicago: Academy Chicago, 1981.

Welter, Barbara. "The Cult of True Womanhood: 1820–1860." In *The American Family in Social Historical Perspective*, ed. Michael Gordon, pp. 313–33. 2d ed. New York: St. Martin's Press, 1978.

Wertheimer, Barbara Mayer. *We Were There: The Story of Working Women in America*. New York: Pantheon Books, 1977.

White, Deborah Gray. "The Cost of Club Work, the Price of Black Feminism." In *Visible Women: New Essays on American Activism*, ed. Nancy A. Hewitt and Suzanne Lebsock, pp. 247–69. Urbana: University of Illinois Press, 1993.

Wiebe, Robert. *Businessmen and Reform: A Study of the Progressive Movement*. 1962; Chicago: Ivan R. Dee, 1989.

Williamson, Joel. *A Rage for Order: Black-White Relations in the American South since Emancipation*. New York: Oxford University Press, 1986.

Wilson, Grace H. *The Religious and Educational Philosophy of the Young Women's Christian Association*. Contributions to Education, no. 554. New York: Teachers College, Columbia University, 1933.

Wolfe, Allis Rosenberg. "Women, Consumerism, and the National Consumers' League in the Progressive Era, 1900–1923." *Labor History* 16, no. 3 (Summer 1975): 378–92.

Index

Denison House (Boston); Shawmut
Avenue Club (Boston)
Boston Trade School for Girls, 111
Boylston Club (Boston), 103
Brooklyn, clubs in, 2, 24, 30, 64, 153
Brooklyn Association of Working
Girls' Clubs, 108
Bryn Mawr College, 139
Buckley, Mary, 103–4
Budlong, Jessie, 173
Buffalo (N.Y.), labor conflict in, 93
Burke, Lizzie, 82–83, 86–87, 94, 162
businesswoman, definition of, 129–
30. *See also* clerical workers

Cameron, Ardis, 6
Campbell, Helen, 77
Camp Holt (Gettysburg, Pa.), parties
for soldiers stationed at, 134
Cannon, William, 11
Canton (Mass.), club in, 95
Carnegie, Mrs. Andrew, 113
carpet mills, walkout at, 43–44, 87
carpet weavers, conditions for, 108
Carpet Weavers' Union, 43–44
Catholic church, sodalities in, 2
Central Labor Union (New York), 43
Chapin, Maria, 72
charity: attitudes toward, 19, 28, 31–
32, 38, 78; and cooperative efforts,
2–3; definition of, 28; domesticity
emphasized in, 57, 65
Charity Organization Societies:
friendly visitors from, 18, 32, 65–
66, 146; leaders for, 17, 97; as
upper-class meeting ground, 3, 28
Chicago: clubs in, 2, 20, 69, 86, 100,
106–7; labor reform in, 85–86, 91,
106–7; schools in, 69; sponsors in,
17, 69. *See also* Hull House (Chicago)
Chicago Association of Young
Women's Clubs, 100, 107
Chicago School of Domestic Arts and
Sciences, 69
Children's Aid Society, 2–3

Children's Dressmaking Company
(New York), 79, 97, 112
churches, women's organizations in,
2–3. *See also* Episcopal church
cigar industry, strike in, 87–88
Cigar Makers' Union, 11, 85, 88
Cincinnati (Ohio), club in, 50
civics, classes in, 50–51, 141
The Clansman (Dixon), 131
class. *See* social class
clerical workers: attitudes toward,
129–30; class status of, 194n16;
conditions for, 44, 79, 108, 113;
employment agency for, 107;
prevalence of, 113, 130; training for,
50, 79, 129
clothing: attitudes toward, 10, 43–44;
and pin money issue, 101–2;
recommendations for, 19–20, 42–44;
and self-representation, 78
club conventions: goals, policies, and
programs discussed at, 26, 30–32,
34–35, 48–53, 58–60, 62; labor
issues discussed at, 101–6, 108, 142;
and labor reform, 98–99; and
movement growth and contraction,
2, 108, 142; and NLWW founding,
108–10; NLWW name change
discussed at, 139
club meeting rooms: atmosphere in,
23–24, 37–38, 46–48, 52–54, 71, 95–
96, 123–24; behavior in, 38–41;
clothing worn to, 42–43; parental
approval of, 23; rental of, 2, 19;
supplied by employers, 19, 116–17,
135, 141. *See also* vacation lodges
(club)
club members: assistance for, 79–80,
97–99; autonomy of, 61; characteristics of, 3, 19–21, 113, 130, 137–38;
criticisms of, 40–41, 109–10, 125;
essays and articles by, 155–59, 160–
67; on homemaking, 55–60;
influence by, 47–48, 52–53, 84–85,
109–10, 118–19, 122–27, 126–27,
145–48; and labor unions, 82–83,

86–87, 87–88, 90, 94, 103–4; as leaders, 30, 47, 50, 72–73, 121–23, 126, 146–47; on marriage, 65–71; and politics, 89; prejudices of, 20–22, 135–40, 145, 148–49; and self-government, 29–31, 119, 122–27; and self-support, 31–32, 127, 135, 141; on sexual conduct, 25–26, 44–46; solidarity of, 21–22, 26, 28, 34; survey of, 113, 180n20; on treating, 61–62, 64. *See also* education; recreation; respectability; sisterhood

club programs: control of, 30–31, 47–49, 109–10; on economics, 95–96; and exclusivity, 20–21; focus of, 24–28, 48–50, 70–71; implications of, 3–4; on labor issues, 83–85, 93–94, 106; politics in, 89–90; racism in, 135–36, 148; samples of, 153–54, 174–76; on social reform, 127–28. *See also* practical classes; practical talks; recreation; self-improvement

clubs. *See* working girls' clubs; *names of specific clubs*

club sponsors: characteristics of, 16–18, 37–38, 47, 57–59; and cooperation, 33–36, 119–20; goals of, 18, 30–31, 56–59, 114, 120, 123–24, 146; and governance, 29–31, 123–25; on homemaking, 55–60; and labor issues, 77–78, 80–85, 91–92, 96–99, 100–106, 109; and marriage, 65, 69–70, 72–73; members' trust in, 78–79; on recreation, 51–52, 62–65, 118–19; role of, 17, 29, 48–50, 53, 109–10, 122, 149–50; and scientific methods, 114–18; self-descriptions of, 74–75, 149–50; on sexual conduct, 45–46; and trade education, 110–14. *See also* etiquette; leisured women; practical talks

Club Worker (journal): on class issues, 119–20; demise of, 142; on democratization, 122; on entertainments, 135–36; on immigrant women, 138–

40; on labor issues, 112, 114; on "oneness," 127, 133; play published in, 124; on race issues, 136–37; on war efforts, 133

coal mines, labor conflict in, 93

College Point (N.Y.), club in, 175

Columbian Exposition and World's Fair (1893), 57

Columbia University, 138

Connecticut Association of Working Girls' Clubs, 108

Consumers' Leagues: investigators from, 106–7; and labor reform, 81–82, 110; leaders for, 17, 117; manufacturers' cooperation with, 118; structure of, 148

cooking, classes in, 19–20, 25, 56

cooperation: as basis for social reform, 133–35; cross-class discourse on, 3, 33–36, 146–47, 149–51; decline of, 119–20, 122, 127–28; and governance issues, 29–31

Cornell University, 57

cotton mill workers, clubs for, 19

craft production, 10–13, 178–79n2. *See also* labor unions

Crane, Stephen, 9

dancing, NLWW rules for, 132

Danielsonville (Conn.), club in, 25, 154

daughters, role of, in working-class families, 10–15, 56, 61

de Graffenried, Clare, 93

democratization: and class relations, 46–48, 52–54; and club programs, 46–52; and governance, 30, 47; limitations on, 122–27, 150; renewed emphasis on, 122–23; reversal of, 118–20, 141, 147–48; and sisterhood, 74–76, 148–49, 151

Denison House (Boston), 3, 97, 98

Denning, Michael, 181n4

department stores: advertising by, 12, 192–93n38; growth of, 12; and labor reform, 106–7, 110; salesclerks in,

Priscilla Murolo is a member of the
U.S. history faculty at Sarah Lawrence College
and affiliated with the master of arts program
in women's history. She writes and speaks on
women's and labor history and belongs
to the editorial collective of the
Radical History Review.

BOOKS IN THE SERIES
WOMEN IN AMERICAN HISTORY

BOOKS IN THE SERIES
THE WORKING CLASS IN AMERICAN HISTORY